The word on *Paradise ...*
America's finest writers:

An ordinary family lived an extraordinary adventure. In their eating, praying, and loving, it becomes clear that readers can, too.

Margot Page's intelligent and witty prose style is at its best; every word seems uniquely chosen. The pages of *Paradise Imperfect* brim with possibility, inspiration, and even a bit of hilarious how-to.

—Marcelle Soviero, Editor-in-Chief,
Brain, Child: The Magazine for Thinking Mothers

"Travel is often glamorous and sometimes inconvenient, but at its best, it changes us. *Paradise Imperfect* is a rare and candid look at what happens— internally as well as externally—when this family pulls up stakes. It's a story about people as much as it is about place, and Margot Page describes the rain forest butterflies and her own family's transformation with equal honesty and affection.

It's a travel story, but it's also a love letter to the tangled and beautiful mess that comes from taking big chances. A truly refreshing voice in the landscape of shiny travel writing."

— Pam Mandel, award-winning travel writer,
blogger at nerdseyeview.com

"Hilarious and heartfelt. With keen observation and dry wit, Page puts to words the things the rest of us have only suspected and half-thought."

—Theo Nestor, author of *Writing is my Drink*

"Delightful and immensely readable. Margot Page's memoir reminds me of Anne Lamott and Barbara Kingsolver—the power, the beauty, and the accessibility of their prose—yet Page's brash charm and wry humor are her own. Feeling out of step with the super-vigilant parenting culture of the metropolis, Page felt suddenly done with it all. *Paradise Imperfect* is the story of how she moved her family to Central America, and her insights into the nature of family, faith, friendship, do-gooderism, poverty, and materialism are both morally complex and surprisingly, poignantly hilarious."

— **Bob Shacochis, winner of the of the National Book Award, author of *The Woman Who Lost Her Soul***

"Margot Page's writing brings together three elements all too rarely found in combination: fierce intelligence; genuine, irresistible funniness; and authentic sweetness. In *Paradise Imperfect*, Page—an overextended, oft-frustrated working mom—spirits her husband and three children away to the misty forests of Costa Rica. In the year she and her family spend there, Page learns about slowing down, about being a less-than-perfect mom, and about the possibilities that arise from having and doing a lot less.

All this she does in prose that is hilarious, heartfelt, and never less than gorgeous."

— **Claire Dederer, author of *Poser: My Life in Twenty-Three Yoga Poses***

Paradise Imperfect

An American family moves to the Costa Rican mountains

Yellow House Press
Seattle, Washington USA

The chapter "¡Hola, Jerry! ¿Donde esta George?" first appeared in the Spring, 2012 issue of Brain, Child *magazine.*
Some parts of Paradise Imperfect *appeared in the story "Disappearing Act," published in the 2013 Teen Edition of* Brain, Child *magazine.*

ISBN 978-0-6158936-4-8 (pbk)
ISBN 978-0-9912471-1-0 (Kindle)
ISBN 978-0-9912471-2-7 (epub)

for

Anthony, Hannah, Harry, and Ivy

Love you madly

and for

Andy Walker and Levi Mann

who made the world sweeter
and left it much too soon

Author's Note

Paradise Imperfect is a memoir, and my memory is surely imperfect. But if I'm going to search for meaning—and it appears that I am—I have to start with what, to the best of my recollection, happened.

So: These things happened. The people are real. Most names have been changed and some chronology scrambled, for the sake of story.

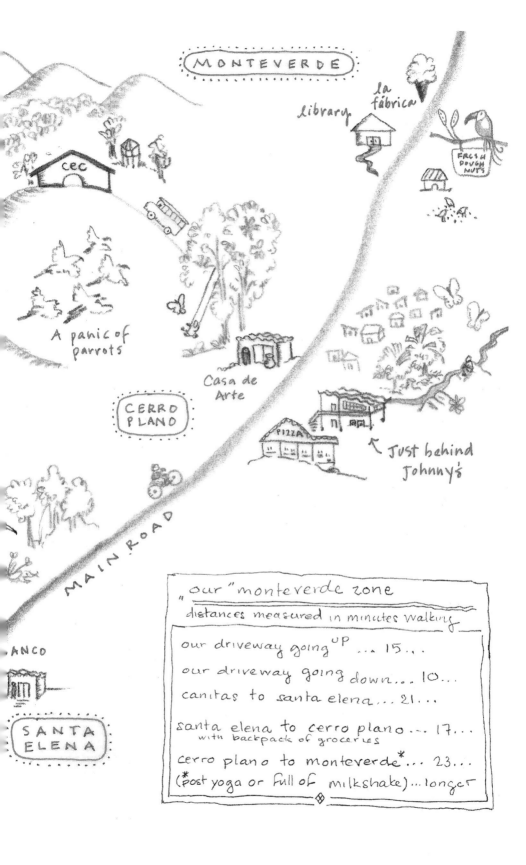

MONTEVERDE

la fábrica

library

FRESH DOUGH NUTS

cec

A panic of parrots

Casa de Arte

CERRO PLANO

PIZZA

← Just behind Johnny's

MAIN ROAD

ANCO

SANTA ELENA

our "monteverde zone

distances measured in minutes walking

our driveway going up ... 15 ...

our driveway going down ... 10 ...

canitas to santa elena ... 21 ...

santa elena to cerro plano ... 17 ...
with backpack of groceries

cerro plano to monteverde* ... 23 ...

(*post yoga or full of milkshake) ... longer

Contents

Prologue

Our neighbor's dairy cows prowled their side of the post-and-wire fence, making big, brown, covetous eyes at the nascent orchard. "Sorry," I told them. "Not today."

Anthony and I had fixed a gap just this morning, using a whole spool of wire. Cow deterrence was new to us, and we wanted to be thorough.

I flopped my left leg over the edge of the hammock, set myself swinging, and turned to the view.

From my perch near the top of the Tilarán Range, first I saw yard. Punctuated by the sideways parentheses of a laundry line so long it needed an extra post between its two ends, our machete-mown meadow sloped down and away. Past the friendly flutter of my family's clean socks, thirty avocado saplings held their own. Then fence, then cows.

On the downhill side of their pasture, I could just make out the variegated edge of the rain forest—a cool, wet tangle of passion flowers and strangler figs. Individual trees blurred to furry green foothills, unrolling toward the flatlands until they resolved, finally, into the sparkling blue band of the Gulf of Nicoya.

Flapping laundry to the slow-flexing muscle of the mighty Pacific: Those were my boundaries.

Each day in the foothills, invisible droplets rallied into visible gray, and together they climbed the mountain. In reverse my view would narrow. The blue Gulf disappeared and then the rolling, dark green. An hour later, the cows slipped into the drippy mist. Finally, the front yard and the laundry line would vanish.

That early afternoon in January, 2004, I was alone at our house when I noticed the Gulf was gone. *This could be the moment.*

I'd hauled my family to Costa Rica six months before, for a backpack full of reasons that had seemed pretty genius at the time: Slow down, learn Spanish. Entertain the possibility that select soccer was not the pinnacle of human evolution. But lately a niggling suspicion had begun to bloom, the thought that my excellent reasons were just part of the story.   I'd awakened that morning with a strange certainty: I was in for some kind of enlightenment.

Looking down the mountain at the disappearing world, I felt it again. *Today I'm going to learn something,* I thought, and my anticipation climbed along with the gray.

Costa Rica had something to tell me.

 I'd better get some snack.

Inside, I set two homemade tortillas on a plate and sliced an avocado in half, salting the hole where the pit had been. I grabbed a spoon and parked myself at the window.

Now the pasture was gone, and the scheming cows. Any moment, it would just be me and my avo, inside a white cloud. I set down the plate and closed my eyes. I tipped my head up in a posture I hoped was receptive in a non-showoffy way. I listened.

Before

1

Breaking Point

Seven months before, I'd been driving toward daycare, mentally sorting and pinning. My life was about making things work, and mostly they bowed to my efforts. This week, though, I'd been cutting it close. So far today, I:

- had procured zero items for Hannah's middle-school auction—just as I had yesterday, and the day before that,
- had forgotten to pack a snack for Harry to eat between school and practice, and
- was right on track for making Ivy the last child at daycare to be picked up.

Bad-mother hat trick!

At Hilltop, late charges kicked in at six and accrued by the minute. You made payment directly to the teacher who had to stay late, underscoring that you weren't just late, you were *rude*. I was grateful for my work carpool. Through the magic of the HOV lane, we hit the bridge by 5:33. I dropped my buddies at Tully's, glad I was the driver today: Not switching cars would save me a solid ninety seconds. As Mike waved and headed home, I sped off toward Hilltop spinning a fantasy of his life. His stay-at-home wife Amy would be stirring something delicious, made of organic local vegetables. Beef from a hand-raised cow that had almost certainly been read to in its formative years.

I mentally rummaged our fridge. I might not get to be Amy, but I wasn't going to be take-out mom, either. I carried a list in my head of how long it had been since I'd made spaghetti with meatballs for Harry, or cheesy bread for Hannah.

5:45. I gunned it down Aloha Street and thought about last weekend's tournament.

Not content to play every sport, my nine-year-old son had recently entered the freaky netherworld of youth chess. Last Saturday, the air in the gym was already humming with focus as I tiptoed in late. Two hundred heads bent over boards, but I spotted Harry easily by his red hair and inability to sit still.

Chess spectating from the bleachers is not riveting; as my mind wandered I realized that my son's latest obsession provided the perfect metaphor for my own life.

Every day was a chess game. If I could think enough moves ahead, I could prepare a defense against this possibility or that one. Making it to bedtime with everything done and everyone happy—that was the win. I just needed to be able to see my way to the endgame. (It wasn't exactly clear to me who my opponent was. No matter; I knew there was one.)

Today, being late to daycare would put me at least a couple of rooks down. But I was making good time and dared to hope. Then, twelve blocks from Hilltop at 5:56, a yellow light. The shiny new Prius in front of me was almost at the crosswalk, but on came the brake lights. *Come on, Prius Man! We can make it… SHIT!*

I had been through a fair amount of marriage counseling by this time, so I knew how rhetorical questions (e.g., "What the hell is your problem?") are not always helpful. Real progress occurs only when we approach conflict with curiosity. I took a cleansing breath and spoke to Prius Man gently, with great interest:

"Why," I asked conversationally, through teeth that were almost not clenched, "must you be such a pussy?" I issued a sheepish apology to my mother's generation of feminists and amended to "coward."

But it was a long light, possibly the longest in history. At 5:58 I, decided to reclaim the word. *I am going to kill that pussy in the Prius,* I vowed. *I refuse to be put in checkmate by some idiot who cannot work a stoplight.* On the corner, a group of sign wavers urged me to Support Our Troops, Bring Them Home. I agreed with the sentiment, but I really had to pick up my kid.

My kid. For a second the frantic stopped. The chess game fell away and I felt only the ache. Five days a week, I left my children. The light changed, and the Prius sprang noiselessly into action.

I sprinted into Hilltop at six exactly. "Mommy, Mommy, Mommy!" Ivy launched herself at me. She was light as a bird, skinny arms and legs winding and tightening in the death grip that was the best moment of any weekday. Hugging back, I noticed Alanna playing quietly by the bookshelves. *I was beating Alanna's mom at working mother!* At 6:01 I could afford to be magnanimous. "How's it going, sweetie?" I asked Alanna, not patronizing at all.

This time of day required particularly strategic moves. Ivy never felt hungry and was too contrary to take any food offered outright. But when this kid needed to eat, she became a tornado: anything in her path was going to end up rubble. (Everyone told me the third child is the easy one, but the first time Ivy said "I hate you, Mommy!" she was 22 months old. I had suggested she put on some socks.) In the car, I got Ivy chattering while I steered with one hand and grabbed a granola bar from the glove box with the other. In case Ivy was paying attention, I took a bite to show I was hungry—nobody was accusing *her*—then reached back and abandoned the bar on the back seat without comment. Ivy picked it up mid-chatter, and I started to unclench.

I'd grab Harry from baseball and make dinner. Where was Hannah? Right—library. She'd take the bus home.

Fifteen minutes later, I had pasta water on the stove and was starting the daily rummage. Most days I just looked through backpacks for permission slips and overdue homework, but today a tangy odor in the hallway indicated that, somewhere, down deep, an orange was turning soft and gray. I pulled a second-grade math assignment from the bottom of Harry's backpack—corrections that needed a parental signature. Harry was currently winding up his third-grade year. *Oops.*

"Are you remembering we have Carl and Tammy's?" Anthony came in the door and set his car key precisely on its hook. Anthony's dark hair was trying to recede, but the youthful openness of his face kept everything around it from looking older.

"Oh no. Oh jeez. No, I spaced that completely." Who has people over on a weeknight?

Dinner with a work teammate and his family had sounded fun, back before I'd spent the last two hours in and out of the car. Hail Mary pass: "Maybe it'd be a relief for them if we said we couldn't make it?" I suggested.

Fumbled. No matter the plan, Anthony likes to stick to it.

"We said we'd go."

"Yeah, okay. I'll like it once we get there."

Hannah arrived, scuffed off her shoes. She dropped her backpack in the middle of the hallway, wincing as the pack caught on her ponytail and took a few brown hairs with it to the floor. On hearing the news of dinner, Hannah sighed and shoved her feet back in her shoes.

"We have to *walk?*"

Put Harry in an athletic contest of any kind and he couldn't stop running. Feet as transportation? He protested on principle.

But Harry's desire to win, coupled with an innate sunniness that assumed everyone in the world had the best motives, made our son incredibly easy to manipulate.

"Race you up the hill," said Anthony. Harry, still in cleats, took off on the grassy parking strips.

Hannah, Ivy, and I followed. I asked Hannah about her day. Turned out it was, like so many before it, "Fine, thanks."

Hannah was twelve but looked ten. It had started to bother her that she kept on looking like Hannah while her sixth-grade classmates had morphed into breastier, curvier versions of their fifth-grade selves. Her best friend, Lucy, was suddenly five inches taller and getting her period. At first Hannah had wailed to me about her body's adamant refusal to adolesce, but lately she kept to herself. As we headed up the hill, I took the opportunity to do some Parenting.

"Did you know," I kept my voice casual. "That Daddy's first driver's license shows him as five-foot-four and ninety-five pounds?"

No response.

"I'm just saying. Some people start growing late. By the time I met your dad, he was six feet tall."

I watched her out of the corner of my eye. Fine, curly wisps had escaped her mostly-straight ponytail and come forward to frame her freckles.

"Yep," she said. "I also know that you started high school flat as a board. And Mom? I really am okay."

She licked her palms and slicked her wispies ruthlessly back.

Blocks don't measure the true distance between the top of Seattle's Capitol Hill and our street, halfway down the side of it. It's the difference between recessed mahogany built-ins and the Ikea Billy collection, between Pottery Barn Kids and Target, between starting at Microsoft in the eighties and starting when I had, in 1997.

Seattle in 2003 could make a person crazy. It was post-dot-com boom, pre-Facebook. Early enough in high-tech history that the overnight millionaires were still getting press, but late enough that I was never going to be one of them. It was an environment that made a person constantly aware of how rich *other people* were.

We're doing fine, I continually reminded myself, and tried not to get weird about all the wealth around me. Tonight would be practice.

Harry had no concept of getting weird about it: He just wanted, unequivocally, to be insanely wealthy. As the kids found each other and ran around, he came back periodically to report his findings. "Mom, their TV takes up a whole wall! And *yes!* Xbox!" (Harry never failed to report on the existence of video games, since his parents didn't love him enough to provide same.) "*And* they have a *trampoline!* Man, we are totally poor compared to these guys!"

I made a mental note to draw for Harry the admittedly fine line between *poverty* and *lack of trampoline.* Right now, I was making my own tasteful, mature observations.

Carl and Tammy's living room was all effortless confidence. No need to be Martha-Stewart matchy. Just the haphazard perfection that results when the little figurine you picked up in Nepal, the prayer totem from the ashram, and the oversized black-and-white art shots of the children tie together perfectly with the simple addition of an oversized sofa from Restoration Hardware.

We're doing fine.

Tammy was talking to me. I complimented a modernist painting, and she told me how much she enjoyed the couple of afternoons a week she spent making and collecting art.

"I was a litigator before we had Claire," she laughed. "The gallery keeps me sane, after singing 'Wheels on the Bus' forty times a morning!"

By and large, the Microsoft wives I knew were lovely, intelligent, giving people. They used their considerable skills and high-end educations to organize the hell out of PTA meetings that I rarely had time to attend, and to support the heroic teachers in our underfunded public-school classrooms. They meant no harm and did quite a lot of good.

But I never felt safe around them. As mothers, none of us—them or me—had quite figured out how to reconcile our roles in the world with what we'd been told we were supposed to want. It made us wary of each other. I suspected we were all being more defensive than we wanted to be, but none of us knew how to stop. Those of us with jobs outside the home were desperate for everyone to know we loved our children. And the stay-at-home moms seemed to shimmy every conversation around to how smart they were, and how deeply right was their decision to stay home.

I had had a hundred conversations that went, if you stripped away the fluffy niceties, about like this:

Woman with Full-Time job: *I sure do love my children.*

Stay-at-Home Mom: *I love mine enough to give up my career, although I am extremely brilliant and capable. Because mothering is the Most Important Work of all.*

WwFTJ: *Have I mentioned that my job is in fact an expression of my love for my children?*

SaHM: *My daughter will know that it takes extraordinary strength to put family first, when our culture tells us that smart women should all have careers.*

How were we all not out of breath every minute, working so hard to feel okay?

Now, Tammy was perched on the grape-juice-stained arm of her fifteen-thousand-dollar sofa:

"Of course, I know career is *important*." She laid an understanding hand on my arm. "But I really want to spend time with my children. These years go by *so fast*."

I froze. As if I didn't know. As if I didn't want that, too.

"Oh, not me!" I later wished I had said, just to see her face. "I don't really like my kids that much! Thank God for Microsoft!"

But I just nodded and agreed—yes, yes, unbelievably fast. Precious. Yes. *Checkmate.*

I bit the insides of my cheeks and got through the evening. Harry spent three happy hours in front of the Xbox, stopping only to ask Ivy why she *always* had to get in the *way*. I wasn't sure where Hannah ended up, but we all made it out gracefully enough.

Back at home I cried on Anthony, who was absorbent.

I hated the implication that I was at work not because we needed my paycheck, but because I just didn't want to stay home. That I was putting in fifty- or sixty-hour weeks in Redmond because I found it more fulfilling to ship another version of what-the-hell-ever than to hear Ivy's first word. I missed my kids, hard, every single day. But I always knew—and Tammy had verified— that many people would look at my life and think:

When it came time to choose, Margot picked career. She likes to feel smart in meetings while other people raise her children.

I wanted to call everyone in the world, plead my case: *Some mothers love our kids by funding them,* I would say. *Sometimes that's the best way we can do it. It doesn't mean we wanted to spend our lives in a conference room.*

I said to Anthony:

"What if the kids never know how much I love them? What if all they remember is that their mother was gone most of the time, and then she raced home tired and awful? What if they think I *wanted* to spend their childhoods at a whiteboard?"

"The kids know you love them."

"We won't know I've wrecked them until I've already done it," I said darkly.

"The kids are fine."

I am perfectly capable of recognizing that I'm being whiny and obnoxious while continuing to whine and be obnoxious. I felt like the mirror-image of those women who talked about being trapped in perfect-mother syndrome. I was dying to be a perfect mother.

"I just can't do it and work in high tech."

I paused for breath and in case there was a response. That was the rub, of course. "So quit your job" was the obvious answer, but feeble—we both knew our family couldn't live on Anthony's income.

The so-called mommy wars were confusing to me. The anguished voices debating whether it was better for a mother to choose home or career never seemed to note what a profound gift it was to be choosing at all.

My husband examined the ceiling, which I took as invitation to continue my oratorio.

"I want to make hot breakfasts and always have finger paint on my clothes. I want to give each kid a patch of garden and help them turn our homegrown produce into delicious gift items." I would tie them with raffia, and bring them as hostess gifts. (Dammit. I hadn't brought Tammy a hostess gift.)

Anthony's face manifests confusion like a cartoon. All he's missing are a few question marks sprinkled above his head. Sometimes, when he's wearing his puzzled look, I imagine (because I am insane) that his face is actually the source of the problem. That if I could just pull his brow smooth, close his gaping mouth, and uncock his head, that would do the trick. I considered now whether to test this hypothesis. Too late.

"But...there's plum jam in the basement." Anthony focused on the specifics, which had answers, rather than on the sadness behind them, which did not. My intensity baffled him, always. "And wait...you did the garden thing, too."

"April was impossible," I sulked. "Everything got weedy and sluggy and unmiraculous." I was powerless to stop my own tantrum; Ivy with no 6 p.m. granola bar.

Anthony had given my frustration as much try as he had in him. "Bummer."

We all have our gifts, and one of Anthony's is sleeping. I knew I had about fifteen seconds before he'd be out. If there was anything else I needed to complain about, I'd have to hurry to get it in under the wire.

"Does it seem weird to you how much our family doesn't hang out together?"

"Ummm . . ."

"Seriously. The kids barely even interact. Everyone has their own friends and their own activities. You and I show up to watch, then we all meet up for dinner and vacations."

This was gross hyperbole, with truth at its core. Our children differed completely in age and temperament, and our life made it easy for them to slot themselves. There were athletic kids for Harry to hang out with, booky ones for Hannah, little ones for Ivy. With an eight-year range between eldest and youngest, we could barely find a movie everyone could enjoy. I spent workdays missing the kids, but then when I was with them—zooming around town, *making our lives work*—it wasn't quite the togetherness I fantasized about.

Anthony was still formulating a response.

"Oh, also," I remembered, "Harry thinks we're poor. He was wearing sixty-dollar cleats when he mentioned this."

Anthony laughed, and then he slept. I set the alarm for six, and began laying the groundwork for my own best shot at losing consciousness: I lay on my side tilted forward, a pillow between my knees and one scrunched by my chest with my top arm holding it tight. My head rested on a third, which I squished thick and supportive under my neck.

I took comfort in a mental to-do list. I'd sleep better with everything laid out, my moves plotted for the next few days.

- Finish spec for Thursday review
- Grilled bread salad for Ivy
- Support our troops (bring them home)
- Divide the rhubarb
- Stop turning everything into a list—you're acting like a crazy person.

Suddenly it occurred to me that a radical change might be warranted. I had an idea. Or an aneurysm, or something.

"Wait," I said aloud and poked Anthony in the shoulder. He'd closed his eyes almost a minute ago, so naturally he was deep in a REM cycle. I poked him again.

"I think we should move to Costa Rica."

Anthony struggled to his elbows, tried to shake off the groggy.

"Wait...what?"

"Seriously. Hannah will be in high school in two years. It'll be too late. We need to go now."

Anthony sat up in bed and was silent for a long moment. Then he said this: "Hmmm. Yeah. Let's." And went back to sleep.

I sat up, kicked away the extra pillows, and began revising my list.

2

Our Life in Nine Conversations

What makes a person know with absolute clarity what must be done next? What gives her the freedom to step up and out—not of a simple, unencumbered life, but of a life filled with connection and obligation?

I had awakened that morning to a normal day and had lived it normally. By its end I was in a funk, but that was just part of the picture. Most things were pretty good. Three interesting, involved kids who didn't beat on each other more than anyone else's. A tree house and backyard chickens, here in the middle of the city. A decent living. There was nothing to flee, here. No unnamed longings or secret despairs. Why was I suddenly done? What snapped that night that had been holding fast in the morning?

And was Anthony done, too? Or was his unquestioning willingness simply a measure of his trusting good nature?

Anthony's tri-syllabic thumbs up was typical. Our marriage was almost thirteen years old, and I couldn't think of a single pivotal conversation during which Anthony had spoken more than fifty words.

Inevitably, when I got close enough to a friend who knew us both, the question came:

"So. You and Anthony. Explain."

What I had was this story.

Anthony and I had started dating a year after I'd graduated from college. I'd spent a year teaching at a Massachusetts boarding school, and was regrouping at home and dating a couple of guys (my first and, it would turn out, only go at non-exclusive dating). My dad had taken to calling them, collectively, "MM's swains" and referring to them by haircut. Anthony and I had seen each other a few times when he did me the favor of stopping by my father's office to pick up a book I wanted to borrow. The two had never met, though my dad had seen Anthony in passing. They shared the same deadpan humor, a fact I'd mentioned to neither. I was curious to hear what my father would think of this guy.

When I thought Anthony would be safely out of the office, I set down my Diet Coke to dial my dad and get the verdict. It turned out Anthony had only just arrived.

"Your buzzcut swain is here," my father said. "Do you want to talk to him?"

"I like to think of him as my perfect-teeth swain. And sure."

I heard my dad hand the phone over to my sort-of boyfriend. Standing right next to his sort-of girlfriend's father, whom he had just met, Anthony took the phone and said, sternly and without missing a beat, "I thought I told you never to call me here."

Life is a mystery, love is a delight, and faith defies logic. On many obvious levels, Anthony and I didn't make sense. No one would connect the dots between us and say *aha*.

But to be with Anthony was to never know when my Diet Coke might come shooting out of my nose.

We dated for about a year and then broke up. Either I was wound too tightly or he was too laid back; either I needed too many words or he needed too few; either I wanted too much connection or he was too fundamentally solitary. On any spectrum, Anthony and I waved to each other from its farthest ends. Whether it was a too-muchness in me or a too-little in him didn't really matter; it seemed a poor setup for the long term. But we still made each other laugh and the sex was great; the breakup didn't really take. We were in a nebulous, friends-with-occasional-benefits zone when I found myself constantly sleepy. I took a test. Holding the white stick gingerly so as to avoid the pee, I watched as a pair of blue lines bloomed instead of the prayed-for single.

If you're thirty-six, professional, and can hear the clock ticking, unplanned single motherhood is kind of edgy and hip and brave. At twenty-four and barely employed, I was just tacky.

It wasn't what my people did.

I'd grown up solidly middle class, in a Seattle that didn't even pretend to be a real city (back before Microsoft, Starbucks, Amazon). I'd gone from there to a fancy liberal arts college, and my new friends spent their twenties traveling and forming bands, going to grad school and making art, being poor until they decided to knock that shit off and become lawyers.

We had all been blessed with choices on a scale beyond any our parents— especially our mothers— had known. I'd chosen my own college and taken my pick of majors. Now, I was marginally employed by choice, while I weighed the relative merits of the Peace Corps, grad school, or traveling randomly until I ran out of money. The Trans-Siberian Railway seemed like it might be worth my time.

But on the day of the two lines, I knew that my first true choosing, the first that mattered, had arrived. I closed my eyes and gripped my pee stick.

I would have this baby. I would be its mother.

I set aside dreams of Russia and trains and masters programs. I would learn instead how to snap a baby into a stretchy little suit. How to fund a family. How to be grown up.

Two lines. The adventures I'd been planning for the rest of my twenties became, in that instant, the kinds of things other people did.

I asked Anthony if we could meet on his lunch break.

A freakishly slow eater, Anthony usually packed his lunch so as not to waste valuable chewing time standing in a line. We headed to West Queen Anne Playfield, two blocks from the market research office where he worked the reception desk. The brown paper bag in Anthony's hand made him look even more impossibly young than his short, dark hair and open, guileless face. *This cannot be happening.*

The March day was sunny and ass-freezingly cold—at least it would keep me awake. We found a splintery park bench, and in atypical (for me) silence watched a team of eight-year-olds trying to catch baseballs. We did not find them particularly cute.

I didn't know what to do with my hands. At last I settled on biting the nails of one and putting the other on Anthony's knee. Too high-drama—I pulled it back. I made a few false starts, taking a deep breath then doing nothing with it. I shifted, and began to use what was left of my fingernails to pick at splinters on the bench. Anthony was patient, as always. He covered my cold hand with his warm one and waited for me to spit it out.

Blue-lipped and exhausted, I finally explained the existence of an embryo, and that it was going to become a full-on baby. I explained that the baby part and the Margot-as-mother part were nonnegotiable—my body, my choice. I said we should figure out whether, and how, Anthony might want to be involved.

He was very quiet.

Early in our relationship, when pregnancy had been more of a theoretical state to me than a physical one, I'd somehow had the presence of mind to talk with Anthony about my stance on abortion. Politically: yes. Personally: not for me. Having that conversation in our history meant there was never any question that I had somehow engaged in a bunch of good-time sex, then changed the rules. I don't know how important this was or wasn't to Anthony, but it was critical to me.

Now, I told Anthony that I wanted him to be only as present, emotionally and financially, as he wanted to be, but that I needed him to figure it out in the next several months and stick with it.

"I don't want a daddy popping in and out of this baby's life. I know I don't know what I'm doing. I'm freaking terrified of how much I don't know what I'm doing. But whatever I'm going to provide, it's going to be something this baby can count on."

Anthony held my hand and said that makes sense. He touched my cheek and said, "We'll figure something out. Let's get you inside." Then, as he did every day, Anthony folded his paper bag so he could reuse it tomorrow.

I found a freelance tech-writing gig, while Anthony and I worked to figure out a plan for ourselves. For all of our differences, he and I lucked out by sharing some core convictions. One was that pregnancy was an insane reason for two people to get married.

"So you're saying no shotgun, right?" Anthony asked.

"No shotgun. And we'll never lie to this baby about its origins. Ever. There's nothing shameful here."

"Also," I added, "I will kick the shins of anyone who uses the word 'mistake.'"

Anthony and I considered vocabulary options.

"I think we can say 'surprise,' though," he said.

"Yes. Perfect. Surprise."

My planning instinct was beginning to shove aside the abject terror instinct. This was, in terms of getting through the day, helpful.

That summer, living together in a strange, but strangely okay, limbo, Anthony and I both happened to wake up one morning with a solidly permanent feeling. I was seven months pregnant when we exchanged rings on the north bluff of Discovery Park, overlooking a sparkling Puget Sound.

Hannah's birth that fall set off a chain reaction of decisions that Anthony and I had never set out to make. But within our real and often painful struggles—money and roles, personalities and sleeplessness, not knowing which way was up much of the time—the two of us loved being parents. We were just young enough to think we'd invented it; that before us, no two people had been quite so unable to stop staring at their sleeping child. Or, for that matter, their awake one.

"I know everyone thinks their baby is beautiful," I said one day when Hannah was about four months old. I had her sitting in the bathroom sink. She liked it there; it helped her sit up, and she loved to put her mouth on the cool, smooth knob of the faucet. I was brushing my teeth over the shower, as had become my custom.

I continued about other people's babies. "And I'm sure they're really fine. But Hannah is, objectively, unusually gorgeous. It's only surprising because the two of us are so ordinary."

"I don't feel bad for the other babies," said Anthony, leaning into the stall and spitting expertly down the drain. "They're little and don't know. But I worry about the parents. It must be hard to look at Hannah and suddenly figure out you got an ugly baby."

Over the next few years, I created a decent little business, doing freelance writing and project management for high-tech companies. The only thing I wasn't working on was my marriage. If I'd thought I needed to justify this, I would have said, "Well, neither is Anthony." Hah!

Was this how it was supposed to be? I had no idea and nothing to compare it to.

Our college friends were light years from parenting and had no concept of what our lives were like. When Hannah was nearly three and I was still walking gingerly from giving birth to Harry, a pal of Anthony's came to crash on our couch for a week while he contemplated maybe going to grad school or something. He threaded his way between toddler toys and breastfeeding books to Hannah's bedroom one night, where I'd been scratching her back for so long I could barely feel one arm. In the other, I held a nursing newborn. It was nearly 10 p.m.

Colin peeked in the door. "So, do you guys want to grab like a babysitter or something, meet up with some people for a drink?"

Those were our old friends. My new ones, the mommy-baby-groupers, hadn't messed with the order of operations the way we had. All the other parents seemed like spiritual soul mates who found each other, then started buying furniture. They'd spent a decade building up savings accounts and taking tantric sex classes before they traded in birth control for ovulation predictor kits. I knew our marriage would never look like theirs.

That night, after Colin went out, I dared for the first time to ask the question:

"Are you ever sorry we did it this way?"

"Of course not."

"No seriously—you could be out drinking with Colin and Jack right now, getting laid later, and sleeping in tomorrow. Or you could be married to someone more like you—calm and quiet and not insane. Really, you don't have regrets?"

"Well, the getting laid part sounds nice."

The world of software into which I'd stumbled didn't hold a lot of interest for me, but I worked my ass off and the money was fine. Eventually, I ended up where everyone in high tech did back then. I knew in the first week that Microsoft was a world of its own.

The hallways were filled with twenty-three-year-olds; I was ancient at twenty-nine. My third day, I made small talk with a teammate so fresh from biz school she was still practically clutching her diploma. Jenny asked about Hannah and Harry, whose pictures she'd noticed on my desk. I told her their ages and how stupendously adorable and perfect they were, and she said she couldn't wait to have kids.

"Do you think that'll happen soon?" I asked politely. The rock on her finger was hard to miss.

"Oh no. No. Not while I'm working," she said to me. "My fiancé and I talked about it; we're going to wait to have children until we retire."

So. I spent my days with the hyperambitious, and then I came home to Anthony. In the years since I'd met him in the park with my surprising news, Anthony had moved to a new role and a new desk at the little market-research company, but was still earning barely more than when he'd been answering the phone. He was cool with it.

I wasn't troubled so much by Anthony's lack of ambition—he was smart and funny and handsome and a great dad, which is a pretty winning package. But I hated what that lack meant for me. It was a delicate subject, so of course I approached it with my trademark empathy and understanding.

"Do you think it's right that I earn all the money?"

"No."

"Well, what are you going to do about it?"

"I don't know."

"That's not an answer! You have to think! I can't do all the thinking for all of us, all the time. I am So. Fucking. Tired. If this keeps up, by the time Harry can talk he won't know who I am."

Silence.

"Do you think I should have to do all the problem solving around this? Am I somehow misguided, in believing that's hardly a partnership? Feel free to correct me here. Have I gotten something wrong?"

"No."

"We both know you're not stupid. Why won't you think? Why won't you help? Why won't you *step the fuck up*?"

Unanswerable questions. So Anthony didn't answer.

After a few years and a wizard marriage counselor, I stopped the haranguing. I never got okay with the earning situation, but I ended up in a place that kind of worked. Somewhere slightly more cheerful than resignation, far less self-actualized than true acceptance. By the time Harry was four, there was just one thing missing.

"I know it's crazy. I just feel like...we're not done. Like there's another person before we're *us*."

"Um, yesterday you said we don't have enough money or time, and we should at least have one or the other." Anthony is a good-sense machine. "You said that every so often you hate being married."

Well, who doesn't?

It was a pickle. I didn't want to argue my way into a baby, but I also didn't know what to do with this bedrock certainty that there was another person out there for our family. My thinking was further complicated by strong convictions about world population: We all had the right to replace ourselves, but no more. But my pal Victoria had promised never to procreate, and when I asked if I could have her allotment, she was more than gracious.

"If anyone should be putting more people in the world, it's you guys," she said.

Well. What a nice thing to say.

"You're completely right about all the reasons not to," I said to Anthony, a couple of weeks into my ongoing monologue on the topic. "But I think they're smoke. I think what's really going on is that you just hate change."

Anthony turned this over for a long minute.

"You're right," he said, pulling me up off the couch. "I trust you. Let's go."

Two parents can get a lot done without talking much, especially if one of them is a driven maniac and the other is totally willing to go along with whatever. And I loved being a family.

By the spring of 2000, we could finally afford a faraway vacation. Hannah and Harry, nine and six, were old enough to learn the importance of doing work for others, something I had so far failed to weave into the fabric of our daily lives. A group called Global Volunteers willing to take us, even toting twenty-month-old Ivy, on one of their "volunteer vacations." (You work hard and pay for the privilege.)

In Monteverde, Costa Rica, four of us worked on trails in the rainforest with a group of twelve other volunteers. Ivy, who still worked best with tools that came in primary colors, got babysat nearby. In the afternoons, she toddled from one volunteer to another, being cute.

That week, amid the trails and the toddling and the making sure Harry didn't nail himself to anything, I got a giant crush on Costa Rica. It started when I learned a bit of its twentieth-century history: In 1949, the country's leadership noticed that they had enough money for an army or decent schools, but not both. When the Army got the boot, someone supposedly said, "We will replace the army of soldiers with an army of teachers." Since then, Costa Rica has managed to provide both education and a lack of crackpot dictators to its citizenry. The country's crime rate is negligible and its literacy, high. I understood why Costa Ricans could sound the tiniest bit smug when they talked about their neighbors on the isthmus.

We visited a K-12 school in Monteverde, which was created for *Ticos*—native Costa Ricans. *Tico* is a friendly term, not at all pejorative. (*Gringo*—or

Gringa, for the girls—can be disparaging, but if you are one, you get to use it.) The school was made for locals but welcomed international students. The campus had modest buildings in a lavish setting: over a hundred acres perched high on a hilltop, overlooking a clean, green world.

At the lower school, butterflies congregated on bushes scattered among swing-sets and slides. A pathway through lush forest led to the upper school, with a clearing between for a soccer pitch. Hummingbird feeders, hanging from the eaves, ringed individual classroom buildings. Everyone seemed relaxed.

"Wouldn't it be incredible," I said to Anthony, "to spend a whole year here, and send the kids to this school?"

"It would," he answered. "Someday."

We went home. We kept working the jobs and raising the children, though I felt increasingly out of step with the super-vigilant parenting culture that surrounded us. This made me prickly and defensive.

"I don't think I'm a careless parent," I said to Anthony, who already agreed with me. "I think I'm a careful parent."

"I think so, too."

"I just...don't you think does children a huge disservice when we teach them the world is out to get them?"

"I do."

Hannah had just finished fifth grade, and I'd decided it was time for her to learn to take the city bus. I created a scavenger hunt that would take her and her friend Lucy to all of their usual places—school, each other's houses, a movie theatre. After they negotiated this successfully, we'd give Hannah a bus pass and some freedom.

"I feel like the good mothers shake their heads behind my back," I said to Anthony. "Like parental love is somehow measured by how many miles I put on the car."

I couldn't stop picturing the other mothers, clucking their tongues at the poor bus-stop girl as they Volvo'd past. Thinking I was neglecting my daughter when in fact I was trying to give her a gift.

"Who cares what they think?" Anthony said. He reminded me that Lizzie, Lucy's mom, was an excellent mother *and* was totally down with the bus-pass plan. We moved forward.

We'd made a life! Who knew you could just *do* that?

It was a life I loved deeply. If, over the years, I felt trapped by the trials that came with having babies before I had a savings account, by working long hours in order to meet everyone's needs, by having daycare teachers witness more of my children's firsts than I did, I mostly brushed it off. Except for a couple of nasty years and the occasional bad dinner party, I had concentrated on the many good parts.

But would I have hauled my entire family to Central America if I'd gotten there myself as a twenty-something backpacker, instead of spending those years changing diapers? I don't know.

I do know that, from the moment I became a parent, I always had a list in my head of the things I wanted to do *once I had some time*. My list was not particularly creative and was certainly not unique: More time with my hands in the garden and my nose in a book. More cooking and baking. More time to be a mother, a partner, a person. By 2003 I longed for a life that was as rich and full as the one we had—but with a bit less commotion.

Thirteen years before, Anthony and I had chosen each other. In terror and in hope, and with a level of gameness that was idiotic or charming, depending on the light. In the years that followed, we continued to choose each other— over and over, sometimes surprising ourselves. We chose to have another baby, and then another still. (I kept waiting for one of our many child-free friends to quietly slip me a pamphlet, murmuring, "I just thought you might want to know why this keeps happening to you.")

In the middle of the night, over a decade after that first big-kid choice, I poked Anthony awake and we made another: we would quit our jobs, cross our fingers, and jump—right off the edge of our lives.

Now, as enlightened, empowering, twenty-first-century parents, we just had to trick the children into agreeing.

3

On the Tarmac

I'd assumed the entire universe unwrapped its school supplies at the start of September.

Not so! The morning after Anthony's and my midnight exchange, I learned that the little mountaintop school in Costa Rica we'd visited three years before would start its new academic year in mid-July, just under eight weeks away.

We usually tried to ensure everyone felt heard in family decisions. This was practical as well as philosophical—the whole thing would crash and burn if the kids didn't buy in. I dug a piece of white poster board out of the space beneath the stairs, where I conducted a perpetually losing battle to keep art supplies organized, and found colored Sharpies in the kitchen drawer. I headed the poster board MOVING TO COSTA RICA and called a Family Meeting to Consider a Thrilling Adventure.

Pros on the left, Cons on the right. I transcribed everything verbatim, adding asterisks and possible mitigations to Cons. (Middle management, anyone? Don't let anyone tell you you aren't yourself in every single action.)

I'D REALLY MISS MY FRIENDS → Pick a couple of favorites and talk to their parents—visiting possible?

I DON'T WANT TO MISS BASEBALL SEASON!! → The last tournament ends the day before the first day of school in CR. Doable?

I left the poster board hanging in the living room. With a pen, so any of us could add to it.

I do not do secrecy well. In the days that followed my nocturnal brainwave/ ruptured blood vessel, I told two friends what we were contemplating. I chose Victoria because I wanted encouragement and Lizzie because it felt like a betrayal not to.

Vic was my closest friend-without-children. A brilliant painter and committed adventurer, Vic had never, to my knowledge, let anything keep her from doing exactly what she wanted to do. Vic would help me be brave.

"So we're thinking of going to Costa Rica for a year, the whole family. We know of a school, and..."

"Outstanding. Do it."

"Well, it's kind of complicated, pulling the kids away from everything they know. Hannah's at such a tricky age."

"Margot. No-brainer. Do it."

"And work. We'd have to quit. Coming back, we might not be able to find..."

"Go. Get out of here. Why are you still talking to me?"

Telling Lizzie was a whole other thing.

I'd met Lizzie in the vegetable patch at McGilvra Elementary, the day our daughters started kindergarten. Lizzie and I had bonded the bond of two mothers who aren't usually crazy but find themselves working hard not to cry.

Hannah and Lucy, now in middle school, had been inseparable since that day in the garden, and Lizzie was my closest mom friend. Her son, Galen, was Harry's buddy. Even our husbands got along. Whether there was a movie to see or a weekend to plot, Lizzie, Nick, Lucy, and Galen were our go-to people. It was a measure of our friendship that I didn't hold it against Lizzie that she never offered to produce her own third, a homegrown playmate for Ivy.

When I told Lizzie what we were considering, her eyes welled. She waved her hand in front of her face, and said, "No, no, no. Ignore me. It sounds amazing. Really. I'm so excited for you guys."

Five days after we'd begun our poster board, the margins were full—an answer for every Con. That evening, we'd stopped at home between Harry's baseball game and dinner at my mom's. On impulse I grabbed the sign as we ran out the door. The twenty-five minutes between home and Grandma's would be enough to get the decision ball rolling.

We piled into the ancient Toyota Previa, the only stick shift minivan anyone had ever seen.

Anthony drove. I rode shotgun, turning around to face Hannah in the middle seat and Harry in the way back. (Ivy was missing from her customary spot next to Hannah, having slept at her grandparents' the night before. Perfect. At four, Ivy was too young to contribute anyway—we'd tell her something thrilling: "There'll be horses!" Ivy would be fine.) I held up the poster board like a teacher and poised my Sharpie to begin running through the lists.

"So. How do you guys want to talk about this?"

Pause—not a long one.

Harry: "I think we should just go."

Hannah added logic: "We thought of every reason not to, and none of them were really that good."

Anthony and I looked at each other. Was it really that easy?

It was.

We were six blocks from our house, not even to the freeway yet. But we were off.

When people asked how we *explored* the idea of moving to Costa Rica, I told them the minivan story: We just decided to. Seven weeks later, we went.

In between, we fielded a lot of questions. Most were about the financing.

People who were just making ends meet asked detailed questions. Our favorite clerk at the video store, who kindly ferreted out every popular DVD with a Spanish-language soundtrack, had a hundred: How much had we saved (nothing), how much would we need to earn while we were there (unclear), were we Microsoft millionaires (not by a very long shot), what would our rent be ($400/month).

But the Audi-and-Escalade crowd—we knew many, thanks as much to Harry's career as a miniature elite athlete as to my career building software— displayed no interest in the finances of how this was all going to go down. They asked about school (yes), how we'd learn Spanish (osmosis?), and whether we were worried about safety (no). Same with our trustafarian pals, the ones with ancient cars and no discernible need to produce income...except these guys didn't touch the safety question. I think they feared it was vaguely racist, or at least that it displayed an inappropriate level of ethnocentrism.

We also got a lot of code:

"Wow, that's great! How will you, um...will you work?"

"Is this something you've been saving toward for a long time?"

"That is so cool you can afford to do that. So you left Microsoft...when did you start?" (Hint: *When did you start?* is Pacific Northwest for asking Microsofties whether they hit the jackpot. If the answer is any time before 1994, chances are your pal could buy you your house. Under those same conditions but with a pre-1990 start date and no vitriolic divorce, she should buy you an island. I started in 1997, and left with a whole lot of worthless stock options. But the paycheck was regular; we'd always found it useful.)

When people asked their questions, coded or not, Anthony and I answered. We were our own Freedom of Information Act.

- No, we are not independently wealthy. We could never stop working and stay in Seattle for a year unless we gave up luxuries like food and a roof.
- But we're incredibly fortunate, no question, and we bought our house at a good time. We'll live on about $850 a month, which is the difference between our mortgage payment and what we can get in rent.
- One reason we're going to Costa Rica instead of, say, Paris, is that the cost of living difference works in our favor.
- If we want to travel once we're down there, we'll have to find some work. But we're not going to worry about that yet. Mostly because we need to pack.

Staying alive in the competitive, fast-changing world of technology had required that I become deeply organized. Or maybe I stuck around high-intensity high-tech because an innate drive to write things down and then cross them off made me a decent fit. Either way: You can perhaps imagine how, listmakingwise, moving a family of five to a whole different country was something of a mountaintop experience.

We decided that Anthony would work until the last minute, and I'd quit now and get us the hell out of Dodge.

As I'd begun to predict from my first Lizzie encounter, the hardest thing about my moving-to-Central-America list wasn't its length or the logistical nightmares it contained. Getting the kids enrolled in school, renting out our house, and finding an orthodontist in a language I did not speak were nothing compared to telling people we loved that we were leaving.

Anthony and I are Puget Sound natives. The fact that we had relatives crawling all over our lives wasn't always easy, but it was us. To the grandparents, there was much explaining of the difference between Nicaragua under General Somoza and a Quaker-founded town in army-free Costa Rica. I promised my mother repeatedly that I would not be foolhardy with the grandchildren. I tried to remember that some things a person just needs to say out loud. Even if she's implying that, without a reminder, I might ask a guerrilla to babysit the children.

"Costa Rica isn't like that," I told her. "Think of it as Central America Lite."

My sister was less panicked, but still sad. The two of us had grown up as enemies, or maybe just foreigners. After she followed her *magna cum laude* in Economics with an Ivy League Ph.D. (oh, she just *would*), Erin had become a consultant in D.C. (of *course*). But as she started making a career and I started making babies, we'd grown on one another. My sister had been a world-class long-distance auntie for Harry and Hannah, but my third pregnancy pushed her past a tipping point. In Ivy's infancy, Erin ditched an other-Washington salary and loads of prestige for a Seattle quality of life. She'd been such a presence for Ivy that her youngest niece's r-less pronunciation of her name stuck for all of us. How would we leave Auntie En?

And friends. Lizzie wouldn't be surprised—she'd heard the way I was talking. But she burst into tears and told me, working hard to smile, congratulations. Child-free Vic happened to be on the scene. Lizzie and I talked about ways to keep our daughters in touch, and what it would be like for them to tackle seventh grade without each other.

Vic fled.

But that night, I got an email.

"You know," Vic wrote, "as a less-encumbered girl, it's possible I didn't have my head around exactly how big a deal this would be for a family."

Before we left, Vic painted a beautiful watercolor, filled with tiny homey things: boots and houses, mittens and steaming mugs, and an inscription up the side: *A lot of places can feel like home.*

The painting was little and easy to pack. I knew I would find a place for it, wherever we were, for a very long time.

I was relieved when word of our plan started to spread. The excitement of our wider circles moved the enterprise back into the Adventure column; it had been filed, for a few days, under Abandonment.

Place to live: check.

A guy from the States would rent us the top part of a duplex he owned. He typically used it to house nature guides who worked for his ecotourism business, but he could make better money from us. We committed for three months sight unseen, having neither the time, money, nor interest for a house-hunting expedition. When Dave sent us our mailing address, it read:

Just Behind Pizzeria de Johnny
Cerro Plano
Puntarenas, Costa Rica

Perfect.

Orthodontia would be my first foray into dealing with medical care in Costa Rica. Our Seattle dentist had found us a name and number in a secret book they all have, which lists every orthodontist in the universe. Using my single week of Spanish instruction (but it was an *intensive* week), I spent an entire afternoon composing my letter to Dr. de la Rosa. My brain bled. I stomped around the house, then buckled back down. I looked up verb tenses—*I can't misconjugate in front of the orthodontist!* Finally, I clicked "Send" on a three-paragraph marvel that said, basically,

"My daughter has braces. Can you please watch them for us?"

Before I had time to mop my brow, the reply dinged into my inbox. I steeled myself for a new round of translation.

The email began:

Hi Margot,

It would be a pleasure to continue Hannah's treatment once you get here. There is a standardized transfer protocol and I am sure Dr. Murata will help you with that. He and I can be in touch ahead of your travels to Costa Rica.

I got my orthodontic training at the University of Washington in Seattle, graduated in 1992. I loved Seattle, it is a great city...

My exchange with Dr. de la Rosa was the first surprise of many of that particular nature: I would prepare carefully for something, only to have it turn out to be a nonevent. To keep balance in my universe, some leave-taking tasks that I assumed would be straightforward turned out to be anything but.

It would be difficult to overstate the pain in the ass that was the Seattle public school system. Harry's spot in his much-desired school was in no way guaranteed if he left it, and we'd be in Monteverde when it came time to sign him back up. The district offices were half an hour away and on the way to absolutely nowhere. I pleaded, gnashed teeth, came near to tears, and got nowhere. Finally, "Harry, fifth grade" joined "M. & A. get jobs" on the list of things we'd have to deal with when we got back.

When I wasn't winding myself up in red tape, I worked on packing up a house that hadn't been de-cluttered since...ever. One day, Lizzie found me kneeling by the bathtub, into which I had emptied every shelf and drawer from both bathrooms. She knelt beside me and fished out a gummy collection of ancient hotel soaps.

"Being at your house always makes me feel better about mine," she said, and I stuck out my tongue at her. We hovered over the tub, separating spent Chapstick tubes from save-worthy bottles of fancy conditioner.

"So I've been wondering," Lizzie said. "No jobs, nothing but time...does it make you nervous? Have you and Anthony ever even been around each other 24/7?"

"No time for nervous," I said. "Hey, hand me that box. When we come back, it'll be Toiletry Christmas."

One week later, we were ready to leave the country. We had to be—some people were coming to live in our house.

July – September

4

Takeoff

Take, Store, Get Rid Of. One hundred percent of children got less clingy about their belongings when told they could pocket the proceeds from a yard sale.

Everyone had been allotted a single trunk and daypack. (I knew how Harry's mind worked, and made some minimal clothing requirements.) One at a time I watched each of us try to stuff three trunks' worth of life into one trunk's worth of space. Harry left his baseball bat but brought his mitt and roll-up chessboard. Hannah sacrificed four of ten books in order to fit a handmade calendar gifted by Lucy. It featured countdowns marking milestones until Hannah's return and was thick with pictures of the two of them from kindergarten on.

From Ivy's piles of stuffed animals, it was always going to be Bloody who made the cut. Ivy had named her floppy stuffed elephant "Audrey" at age two but changed it to Bloody a year later. If you asked her why, she'd shrug, tell you, "Bloody sounds pwetty," and walk away. Why were people such idiots?

My own big tradeoff was kitchen oriented. Colander or waffle iron? Our family had an unnatural relationship with yeast-raised waffles. They were our primary comfort food, and we might need comfort. But who can survive without noodles? Okay, colander.

Anthony had the same space requirements as the rest of us, but if he made a painful tradeoff he did not mention it.

My trunk was also the family space, and I packed it with a mixture of items sentimental and practical. Vic's painting. Three DVDs, chosen for their Spanish-language soundtracks (much harder to find than French, I discovered. The planet might have five times as many Spanish speakers as French, but France has infinitely more Cannes):

- *Newsies*
- *The Princess Bride*
- *12 Angry Men*

Anthony and I had decided on a staggered departure. He and Hannah would do recon and setup, leaving on a Monday night in early July and arriving in San José midmorning. At the airport, they would hire a driver and van for the final leg of the journey: four hours up a winding dirt road to Monteverde and the house Just Behind Johnny's Pizzeria.

While those two were setting up life behind Johnny's, I would scrub Seattle cupboards, get keys made for tenants, and watch Harry's final baseball tournament. Getting Harry to this event was a deal we'd made from the poster board, which had become our leave-taking Ten Commandments.

At last the winnowing was done, the basement stacked to the ceiling. The tenants had wanted our beanbag chairs, sewn by my mother back when we could afford furniture or diapers, but not both, so those remained. Our five trunks formed a line down the center of the living and dining rooms. We'd use them as a buffet at today's goodbye party. Tonight, Anthony and Hannah would fly away.

When I have a summer party, I like a thing to do. This year, we made stepping stones. I'd gathered all kinds of junk to put in them—coins and beads and keys. Even an old copper garden spigot, appropriated immediately by Vic. She combined it with a blue costume-jewelry necklace to make the most effortlessly artistic stepping stone ever: a greened-copper spigot dispensing blue water in a beady stream. I hated her a little, looking at my awkward coins-n-keys concoction, but what are you going to do? Some of us are arty, and some of us are me.

At dusk, we lined up the stepping stones and took pictures. My throat constricted at the sight of this concrete quilt, a patch for every person I would miss.

Two hours later, Hannah and Anthony left with the trunks. A group of us waved goodbye at security and were walking back to the car when Ivy announced with great seriousness that she was really excited about Costa Rica, Mommy, but she would be talking in English there. Only English.

I picked up her hand, tucked a stray lock of hair behind her ear, and set her straight. "Honey, I know you *think* you don't want to learn, but we'll find ways to make it really fun!"

Ivy snatched her hand away and shook her hair back in front of her face.

Ivy, Mommy, Spanish. It was *on*.

With pages of to-dos, I'd mostly managed to not to feel the feelings. Then, after four days of running errands and hustling details, I got an email from Anthony:

> I'm vying for the self-appointed moniker of Crazy Can Man of Monteverde. I guess if I want it, I can have it. I try to pick up cans that I see along the road to town and take them to the recycling center (which is, by the way, in our front yard). Today a Tico saw me carrying some cans home in the rain and, in Spanish, he said, "Thanks, tourist." Then I felt very proud. But also I wanted him to know that I'm a community member so I replied, also in Spanish, "My house here" and pointed. Thank God I was so close to home. Otherwise, I wouldn't have known how to convince him how local I am.
>
> Hannah made up an alert system. When she sees a can, she'll let me know by sounding the alarm: "Crazy Can Man, woop woop!" The woops are high pitched but quick. You'll learn.

Somehow, my husband angling for Village Eccentric in a faraway land drove it home for me: We really were leaving everything we knew.

And then I did the walkthrough.

The tenant walkthrough is Routine Procedure, of course. The renters get to nose around and make a note of every imperfection, so they don't get stuck with a bill at the other end. Completely reasonable. I'd done it a hundred times.

They wrote down all the wrong things.

Those crescent-shaped scratches on the wood floors, every two feet from stairway to kitchen? Harry was three when he tried to do the firefighter pole one-handed. The resulting snapped tibia gave Anthony and me our first inkling that we'd spawned the most relentlessly optimistic person on the planet. For six weeks, Harry scooted around on his little butt, scraping his lime-green cast before him and saying things like, "Isn't it good I got a broken leg, Mommy? Now you can always hear me coming!"

Those scrapes are an enhancement. You should pay extra to get to walk on those.

That dent in the drywall? Lord. I was such a wreck that year I could hardly see straight. Tired of feeling like a terrible mother for working full time and a terrible employee for always running out to take a child to <fill in the blank>. But it was just the wall I kicked that awful night, don't you see? Don't put that dent on your list of flaws. Make a new heading: *Things That Remind Us That It Gets Better.*

That pockmarked place in the linoleum under the cutting board, where I always drop knives? You can have that.

On the bleachers, our last day in town, I chatted with the other mothers as we cheered for our sun-kissed sons. I watched twelve hours of baseball, sitting three miles and thirteen years from the day Anthony and I had shivered on a bench, unimpressed by the foreign world of little-boy sports.

Now I was part of that world. I loved those little boys. And before we left, several moms told me how much they loved mine.

"That child will have all of Costa Rica in the palm of his hand," said Beth, a longtime bleacher pal. Other parents laughed and nodded.

Harry had inherited Anthony's affable charm but none of his counteracting reserve. Harry loved the world exuberantly, and it loved him right back. Sometimes I worried about this, in a puritanical, make-lemonade-out-of-lemons kind of way. A childhood filled with unbridled adoration—isn't that how you build a crazed narcissist?

Still, heading into a year that was sure to knock us all around a little, I was grateful for his Harryness. Harry, of all of us, would always be fine.

At the bottom of the ninth, Beth asked why we were doing this crazy thing. Out of the host of reasons, I picked the one that had ended up shining brightest for me those last few weeks.

"It's just...there are so many ways to live a life," I told her. I tried not to sound preachy. "Lately it seems like the overall mood is that the U.S. has everything wired, that the most the world can hope for is to be like us. But there are a million good ways to live a life. I want us to see that."

"Makes sense to me," Beth said.

As if to underline the insane scheduling we were hoping to escape, we would go straight from Harry's final inning to the airport, then start school in Monteverde the next day. We got hugs from teammates and parents, and off we went.

At five we mostly have playmates, not soulmates, and very little sense of time. For Ivy's goodbyes, we parents had colluded to keep it light. Ivy reinforced the idea that farewell was more darling than sad by still not having her r's:

"Bye, Sophie! See you next yeaw! Wite to me in Costa Wica!"

But Erin and Lizzie, who delivered us from the dugout to the airport, had been holding this child from the day she arrived to be held, and they knew how long a year was. Ivy studied their faces and finally understood that all this was bigger than she'd been led to believe. ("There'll be horses!")

The soulless cattle-lines of post-9/11 security were the worst combination of bureaucracy and sadness, like if your first true love broke up with you at the DMV. Lizzie and Erin stayed with us as we wended our way through that awful time and space, and at the final second Lizzie picked Ivy up for one last hug. Ivy clung with arms and hands and legs and began to sob. The Security lady looked at us through narrowed eyes that were conveyor-belt black. She seemed ready to intervene and...what? I didn't want to know. I peeled Ivy off and carried her bodily toward our fabulous new life.

5

Arrival

We've all heard of the tropics, but geographers, when they're being official, call the latitudes that hold Costa Rica the Torrid Zone. *Aptly chosen, geographers,* I thought, as we stepped through the sliding doors of the San Juan Santamaria airport and into what I would forever after think of as the torrids.

Anthony had set up the same driver for us that he and Hannah had found the week before. Most of the year we planned to take public transportation, but this first day I was grateful to have air conditioning waiting for us in the form of Marco Tulio's van.

The hot, sticky plain we set out on is called the Central Valley. To the north, things rise pretty sharply to the vast, green range called the *Cordillera de Tilarán.* It was to the tops of these mountains, far above the heat, that we were heading. The Monteverde rainforest sits at an altitude that, in Washington's Cascade Mountains, would be a ski slope. But Monteverde daytime highs are about sixty-five to eighty degrees, all year, occasionally warmer, occasionally cooler, but never by much. With bright blue skies and soft gray mists, Monteverde boasted a climate recognizable to sissies from Seattle like us.

"Pura vida!" Marco Tulio said to us as he hoisted our stuff to the roof of his van.

Pura vida is the informal Costa Rican motto. Literally: "pure life," but in use it's closest to "It's all good" or "No worries," or "I like you and I hope you have a wonderful day." *Pura vida* was greeting and goodbye, a general statement of goodness. When a Tico said *pura vida* to me, I felt like I'd been blessed.

Marco Tulio and I chatted until we'd exhausted his English and my Spanish—about five minutes. By the time he turned off the Pan-American highway, taking us up the winding, dirt road that grew greener as we climbed, it was just *"Mira, Señora,"* and Marco would point out something he thought I should see. I was grateful to glimpse the toucan and tried not to be insulted when he pointed out a cow. Most exotic was the sloth, motionless in a treetop. Marco slowed way down so we could get a good look. He gestured to tell me how many hours a day this animal sleeps: He flashed fingers that added to eighteen, then closed his eyes and rested his cheek on pressed-together hands, even snoring a little in an elaborate nap-time pantomime. The rest of the time, Marco gestured, the sloth moves from tree to tree, eating.

Soon after, a flock of parrots shrieked overhead, high and fast and green. Harry ducked this way and that, covering his head but peeking up. Were we under some kind of attack?

When five minutes later we heard a second flock approaching, I had caught the parrots' urgency. I gesticulated to Marco, a series of complex hand movements that he cleverly and accurately interpreted as, "PLEASE CAN WE STOP? I MUST GET OUT AND LOOK AT THE PARROTS!"

The second flock passed over as noisily as the first. Where were they going, and what was wrong? We'd just have to wonder, because, we were learning, parrots never stop to tell you anything. Parrots are always in a panic, sounding the alarm that the world is coming apart. There's a lot to get done before Armageddon, and the parrots must get on it immediately.

"Emergency! Emergency!" they told us.

Parrots don't soar like your bigger birds. Parrots are all flappetty flap, squawketty squawk, motion and sound.

Later, I did a little research. "Parrots are often highly vocal," said the tactful scientist.

Psittaciformes is the parrots' science name, and they're reputed to be among the most intelligent of birds. That probably explains why they're so panicked all the time; they have all that important, smart-people shit to do.

Your sloth is relatively stupid, I wanted to tell Marco Tulio, but couldn't figure out the gestures. *You can tell because he just hangs out relaxing for eighteen hours, and then he has snack.*

We drove past a few waterfalls, but either Marco was worried I'd make him stop again, or he figured I could find them for myself. The kids had fallen asleep shortly after we realized that the parrots were overreacting.

Harry and Ivy were so eager to be done traveling that they would have been delighted with a cardboard box to live in. So our Just-Behind-Johnny's house, with its walls and roof and sink and everything, was a paradise. Right away, Ivy knew which bed was hers by the photos of her favorite people that Hannah had taped above it. Mariners colors were flying on Harry's side of the room. The bedroom smelled a little dank to me, but the kids didn't seem bothered.

Hannah glowed as she showed off her own bedroom—a luxury she hadn't had for years.

The kids appreciated the cracks between two boards in the living room, where our top-floor unit had an overhang above an outdoor laundry area. Hannah showed us how to lie on our tummies to squint through and see the washer and dryer below. Handy!

We occupied the top floor of a two-story house. Downstairs lived Julio, who managed the property for our distant landlord. Julio lived with his wife, Elizabeth, and their small son, whose name we missed in the flood of unfamiliar words. Our families shared no spoken language, but all of us smiled a lot. Apparently Julio had managed to warn Anthony via pantomime that the dryer would give you an impressive electrical shock if you touched the metal while removing wet clothing.

"But I forgot," said Anthony, wincing.

Anthony wasn't kidding about the recycling center. This *Centro de Acopio* served the entire community, and sat right next door to our duplex – convenient for the Crazy Can Man.

On the non-*Centro* side of our house, a little stream with a waterfall ran between us and the pizzeria. When it rained, our stream ran brown and full and fast. When the rain stopped, the water cleared. Harry immediately claimed an "alone spot" on a large boulder by the stream, to "just sit and do some thinking." Anthony and I guessed that the first thing Harry would do with his retreat spot would be to invite everyone he met over to see it.

Hannah showed us the banana tree outside her bedroom window. We marveled.

For dinner that first night, we walked twenty yards around to the front of Johnny's and ate pizza.

Before bed, I carefully tacked up Vic's painting with the four thumbtacks I had brought for exactly this purpose. (Remembered to bring to Costa Rica: four thumbtacks. Forgot: driver's license.)

Tomorrow, school would start. Too exhausted to be anxious, we all fell right to sleep.

6

A School in the Sky

We awoke to drizzle the next morning; at least that was familiar. Hannah appeared less queasy than her siblings did about the first day of school. Either her extra week in town had been calming, or she was an excellent faker.

Anthony and Hannah had acquired the school uniform, a simple jeans/school t-shirt combo, for all three kids: blue shirts for the younger kids and maroon for Hannah. She'd be in *colégio*—high school—which in Costa Rica covered grades seven through twelve. For Hannah, the uniform relieved the stress that had begun to mount on school mornings in Seattle. The daily attempt to strike the perfect note between *What, clothes?* and *Obviously trying way too hard.*

Ivy, on the other hand, had started putting together her own thrift-store outfits at age three. Now, she claimed she couldn't find her uniform, so would have to wear her own clothes. I reached under her mattress and fished out the shirt. Ivy slammed it down over her head, shoved her arms through, and promptly re-hid it beneath her cow-spotted purple slicker, which she vowed not to remove. She tucked the legs of her jeans into brand-new ladybug boots, antennae poised and ready.

When we handed Harry his uniform shirt, he said, "Thanks. Hey, look out the window—is that an iguana?"

We were the last bus stop on the main road, a hundred yards before the bus turned off. From there it would go straight uphill for a quarter mile to the school.

We were all old hands at school bus—even Ivy, who'd never yet been on one but had been hauled to the stop since infancy to wait with the big kids. So when the ancient, former Greyhound opened its doors, we boarded with reasonable confidence that this part at least, we could manage. But none of us had ever seen anything like this.

Rather than a few wan zombies, as on a Seattle bus, we faced a laughing, chattering sea of children. We craned our heads, looking for empty seats and pretending it didn't feel weird to be the only white people.

I'd been assured via email that it was fine for parents to ride the school bus the first day. The kids agreed I was permitted to climb on casually, as if I was planning to make sure Ivy got a seat. I would beat it immediately if there were no other mommies. Anthony had already agreed to walk.

The school bus appeared to be carrying not just mothers, but fathers and neighbors as well. Later, I would come to understand that the morning bus runs were a vital piece of the area's transportation network. Farmers headed to the dairy with their milk cans, and parents who worked in town hitched an occasional ride on the school's buses; teachers and the school principal rode it routinely.

I looked to the driver for a clue of what should happen next. He gave us a textbook "move on back" thumb, and I wondered whether preschools worldwide sing "The Wheels on the Bus."

I caught a glimpse of Hannah's face as she pushed up the aisle. Every freckle stood out on her blanched skin. Her jaw was set. I knew in that moment that all day, Hannah would be making a choice: She could act like she had this wired—or she could flee, grab a book, find somewhere small to hide, and never come out.

I let her concentrate.

Hannah found a seat in the back and Harry in the middle. Ivy and I shared the last available perch, across the aisle and one row up from him. She sat on my lap and sank back into my chest.

As the bus left the stop, I could feel Ivy's terror rising. I chattered, hoping to jolly her out of it.

"Can you believe we got to see a hummingbird, right at the bus stop? He was still there when we left—do you think he takes a different bus?" Ivy would not be jollied. What could I know about the first day of kindergarten? I wasn't going to have to *stay* there.

Hannah had vanished into the sea. Harry looked like he was trying to keep it together, but this small city of children was talking, fast, in a whole other language. Even the most social being has a limit to how many people he can take. It looked like Harry might have, for the first time in his nine years, hit his. Later, when Harry spoke like a local, he and I would talk about that first morning—about how much louder a bus full of chatter sounds when you don't understand any of the words.

Ivy reached back. Harry leaned forward and took her outstretched hand. They held on, across the aisle, for the whole ride.

The *Centro de Educación Creativa* (CEC) was the school we'd visited on our volunteer vacation three years before. It was a hippie-founded affair, brimming with good intentions and not much structure. In the 1980s, a mixed group of people from the States and Costa Rica noted that English proficiency provided a serious leg up in employability for Ticos in the burgeoning tourist industry. They created a school that would provide not only language instruction, but a USA-style, positively-disciplined, whole-learning experience for kids from preschool through high school. Ninety-five percent of the CEC student body was Tico, but most of the faculty came from the States. The CEC was more affordable than the Friends School, the Quaker-run affair a couple of kilometers away. CEC kids were often the children of *taxistas* and waitresses; the Friends' population skewed more toward hotel owners and Gringos.

We'd registered for the CEC from the States, agreeing that Anthony and Hannah would check out the local *escuela publica* as soon as they arrived. When they tried, it was clear the school had never encountered a foreigner looking to register. We stuck with the CEC.

"English in the classroom, Spanish on the playground" was how we'd been told it would go there. For Hannah and Harry, all classes would be conducted in English except for *Civicas* (social studies) and *Literatura.* For those subjects, the school would hook the kids up with a Spanish tutor until they could cope.

Yes, I would preemptively tell our friends. *I moved to Latin America so that my kids could learn Spanish, and then I enrolled them in an English immersion school. Knock yourselves out.*

I took Ivy to class. Anthony would watch Hannah and Harry from a distance.

The year that preceded first grade was called *prepa*, and that's where they'd slotted Ivy. The small classroom had concrete floors, flaking paint and ratty supplies, but still felt more familiar than foreign: A colorful stripe of alphabet lined the top of the walls, and smiling parents cooingly peeled terrified children off their legs.

I was enjoying a little kum-bay-ya musing about how, on the first day of kindergarten, we're all alike, *really*—when something about all those smiling mamas hit me and I realized, uh, *no*. I didn't fit in here at *all*. On Hannah's first day of kindergarten I had been far and away the youngest mom present. Here, in my mid-thirties with a five-year-old, I was ancient. Some of the other moms (I saw no dads) looked like students themselves, and even the legal ones didn't look anything like me. These mamas were uniformly stunning: dangly earrings, sleek dark hair, tight jeans, Clearasil skin.

And then there was me.

Middle-height, middle-weight, middle-aged. My unruly shrubbery of tortilla-blond hair (corn, not flour), could barely be subdued in the urban-mom ponytail—that one where you pull your hair through once, then halfway through again. (As if, what, we were all just *too busy* to follow through on that last tug?)

I was pretty sure I'd looked fine in Seattle—your basic youngish, energetic, I-have-better-things-to-think-about-than-eyeliner mom. I even had an extra piercing up high on my left ear. But I had never once considered whether my eyebrows were the right shape—an oversight that suddenly appalled me. I felt my unpainted toes curl, mortified, into my sandals. Nearly every mom in the room was a colorful, flashing vision of caring how you looked. I wondered how to say "frumpy" in Spanish.

But awkward was nothing compared to petrified, so I tried to get over myself. Ivy had stationed herself behind my (stubby, not-quite-smooth-enough) legs. From there, she watched *prepa* spin up around her.

The two teachers—one native speaker of each language, English and Spanish—alternated days teaching. One day, Isabella would conduct class in Spanish; she was one of those people you liked instantly—warm and innately calm, but also, somehow, twinkly. The next day, Connie, who had just a hint of an accent left from her native Wales, led the class entirely in English. Connie's daughter, Courtney, was the other native English speaker in *prepa*. As 13/15ths of the prepa class was Tico, it made sense that Isabella led class the first day. She encouraged the kids to form a circle on the carpet.

I told Ivy and myself firmly to be brave and sit down, assuring us that everything was going to be fine.

During circle time, Ivy stayed face down in my lap while we did *dias de la semana* (days of the week) and observed that the weather was *muy nuboso y lluvioso* (very cloudy and rainy). Ivy emerged when she recognized the tune to *Cumpleaño Feliz* (Happy Birthday), which we sang for the kids who had had birthdays during the prior month's break. When the song ended, Ivy hid again. I, however, was quite brave when Panchito the Rag Doll came around at circle time. I sat him on the back of Ivy's buried head and told him my name and where I lived. The teachers were lovely and didn't try to coerce Ivy into participating. And she was not alone: The first day of kindergarten *is* the first day of kindergarten, and Ivy wasn't the only one clinging to her *mamá*. Many of her classmates also regarded little Panchito in mute terror.

Everything changed for Ivy when it was time to choose an activity. As soon as she figured out what was going on, she sat straight up and shot her hand in the air. When Isabella smiled at her, Ivy pointed at the puzzle area, grabbed the clothespin with her name on it, and hoofed it over quickly to grab My Little Pony before any of the *urchinos* could lay claim. I kissed her and left. She hardly noticed.

While my lap was full, Anthony had been eyeing the big kids in the Upper School Circle. He reported that he'd seen Hannah smiling and chatting with two other girls, one of whom leaned over and kissed Hannah's cheek in greeting.

I'd thought maybe there'd be less physical difference between Hannah and her peers in Costa Rica, but these girls were even more voluptuous than the Seattle girls. Oh, well. They seemed quite friendly as everyone walked off toward the *colégio* classrooms.

Harry, Anthony noted with surprise, looked more uncomfortable and reserved. His fifth-grade class had fifteen kids, prepping for the *colégio* world by having different teachers throughout the day. He would have one teacher for humanities, one for math, and one for environmental science.

Having all three kids in the same school was itself a dream come true. The addition of butterflies, hummingbirds, and the breezes ruffling the trees made this school feel like magic, a fluttering world in the sky. With our children settled, Anthony and I set out to explore.

The CEC sat on 104 acres of pristine forest and meadows, with sweeping views all the way out to the Pacific Ocean. The school emphasized ecological responsibility and sustainability, and as we headed out on a pathway to the meadows, we walked past huge garden plots and tagged plants that looked like class projects. We walked on into less maintained territory. The path wound around and we followed it. There was nowhere we needed to be. I was wondering aloud whether we were heading away from the school or toward it when we found ourselves outside the middle school.

The fifth- and sixth-grade classrooms were stand-alone little buildings whose backs nestled into the hillside and whose fronts reached out to enjoy the view. Large covered porches marched on stilts toward the ocean. The class could sit outside for discussion, seated at built-in tables, watching as the weather swept over the valley.

"Hard school for a daydreamer," I said.

"Or really, really easy," Anthony answered.

Harry's math teacher, Miss Marti, saw us and motioned us inside for a look.

Harry stood at the blackboard with four other boys, all of whom were taller than he was. The others were messing around, poking each other with chalk, as Harry quietly worked through the division problems, looking straight at the board. For the second time that day I saw that Harry, like his big sister, was working hard to keep it together. I couldn't remember another time the two of them had faced the same challenge, at the same time.

The other boys kept jostling each other. One of the chief jostlers was the most out-of-control gorgeous child I had ever laid eyes on. His wide, dazzling, smile fronted dimples so deep I kind of wanted to poke a pencil into one, eraser-end first. Just for Science, to see if it would stay. Huge dark eyes stood out from his creamy-pale face, surrounded by lashes so thick and so black that I could see them from across the room. Looking at this boy, I could tell that the universe knew Tom Cruise had gotten creepy, and that we needed someone new to light us up. I was looking at a matinee idol before the matinee got him.

"That's Diego," Miss Marti came over. "Insane, right? You get used to it, kind of."

She pointed out the boy next to him, and told us he was Pedro, an exceptionally fantastic kid whom she'd assigned to be Harry's buddy. Pedro would show Harry the ropes, making sure he had someone to sit with at lunch, translating when necessary. Pedro had been making mischief at the board, but now he settled down. He looked over at us, flashing an open smile that was just a regular amount of gorgeous. I liked him. A huge man's watch dwarfed his wrist, and he somehow wore his t-shirt tucked into his jeans without looking prissy. Next to Pedro, a taller boy glowered at the board and shoved his hands in his pockets.

"Stefan's sweet, when you get beyond the swagger," said Miss Marti. "But math really pisses him off."

Harry had finished his problems and looked around briefly. Now he was examining his chalk.

"He looks kind of lost," Anthony said. "It's weird."

Miss Marti assured us that Harry would be fine, but Anthony and I were a bit shaken. It had never occurred to us that Harry could be anything but.

Anthony and I left the boys working a new set of problems and went to spy on Hannah. The kids were all inside. I lurked hopefully, a respectful distance from the classrooms.

"Do you think it would be weird for me to go closer and poke around just a little, just to make sure she's fine?"

Anthony cocked an eyebrow. Right.

We headed down the hill as the clouds came in, and arrived behind Johnny's Pizzeria in a downpour. Dripping all over the floor, we looked at each other.

"Wow. We're here."

"Crazy."

And then the red-eye caught up with me and I fell asleep, still in my wet clothes.

Too soon, I opened my eyes to see Ivy's giant brown ones, peering in my bedroom window. She ran in, jumped on my bed, and said: "I! Love! School!"

According to Anthony, when he met Ivy at the bus stop, she jumped off the last step with both feet, saying "School was GWEAT!" She told me about Courtney, the other non-Tico kindergartner. Courtney didn't speak Spanish either (Seriously? I mean, if ever a name screamed Latina …), and her mommy was the teacher. And one girl Ivy really liked spoke English *and* Spanish. Plus, "There's only one other person with blonde hair in the whole class, Fabiana, and SHE only speaks in SPANISH!"

It would turn out that Courtney was from Seattle. Not only that, but her dad, Graham, and I had attended Garfield High School at the same time. Before they moved to Costa Rica, the family had lived about ten blocks from us on Capitol Hill. Graham and I were all, "Whoa!" but Anthony just said "Wow, it sure took you guys a long time to find each other. What's up with that?"

After school, Diego came over. He told us, dimpling and gesturing, that we should cut our big clump of bananas so they could ripen far from thieving wildlife. Later, Hannah and I went out to do the deed. But as Hannah pulled the clutch of bananas toward us, the whole damn tree came down. With one arm, she felled our banana tree. Was this supposed to happen? Diego hadn't mentioned it. Or maybe he had—how would I know? Regardless, we now had about forty pounds of bananas ripening in the hammock in the guest bedroom and a tree trunk I felt I needed to stash before Julio, our downstairs neighbor/property manager, found us out. Two sucker trees remained standing; maybe I could prop the old tree up between them? Create a drawing of a banana tree, and tack it up outside Hannah's window?

7

Our Towns

For many years, people from the U.S. have moved to the developing world in order to live out their dreams of tranquil affordability. But the place they did it best is Monteverde. This area had the most delightful history of white people I had ever heard.

The Central American isthmus sports several communities where rich (but not quite rich enough, or they'd have stayed in the States) white Americans swooped in and built big houses, then hired poor brown locals to clean them. The lines between expats and locals in these places are thick and rarely blur.

The account of North Americans in Monteverde had a whole different flavor. It went, in brief, like this:

On October 26, 1949, four young Quaker men in Alabama (Quakers in Alabama! Well did you ever?!) refused to register for the draft during the Korean War. When hauled before the law, they explained (very politely, I imagine) to the judge about nonviolence and whatnot, but His Honor was unimpressed. He said, "If you like this country, you should obey the laws of this country, and if you don't like it, you ought to move out." The judge then sentenced them to jail for a year and a day.

The young men emerged after about four months, having been quite well behaved. On the inside, they'd had little to do save discuss what the judge had said, and they deemed his logic sound. They wondered whether there might exist a country whose values more closely matched their own, where they could feel good about the use of their tax dollars. They posed the question to other members of their quiet farming community.

Costa Rica's stable government, sound economy, and simpatico values *vis á vis* the military made Costa Rica appealing. The Quakers, on reconnaissance, heard proud Ticos repeating, "Here we have more teachers than soldiers." The *Cordillera de Tilarán* mountains were high and cool enough to avoid hot, muggy nuisances, such as malaria and yellow fever. And the climate was suitable for dairy farming, which the Quakers already knew how to do.

In late 1950, nine family groups, their members ranging in age from one to eighty-one, moved from Alabama. They bought 3,000 acres of land, of which they divided a third into farming plots and set aside the rest as a watershed. The Quakers, in a fit of understatement, named their new home *Monteverde*—green mountain. (Monteverde had both more green and more mountain than I'd ever seen at once—and I'd come, remember, from Washington State.)

Monteverde came to be the unofficial name of the entire area. The informal "Monteverde zone" named a region that encompassed four little mountain towns, all strung together like a rain forest rosary: Santa Elena had the commerce, Monteverde village had the wildlife, Canitas was the boonies, and our bead was Cerro Plano. It was a regular kind of place.

Cerro Plano sat on the main thoroughfare between Monteverde and Santa Elena. We had Johnny's Pizzeria and a couple of other restaurants, a public elementary school as well as the CEC. Cerro Plano was not a destination in itself, which made it feel, to me, somehow genuine. Real people lived here, getting real things done. And no matter which way we headed from Cerro Plano—up the steep hill to the school, down the steep hill to Santa Elena, or straight back on the road to Monteverde, we shared the road with leaf-cutter ants.

I'd never seen anything balls-to-the-wall industrious as leaf-cutter ants. They actually went marching one by one, hurrah. Up the trees of Cerro Plano and down, all the livelong day, cutting up poisonous leaves.

Leaf-cutter ants were easy to spot because they were carrying bits of leaves above their heads that were easily twice as large as their bodies. So even from our human height we could see the narrow green line, wriggling purposefully down the road.

Leaf-cutter ants live in a caring and mutually beneficial domestic partnership with a fungus. The fungus can't get enough of a certain kind of leaf, but, lacking legs, needs help with acquisition. The ants march to the top of the forest canopy to cut leaves—at great personal peril, as the leaves happen to be deadly poisonous to the ants. Fetching toxic leaves all day leaves the ants little time for home building and maintenance, so their partner becomes an enormous fung-o-cile that provides them both food and living space.

If you followed the ants to the tree they were cutting, you could see the line moving up and down the trunk, some ants going up for leaves some carrying pieces down.

We saw more leaf cutters doing their work in Cerro Plano than we did even in the Monteverde Reserve. The ants must have known Cerro Plano was a workers' town. Not pastoral—that was Monteverde village. We liked our little colony.

On the rosary, Monteverde village was the cross, the beautiful bit out there at the end, connected but a little distant. Without Monteverde, all you had was a string of beads.

Monteverde village continued to be the center of action for the Quaker community. The Friends School, which the Quakers founded in order to educate their own children but which was, Quakerarily, open to all, provided a community library and playing fields. Both the altitude and the property values were higher in Monteverde village than in the rest of the zone. The population of the village, while mixed, had a higher proportion of Quakers and U.S. expats.

The *Monteverde Jubilee Family Album*, a locally published history of the first fifty years of Quaker settlement, is a treasure trove of correspondence and first-hand accounts of life in the village. The book itself is a gem of Quakerness, the community's stories as told through the letters and journals and memories of dozens of people. There is no authoritarian voice, no one storyteller. Beams of cooperation shine from its pages. The way that each group treated the other, newcomer Quakers and existing Tico settlers, made me want to go hug everyone in town. I felt bummed I wasn't Quaker, but by then it seemed kind of too late, and copycatty.

By the 1980s, this Monteverde within Monteverde also sported a rainforest reserve and a biological and educational research institute. The stunning beauty of the area was trumpeted abroad; naturally, a few high-end hotels sprouted up.

But Monteverde village wasn't snobby. It was just—where the Quakers landed. Cloaked in sustainability and concern for the environment, Monteverde had the best forests and foliage. Like any vacation spot worth the trouble to get to, Monteverde village had a place to buy ice cream. The Quakers had settled in to be dairy farmers, as they had been in Alabama. The place where they turned the dairy into products was called *Productores de Monteverde S.A*, but everyone just called it *la fabrica*, or the cheese factory. Walking up to Monteverde for a milkshake became one of the rituals of our year.

Monteverde was where you could do touristy things—take a pottery class, rent horses. But it was not a spoiled Tourist Town. The modest and non-exploitive sensibilities of the Alabaman Quakers had held up well over the last half-century. They sold ice cream but drew the line well before salt water taffy or hummingbird-themed cigarette lighters.

The best part of Monteverde village for us was the library at the Friends School. The Friends kept their library open 24/7; the front door was left unlocked. On a shelf we found a little stack of cards on which to write down our name, number, and what we took. Strictly honor system.

BUT. Get this. If they called you a few times to return a book, and you didn't do it, they put a Friendly little note up at the village bakery, with your name on it, asking you to please return the book because others would like a chance. Holy shit. We went to the Friends library often, but I got a little sweaty whenever Ivy's borrowed *The Boxcar Children* was out of my sight.

Santa Elena was already an established *pueblito* when the Quakers arrived up the road, and remained the big metropolis of the zone. No stop lights or stop signs, but still, three paved blocks. You totally wanted to look both ways when crossing the street.

Any community has to have a place to buy not-charming things, like a hammer, school supplies, socks. Santa Elena was where it all got done. Like any good town center, Santa Elena had a bakery, a hardware store, and a butcher. Vitosi's was the Santa Elena equivalent of a department store, where you bought your school uniforms and training bras. Santa Elena also had several restaurants, a bus station/post office combo, a bookstore with a book exchange, and a bank. And a very young doctor.

Costa Rica offers universal public health insurance and its public health system is very highly rated. We could have gotten a piece of that at the clinic outside of Santa Elena, but somehow it didn't seem quite right to take advantage. Miss Marti had recommended the town's one private-practice doc for our healthcare needs. Dr. Navarro used a lot of product in his hair and said "*¡Tuanis!*" a lot—cool! His office was half exam room, half pharmacy.

Prescription drugs smiled down on us from the locked cases that lined the walls of his waiting area. Dr. Navarro could write his prescriptions in one room, then walk to the next and hand them over. It was the kind of system I was born to love.

Still, we were never quite convinced that Dr. Navarro was a physician and not a canny teenager. Privately, we called him Doctor Doogie. His office was conveniently located a block from Esperanza, the supermarket.

Every visit to Esperanza was a treasure hunt. The cold things could always be found in cold places, and the produce pretty much stayed put. After that, the shelf-stockers apparently looked for an empty space and went for it. In U.S. sizing, Esperanza was midway between a 7-11 and a standard-issue Safeway, so the hunt was not trivial.

Esperanza is a common Spanish girl's name, meaning hope. But the verb *esperar* can also be translated "to wait." For us, both meanings proved apt. Esperanza rarely had everything we wanted, but she always had some of it. Esperanza, that flirt, kept us hoping. And if we didn't find it this time, we waited.

Imported foods for Gringo palates cost a lot, so we mostly stayed away from them. Chocolate chips and peanut butter were our signature extravagance and the biggest crapshoot of our Esperanza experience. The varying presence and location of these items fostered a kind of eternal optimism: *The peanut butter isn't where it was last time, but that doesn't necessarily mean it isn't here! Go look by the regular butter!*

I liked to wander the aisles, but Hannah wanted to think like Esperanza thought. One day early on I sent her to get some yucca, a brown root vegetable that looks disconcertingly like poop. (We'd gotten past it, though, and I was experimenting with various dishes—functionally, yucca was quite potato-like.) Having spent twelve years watching her crazy mother combining errands for maximum efficiency, Hannah considered what else she might pick up since she was at the store anyway. When she got home, she waved her bulging backpack at us.

"So the chocolate chips weren't with the candy bars, which is where I found them last time..."

"Sure—'things that are chocolate.'" Made sense to Harry, too.

"So I looked next to the flour, as in 'baking supplies,' and next to the rice,"

"'Things that are very small,'" Anthony this time.

"Yep, but finally..." Hannah held the pack behind her back. Would it yield chocolate chips or only poop-brown vegetables?

"They were on the Gringo cereal shelf! *With peanut butter right next to them, and marshmallows!* Here's my theory: Once, the stock boy had some very fancy Rice Krispie Treats."

For our kids, Esperanza's biggest revelation was *rompope*—rome-PO-pay. A million times more fun to say than its English equivalent—"eggnog" just makes you sound congested—*rompope* at Esperanza was a year-round miracle. None of us had ever questioned that this particular beverage sprung annually into existence after Thanksgiving and vanished by law each December 26. But *rompope* was total anarchy: It was calendar agnostic, and came in juice boxes! Its deliciousness increased accordingly. We learned to take care to read the small print: *rompope CON ron* and *SIN ron* shared shelf space. It was very easy to unwrap the child-sized straw and jam it into the tiny foil hole, only to end up with a mouthful of highly spiked eggnog. Anthony cheerfully slurped many a rummy juicebox, handed over by a disgusted child.

Esperanza wasn't the only food-shopping option; it was just the grandest. Tiny grocery stores, called *pulperias*, dotted the roads between the towns. For *pulperia*, think 7-11. Now downsize it by about 90%, but make up for the smaller footprint by stacking groceries to the ceiling and narrowing the aisles so you can just squeeze through. Make it owned by someone who lives behind it, or very close. There—*pulperia*.

You were never far from a *pulperia*. They took only cash and sold the essentials: tortericas, dish soap, avocados, mangos. Gum and an ice cream bar. Things to get you through until you could get to town. Behind Johnny's, the nearest *pulperia* was eighty steps away—Harry counted.

Farmers on their way to town would sell you whatever they had—melons or mangos, usually—at a discount, having eliminated the middleman. Finally, there was Gungo the chicken man, who delivered. I'd overheard a couple of moms talking about Gungo on the first day of school but hadn't asked how to get in touch with him. I wouldn't want anyone to think I was new around here.

Grocery shopping was always a thrill, but my favorite place in Santa Elena was the bank. I hoped for long lines.

Two weeks into a life that had no sports, parent-teacher conferences, or work deadlines consuming our afternoons, Harry, Ivy and I ambled to Santa Elena. We wanted to check out the appliance store; the guys who worked there,

Harry'd heard, were often up for a game of chess. And Ivy wanted to buy some bakery treats.

I used to be able to conduct life in plastic and hadn't gotten used to carrying cash. We'd been running about a 5% success rate with the area's single cash machine, so we made a pre-bakery detour to *Banco Nacional.* The armed guard smiled and, as he always did, opened the door for me. *"Buenos dias, Señora."*

I entered the ten-by-eight-foot room. Someone had thought to brighten up its dinginess with lively paintings of children and birds. (I would later learn that these were painted by Ana Ruth, Diego's mom. When I met her, I understood where he'd gotten that smile.) Two lines of bright red electrical tape showed us how to do a single line for the two teller windows.

The line was pretty long—about six people. I took my place at the end, hopefully, and the guard did not disappoint. He took a long look and set about fixing us.

First, he whispered a reminder to one of the less disciplined linestanders among us, and the man moved more precisely between the red lines. The rest of us tidied ourselves up. A very pregnant woman stood in line right in front of me; the guard placed a hand on each of her arms and steered her to the very front of the line.

"Con permiso," he said to the current front-stander, in the gentlest voice.

"Claro! Claro!" came the reply. Of course!

The guard got the waddly lady some water from the ancient machine with the cone-shaped cups. He checked out the line one last time—we looked good. *"Gracias,"* he said to all of us, giving a quick nod. His universe ordered, he resumed his position by the door.

In line, all of us had smiled when he moved the pregnant woman up front, and several people even nodded. *Bien hecho*—well done! Now, the six of us tried to stay worthy of him. We stood straighter, and remembered to greet the teller politely when our turn came.

My courtesy-loving sister would have died over this. If our phone would ever get connected, I'd call Erin and tell her. We were starting to feel the effects of being totally cut off from our old world. Soon I'd take the kids to an internet café, but today they seemed okay.

I withdrew money without incident, and the kids and I headed to the bakery.

We bought pineapple cake. I wasn't a fan; Ivy loved it. Harry played chess with a middle-aged man at the appliance store. Two *muchachos* cheered good moves by both players, teased their elder buddy if Harry took a piece, and argued about who got to play *el ganador*.

The final bead on the Monteverde-zone rosary was Canitas. This tiny village was rural, like Monteverde, but without the luxurious feel. Canitas was modest and quiet. It had farms and families, a *pulperia*—but no reserve, no scientists, no charming ice cream shop. Canitas was on the other side of Santa Elena, away from the reserve. Very little English was spoken there.

It surprised me to find no animosity or competition among these towns. There was no communal agreement that Monteverde was more desirable because of its pastoral beauty, or that Santa Elena ruled because it had the action. Without snobbery around the expensive areas, there was no reverse snobbery or bravado in the more affordable ones. I could hardly get my head around it.

Each town was what it was, and each played a role in the larger community. People lived in the place that suited them best and visited friends and stores all over the zone.

8

Discovery

Before we left Seattle, I'd done exactly enough research to make sure we could meet our basic needs: housing, schooling, orthodontia. Our lack of elementary knowledge about the place we'd landed meant that the whole first month, we felt a lot like Dorothy arriving in Oz. If Oz had been really, really wet.

Rainy season! We'd left Seattle just as the weather was finally getting decent, only to arrive in Monteverde during the deluge.

July in Costa Rica taught me the power of corrugated tin, which tops many buildings in Central America. Corrugated tin raises the drama quotient of all weather, and would make even Pacific Northwest drizzle sound like machine-gun fire. When the skies above Monteverde opened up each day, raindrops as big as the end of your thumb came blobbing onto a village of the stuff. Aural pandemonium.

We couldn't get over the fact that we could be jacketless in a rainstorm and not be cold. We did, however, get wet. (Umbrellas were another item I didn't think to bring to the rainforest—but oh, how we were enjoying those thumbtacks). One night, we were in Santa Elena when the *aguacerro* came. Water ran six inches deep down the streets. We waded and laughed; Ivy was in heaven.

"We LOVE the wain, don't we Hawwy? We ah the wain chiwdwen!" (In Spanish, Ivy's r's rolled like a native speaker's. *Perrrrrro*, Anthony had urged her to repeat one day after she'd commented on a dog. Ivy scowled at him, said, "I don't speak Spanish," and stomped away.)

We were promised that a Monteverde February would be bone-dry and dusty.

One day, during the three-hour stretch between when *prepa* let out and when worthwhile entertainment arrived in the form of her siblings, Ivy wanted to find the secret footpath. The night before, we had seen a family coming out of the woods across the street, laden with bags as if they had Been to Town. We promised ourselves we'd investigate. It would be swell to travel off the road, out of the dust from the locals' *motos* and the omnipresent *turismo* vans.

Our house, with its gravelly, recycling-center front yard, sat across the road from a small, white cottage with a front yard of flowering trees and a mossy, burbling stream that was much more adorable here than it was on our side of the road. To each his own, I guess. A sign said, *Casa de Arte*. I was intrigued by that little house, but Ivy was intrigued by what hung in front of it.

Next to the stream, an old-fashioned wooden swing on twenty-foot ropes dangled from a huge strangler fig. It was a swing of such excellence and old-fashioned sturdiness that you knew, if you pumped hard enough, you could poke through the tangle of forest canopy and burst out into the blue, blue sky.

Ivy had been eyeing the swing and trying to work up the courage to knock on the house's little, arched door, ever since we arrived.

But today we were on a mission. The town-traveling people had emerged from the trees right at the side of the *Casa*'s front yard. We'd start there.

We found the footpath and headed in. After a dozen yards or so, it became clear that any secret footpath was *extremely* secret. Those sneaky locals; where were they coming from last night? Ivy and I headed farther in on the nearest thing to a path we could find and ended up in the jungle, bushwhacking our way across a stream and between the strangler fig trees.

Walking through these woods was like walking on a mattress, the rain forest floor cushioned and soft with rich loamy stuff—dirt and bugs and nature. You could imagine all kinds of organisms beneath your feet, turning the soil.

A few minutes in, we were climbing over a fallen tree. It had rotted, and Ivy fell through. The forest was being untidy and unpredictable. I was lifting her out when she grabbed my hand and pointed, and I stopped thinking about the hidden life beneath us and trained my focus on the very visible life, right in front. A colony of ants had overtaken a tree stump of Volkswagen proportions and built a hill on it. Jagged bits of stump poked up here and there, turrets on an enormous sandcastle. There were dainty white fungi all over the hill/stump, and ants the size of really big ants. Carrying leaves.

Leafcutters!

I'd learned more about these ants, and become even more impressed. They didn't just cultivate the fungus that was both crop and house; they inoculated it, too. The ants carried bacteria on their bodies that acted as an antibiotic, repelling diseases that can attack the fungus. Everyone worked together, and both fungus and colony thrived.

Conceptually, the leafcutters cracked me up. Industrious ants in a symbiotic relationship with a fungus? It's just so obviously the beginning of a bad-relationship joke.

Fascinated, Ivy and I traced a line of ants coming home with their jaggedy leaf bits. I tried to peek inside the stump entrance where they disappeared, hoping to glimpse a gaping fungus mouth.

Then we followed an outgoing line, walking alongside the empty-handed ants for several minutes with no end in sight. The ants didn't turn up a tree, stop for coffee, anything—just kept marching. Ivy decided to help out. She plucked a leaf from a nearby branch, and tore it into careful shreds exactly the right size. She knelt by the line and offered a piece to one ant and then another. But the ants weren't having any—*we're not your charity case!* Finally, Ivy became furious that the stupid bugs wouldn't pick up any of the leaves SHE cut for them, as a FAVOR.

"That is not polite!" she yelled at them, squatting by their line so they'd be sure to hear. Then she stomped away—no mean feat on the squishy rainforest floor.

From the time she could voice an opinion, Ivy had always made me think of the passage in *Peter Pan* where J.M. Barrie explains Tinkerbell:

"Fairies are so small," he wrote, "that they can only feel one emotion at a time."

That was Ivy, body and soul. Now, for a little while, the single emotion consuming her would be fury. It dawned on me that I had the time, this year, not to try to distract her or talk her down. I could simply wait it out.

Ivy stomped expertly to a sunny clearing with a huge boulder in it. I sat down; the sun felt nice.

I saved the little speech I'd been composing back at the anthill, about hard work and industry and everyone doing his or her part. This was sad for me because I had some cogent points that would relate directly to our family life. Instead Ivy and I sat there a while. She fumed, I sunned. Then she remembered the swing at the edge of the woods and popped up, excited and ready to go.

A tiny woman with a pixie haircut stood outside the darling house, smoking. When she saw Ivy, she put her cigarette out, smiled at me, and crouched down. Ivy asked, using lots of English that the pixie could not understand and some pointing, which she could, for permission to use the swing.

"Claro que si! Todos los dias! Todos los dias!" she replied. Yes, of course! Every day!

Her name was Lola, and it turned out she was one of the owners of the *Casa de Arte*. Lola was a wood-sprite of a woman, with paint on her hands and on the man's button-down shirt that reached to her knees. She had on-purpose bedhead and blond highlights, neither of which I'd seen on a Tica, and a couple of piercings in each ear. Her glasses hung on an arty chain, all charms and jaunty angles. Lola was a real-live artist (hence the smoking!). I found myself wishing I had the vocabulary to try to make friends with her. At least I could exploit Ivy. Small children: the universal icebreaker.

Lola lifted Ivy to the swing and gave her a push. I imagined my daughter would in fact be returning *todos los dias*. To bask in Lola, whose coffee-brown eyes held a warmth that balanced the frosted tips of her hair, as well as to swing up and over the creek.

Ivy stretched her toes toward the sky and flung her head backward, grinning upside-down at her new friend. Lola watched, then looked at me and smiled. *"Preciosa,"* she said.

"Gracias," I replied. I put a lot of spin on it, so as to imply, "You look nice and I like your edgy ear situation. I'm new here. Do you want to be my friend?"

Five minutes ago Ivy had told me she hated me for making her come on a walk when I knew the ants were just going to be mean. Yes, Ivy was adorable, but that wasn't the whole story and suddenly the standard mom script wasn't enough. I saw an opening and took it.

"Preciosa...*aveces*," I added. Sometimes.

Lola looked startled, then smiled, then gestured at her open front door. *"Quiere un café?"*

And I chickened out. I couldn't sustain a Spanish conversation. I didn't want to be awkward. I didn't know the rules of invitations and I didn't want to get anything wrong. I pointed across the street and tried to say something about dinner. Ivy finished swinging, and we scuttled away.

When we got home, Julio was outside. The time had come to stumble through a full and mortifying confession with respect to the banana tree.

"*Si, claro. Es normal,*" said Julio.

Banana trees always do that. Apparently, making bananas is a lot of work—the tree makes a single, enormous clump, then falls to the ground.

We were solving mysteries left and right, but still had not figured out how to get a telephone, which meant no Internet access. Apparently phone service was run through Esperanza—you went to a checkout line and filled out a form. Or something. Anthony tried, and the cashier gave him a long and earnest explanation, speaking slowly and kindly. He was so nice that Anthony pretended to understand, and the cashier sent him on his way with a giant smile, "*Pura vida!*"

The thing we most had to learn, the thing our new land really needed us to know, was the language. Not that *The Princess Bride* Spanish soundtrack wasn't useful (*Mi nombre es Inigo Montoya . . .*). And *Newsies* had prepared Harry with "*Huelga! Huelga!*" should he ever need to rally the boys to strike. But even this was not enough.

The first clue we needed to step things up came from Anthony's initial volunteer Tuesday in the *prepa* classroom.

Anthony is not a fastidious man. He wears tube socks with sandals, is as happy eating Apple Jacks as artisan anything, and basically just lets the world operate however it feels like operating. Not much bothers him. Very "*Que Sera, Sera,*" our Anthony.

In fact, Anthony would be happy with *Que Ser, Ser.* Why get bothered about verb tenses? Let the listener figure out whether *What Will Be, Will Be,* or *What Is, Is* or even, *What Was, Was.*

But when it comes to hand washing, my husband is a fussy old woman. No child ever approached our dinner table without being sent off to wash. Whenever I teased him about how seriously he took this, he answered, "It's a question of public health!" (Anthony also refuses to eat raw cookie dough.)

When Anthony saw that the children of *prepa* tended to be lax with their pre-snack hand hygiene, he immediately got busy with our dog-eared—not by him—copy of *501 Spanish Verbs*.

"To wash," third-person plural, imperative: *¡Lavarse!*
Anthony started practicing.

I had decided to look into lessons. The CEC employed a tutor, Ezmeralda, to whip the foreign kids into tip-top *español* shape. Harry and Hannah loved her.

I'd heard Ezme would teach adults, too, for a very reasonable rate. On our second Tuesday in town, I pored over our dictionary, wrote notes, wiped the sweat off my palms, and borrowed the telephone in the school office.

Conversation is harder when it involves no helpful facial cues or hand gestures. On the phone, it's just you and the language. And the other person. And also the phone. But that is *it*.

Once I had stated my business, an understanding voice on the end of the line spoke to me v-e-r-y-s-l-o-w-l-y. Ten minutes later I was set up to receive Spanish tutoring for several hours over the next couple of weeks. But now I wondered: Did I really need it? I mean, I'd had a whole conversation. I'd had to know days of the week, and some numbers, and figure out where to meet her, and everything. I was practically bilingual.

The following Tuesday, Ivy jumped off the bus and hung a glittery sign around my neck. *Dia de la Madre!* I had just gotten my standard U.S. Mother's Day back in May. Yet here it was, just August, and I had a brand-new yarn necklace with a construction-paper placard. Score!

For a second I considered researching Mother's Day dates around the world, creating a multi-year itinerary that optimized opportunities to give me presents and do me favors. But first I had a question for Anthony. The suspense had been killing me all morning.

"So—did they wash?"

Anthony had practiced all week. He'd headed up to *prepa* that morning armed with his conjugation, but now he was vexed.

"It was even worse than last time! I told the kids to wash their hands, and they just laughed at me and didn't bother."

Poor sweetie. It must be hard when there's just one thing in the world you stress about, and no one takes you seriously.

"Do you want to do your sentence on me?" I offered. "I haven't washed for lunch."

Anthony brightened. *"¡Lavarse los monos!"*

The verb was perfect, a masterpiece. But "hands" are *las manos.*" Anthony had told the children to wash their monkeys.

I don't know how most people go about learning a new language, but our family acquired Spanish as caricatures of ourselves, our dominant traits comically supersized. Hannah preferred reading about people to interacting with them: Her written Spanish sprinted ahead of her ability to speak. Ivy maintained her stance from the airport, and despite her perfect rrr's, the very idea of Spanish infuriated her. Harry started with people and sports: He was making soccer playdates before he could reliably communicate his name.

Harry also annoyed the rest of us by not having to actually *learn.* Spanish seemed to want Harry to speak it, and delivered itself to his lips as needed.

Anthony watched us all, amused and unflappable. He had the worst Spanish of the five of us, but he was by far the bravest about using it. Anthony was willing, utterly without pretension, and awful. Everyone rooted for him.

"Hola," Anthony would say. "Umm...Me llamo Antonio. Umm...yo quiero....yo quiero..." and the shopkeeper or hostel owner or man whose taxi was resting on Anthony's foot would start guessing what Anthony might want and help him pronounce the words while the line stacked up behind him. Finally Anthony would get it. His new friend would clap him on the back in hearty congratulation, then back up his taxi or whatever.

My own approach is probably best described as *bull in a china mercado.* I began bashing about in this beautiful language right off, ready to acquire Spanish by brute force. In addition to my Ezmeralda sessions, I'd decided to work my way through the Harry Potter books. I figured that since I already knew these books well in English, I could follow along, picking up vocabulary on the way. I'd already mastered *el armario bajo las escaleras*—the cupboard under the stairs.   I used the newspaper to help with the vocabulary of current events and, for the language of the people, I downloaded pop lyrics from the Internet on the school's computer.

Each evening, the kids and I arranged ourselves around the tiny kitchen table, dictionary in the middle. They'd grind through homework and I'd translate songs or the boy wizard, word by laborious word.

Soon, I could tell my love how I could see his face in the moon, or insist that Uncle Vernon give me my letter.

We'd been in town three weeks when language shifted from nice-to-have to a Priority 1 requirement (I might not speak Spanish, but I still spoke software development). The dank smell in Harry and Ivy's bedroom was produced by a mildewed foam mattress.

"Ivy, I'll give you my whole allowance to trade beds, just for one night."

"Yuck! I don't want to sleep in stink!"

We needed a mattress, we needed it now, and we needed it in Spanish. Surprisingly, the word had not yet come up in any of my study aids. A normal person might have looked it up, but that's not how a bull does it. How hard could it be? I'd already done two songs that morning.

We were three hours from the nearest stop light, and much farther from the equivalent of a Sleep Country, Costa Rica. But I knew where to start because I'd just learned a brand-new universal truth: No matter where you are on our lovely planet, it is impossible to set up even the tiniest dwelling without going to the hardware store every damn day.

The Santa Elena hardware store (*ferretería*) is to Home Depot as tomatoes are to yachting: Any overlap in the experiences is random and not relevant. The *ferretería* was about as big as a Seattle master bedroom. A wall-to-wall counter separated civilians from the merchandise, precluding the browse-then-point approach that I would have preferred.

A few items did live in front of the counter, where anyone could reach them: machetes of all sizes, and the milk cans farmers used to take their product to the dairy. So a person who needed to bushwhack rainforests or deliver milk from his local farm, this person, who presumably had an arsenal of nuanced Spanish at his disposal, got a self-serve hardware experience. Me, I had to find words. Once I did so, one of the sixteen-year-old *muchachos* behind the counter would disappear down one of the skinny aisles. In a while he'd return with my item and a smile that could power the sun.

Another thing about the *ferretería* that never used to happen at Home Depot: On seeing a woman enter the store, the counter boys would trip over themselves to help her, all the while staring openly at her chest. When I spoke, they'd move their eyes up to mine and smile hopefully. I was frankly grateful for any communication I could understand.

On Mattress Day, I craned my neck to peek down the narrow aisles of mystery. There was always something new among the towering boxes. Today I identified rolls of tubing and dishtowels, and corrugated tin roofing in a variety of festive colors. In a store so full of wonders that I could spot magenta roofing even from the wrong side of the counter, it seemed entirely possible I might glimpse a mattress for Harry.

In my language studies, I'd cleared the stage of gross incompetence and the stage where I could communicate a memorized phrase so long as I didn't try to go off road. I was now in what I considered to be Stage Three: substitution and improv. On the fly, I could use common words I knew (say, bed) in place of trickier words I didn't (for example, mattress). Verbs, I'd decided, were implied.

I had only to express this simple idea: "I need to buy a mattress. Can you sell me one here, or would I have more luck in San Jose?" Wielding my fancy new improv skills, I charged.

The giant smiles of four *muchachos* widened impossibly as I gave it my best, Stage Three shot:

"Me ...bed...you...here?" I asked a teenage boy, "or have lucky in San Jose?"

In the early weeks, I fared better with Ezmeralda, since the stakes were lower and I had time to form my thoughts. Ez and I got along great. What's not to like? We were both ready smilers and nodders. We began each session with a rundown of Ezmeralda's love life.

Ezmeralda was, like all of her countrywomen I'd seen so far, utterly gorgeous. She had perfectly plucked eyebrows, unbitten fingernails under clear polish, and an actual beauty mark in the same place as Marilyn Monroe's. She spoke no English. The boys all loved Ezme, but she'd recently settled on just one. I'd say, *"Como está Marcos?"* and we were off to the races.

After the rundown, Ezmeralda would look at me expectantly. I was about a decade older, and married, so this was my cue to offer some sage advice. I did my best. But one day, early on, I was stumped. I used all my tricks for increasing comprehension: I leaned forward and squinted. Very motivated, I worked to squint my ears as well.

I caught this: there was a problem with Marcos. It was one of two things:
EITHER
Ezmeralda was feeling angry at Marcos, because although she had been a little sad and down, and Marcos didn't really care to know why. He just wanted her to act happy.
OR
Ezmeralda was feeling angry and a little sad, because Marcos wouldn't go down on her. She didn't know why, because he knew this act would make her happy.

It took me a minute, but I think my response fit all possibilities:

"*Si, es dificil* sometimes," I reassured her in my excellent Spanglish, "when *hombres no comprenden* what a woman needs."

The Friday of the first week of school, Miss Marti assigned what she called a Bio-poem. The first two words of each line were provided in bold on the worksheet, and the kids were to fill in the rest. Helping in the classroom, I got to read many of the kids' work. The boys were full of pre-adolescent bravado: "**I am** the best goalie in Monteverde." and "**I wonder** when I will start playing for Team *Naçionale.*" Harry's English was fine, so I didn't get to help him. But I'd been curious—what would he pick to brag about?

A few weeks later, fishing for lunchboxes, Anthony found Harry's poem scrunched up at the bottom of his backpack:

I AM

I am the new kid from Seattle

I wonder what the kids are like here

I want to know more Spanish

I pretend I know what's happening, but instead I'm filled with envy for their smiling conversations

I am however learning Spanish very slowly

I understand they have a Spanish tutor here, and I'd like to meet her

I try to do my best in everything, especially in Spanish although I'm not very good

I say "I know what you mean," even when I haven't even understood one word

I dream I'm back in America

I am the new kid from Seattle.

Anthony and I remembered how Harry had looked the first day at the blackboard. He had seemed to get steadily more comfortable, but really, what did we know?

9

A Time to Cook

Harry had learned a new concept in math, and he applied it one September afternoon as he walked in the door. "We have infinite bananas," he said.

The ripening of our banana crop forced the issue of my cultural education, as related to Tico kitchenware. Our "fully-furnished" kitchen had yielded fifteen spoons, twelve cereal bowls, seven salad plates, and a frying pan. We had everything we needed to live on Cheerios and fried eggs. But a balanced banana diet involves all kinds of fanciness—breads, puddings, the occasional savory experiment— and for this I would need equipment.

The things I needed most were:

Measuring cups. I couldn't find them anywhere. However, in each store that I checked, in the place where a sensible person would stash Things That Measure, I inevitably found several sets of funnels in graduated sizes. What were these people moving from one container to the other with such tenacity? And did they never need to know *how much* of it they were transferring?

Mixing bowls. Esperanza carried colanders in dozens of colors, shapes, and sizes. Plastic and aluminum, with lids and without. They had slits, holes, slits-and-holes, and holes grouped to form a flowery vine that wrapped itself around. All this, just to transform what could have been the functional mixing bowl that I needed into a colander I did not.

There seems to be a trend here, I thought, trudging up the hill to Cerro Plano with zero baking supplies and twelve consolation mangoes. Ticos seek things with holes, while I am looking for things that are solid. Is it the torrential rains here? You never want to have anything that the water can't drain out of?

Perhaps it was a lesson in the transitory nature of material objects. Grabby North American me, always wanting to hold on, to measure, so saddled with Western Culture. (I heard people make that actual contrast. As if, what, Central America is in the Orient? Costa Rica is one hair west of Cincinnati.) Perhaps the more relaxed Ticos felt ownership was an illusion, and they reflected this philosophy in their kitchenware.

Who knows? Meanwhile, I stood in my little kitchen-corner, funnel in one hand, colander in the other, thinking: This is going to be a very interesting batch of pancakes.

People joke about the Jewish mother, but she is my soul mate. She can't always put words to her deepest desire, which is to keep her family fed and safe forever. So she stirs her extravagant love into the pot, with the chicken and the carrots. Any apron strings are incidental.

Back when I barely knew how to change Hannah's diaper and was regularly assumed to be her nanny, I was already studying how to create the purest rice cereal a baby ever ate (it involves toasting organic grains in a cast iron pan so that they absorb that vital nutrient. Sweet Jesus.) Hannah rejected my efforts, but couldn't get enough of the Gerber rice flakes, to which Anthony had cheerfully added water.

What started out as a natural enjoyment of cooking had joined forces with an urge to feed that felt primal. But what had perhaps put me over the top was the working mom thing. *I am not there after school, but I made a pot of soup on the weekend...it's there for you when I am not.* For every field trip I missed during the day, a batch of scones came out of the oven at six in the morning. We ate our share of frozen pizzas, but my mac and cheese never came from a box.

When I quit my job, I would finally have world enough and time. Costa Rica was going to be feeding-people heaven.

Early on, Esperanza declared war on my plans. *That's adorable,* thought my grocery store. *How she thinks she'll come down here and become some kind of pin-up mom.*

I could live without measuring cups, but I was going to need a cookie sheet. Esperanza carried one, and she carried it for the duration of our stay in Costa Rica. This cookie sheet was 17" long—an interesting measurement only in the context of our oven, whose interior clocked in at a cozy 14" x 15".

However, Esperanza would sell me *cake* pans of any sizes or shape. A twenty-four-inch round for the bottom of my wedding cake, a six-incher for the top, and all layers between. If I'd wanted to make cake in the shape of a house with a chimney, *Esperanza* had me covered. The house-pan snickered whenever I approached. It mocked my naïve hope (*esperar!*) that a shipment of smallish cookie sheets had just been delivered. Or loaf pans—Hannah had, on a walk, accidentally felled another banana tree.

I got over my cookie-sheet problem by buying a 15" round cake pan from the *Esperanza* wedding collection. I turned it upside down: cookie sheet! I flipped it back over and began turning our never-ending supply of bananas into very cake-shaped banana bread. For reasons of her own, Ivy forbade me to call it banana cake. The one time I did so, Ivy had a cow. *Una vaca.*

Whatever. I was just pleased that I would never have to look at that snotty house-pan again.

In early September, Anthony had set out on a hike to a waterfall and I was waiting for Ivy at the bus stop. The bus was late but I, determined to break character, was cool with it. A clattering pickup truck approached slowly, allowing me a good look at the source of the racket: In the bed of the truck, heavy pots and pans towered in stacked columns. The pillars bounced and swayed drunkenly, thunking against each other as the truck eased itself over the pits and rocks of our road. The driver stopped.

"*¿Necessita algo?*" Need anything?

Did I!

I completed my kitchen with the purchase of a single aluminum soup pot for 4,000 *colones* (ten bucks). I chose this amazing bit of cookware from a teetering stack of its drinking buddies and paid the vendor. (*Oh, spare me your lectures about aluminum and Alzheimer's,* I telepathied to all of Seattle as I handed the money over. *I need a goddamn pot.*) The truck rattled away. I would find out later how lucky I'd been – the pan man passed through just twice a year.

I was hugging my new pot when Ivy's bus arrived. Anthony got home soon after, and I showed him my purchase. He did his best.

"Um, nice pot?"

Yes indeed. From then on, I made pretty much everything in my cake pan and my Alzheimer's pot.

It took me a few months to get good at *gallo pinto*—literally, spotted rooster—the signature food of Costa Rica. *Gallo pinto* is black beans and rice, dressed up with finely chopped red peppers, cilantro, and onion. Sometimes egg—boiled right in with the beans, as I would later learn, or flash-fried in oil separately, then stirred in. Always Salsa Lizano, Costa Rica's secret sauce.

Costa Rican food isn't spicy—it's *flavorful*. And that flavor was frequently Lizano. One of the most Tico things you could buy, Salsa Lizano was concocted in one factory only, right outside San José. Diego taught us to slop it on everything.

"Como los Ticos," he dimpled (and somewhere, an angel got laid).

I tried and failed to figure Lizano out. I read the ingredients, which turned out to be mostly a list of vegetables. But it didn't taste like any one of them. I asked Anthony.

"What is that flavor?"

"Perfection?" We left it at that.

We put it on gallo pinto always, but also on yucca latkes, on top of the *crema* (like sour cream, but runnier). Yucca latkes, fried deep golden and liberally salted, were my best invention and the dinner most often requested by my own kids as well as by any friends they brought over. Every culture speaks fried.

Like any domestic goddess worth her apron, I made breakfast for my family most mornings. And when I didn't, Anthony took the task just as seriously. We toasted bread in the oven, topped it with black beans or avocado. Or poured granola, which I'd made according to a magic recipe shared by the mother of Stefan, the boy who'd glowered at math that first day in Harry's classroom.

American breakfast cereals were special-occasion fare, as they cost about twenty times more than any of the goddess alternatives. Plus, an early splurge had taught us what ants like best.

The morning after we bought the Rice Krispies, Harry woke up first as usual. I heard him through my sleepy fog:

"Hey! Put those back!"

Anthony and I bumbled out of our room, Keystone-Cops style, rubbing sleep out of our eyes and Harry into focus. We followed his pointing finger into the end of the living room that served as our kitchen. A line of crisp rice marched out of the half-inch space beneath the cupboard door, across the room, and down through a crack in the floor.

We ceded that box to the ants, and rarely bought them again.

My final food discovery happened close to home. Our front-yard recycling center had a single employee, who came for about an hour a day to sort things out in the shed and keep everything Costa-Rica tidy. I noticed he often had a cooler bungeed to the back of his *moto*. Women approached him, and I could see money and goods changing hands. I assumed, as anyone would, that our recycling guy was trafficking in black-market body parts.

One August morning, under an impossibly blue sky (I had never lived in the absence of jet trails), I worked up the Spanish to ask what he was selling.

"Pollo, Señora. Le gustaria, de la granja?" I had found Gungo the Chicken Man! Would I like some chicken from his farm?

From then on, every couple of weeks, Gungo brought us two freshly butchered chickens from his farm. Gungo's birds were both like and unlike the chicken I was used to. For example: In my previous experience, a roasting chicken wasn't readily mappable to a walking-around chicken. But Gungo didn't remove his chickens' necks as tactfully as I was used to; they arrived with an inch or two still attached. The rest of the bird oriented itself around that stretch of neck, and I could clearly see: animal. I roasted my chickens or boiled them into soup, using my fabulous, living-on-the-edge-here pot.

That list of things I longed to have time for, with cooking and baking at the top? My wedding pan, Alzheimer's pot, and I began in earnest to make that list my bitch.

10

Little House on the Plano

W e hadn't caught the name of Julio's son during introductions, and by August we were too embarrassed to ask the name of a child we saw several times a day. Ivy called him "That Little Boy That's Two." (In formal situations. For everyday use, he was just Boy.) Whenever Ivy was outside, Boy ran outside to look at her. But he ran right back in if she tried to speak; moments later, we'd see him peeping through the curtains.

One day in mid-August, the rain was taking a break when we met Ivy at the bus stop outside our house. Boy ran out as usual, Ivy said her *hóla*, and Boy took a step in her direction. Hope welled in Ivy, and she made a plan. She reached into her backpack and handed him a pretzel, then created a long line of them going up the stairs toward our house.

Anthony and I parked ourselves near the stream and tried to look like we weren't spying.

"Is this what stay-at-home parents do all the time?" I asked him.

"Must be. I wish we had some popcorn."

Lizzie had been right: except for a single, ten-day bike trip when we were dating, Anthony and I had never spent so much time together. For years, our conversation had skewed heavily parental; things like, "Seriously, I'm pretty sure we're supposed to get them immunized." The two of us weren't really practiced in deep conversation.

No matter—we'd get the hang of it. In the meantime, we used our newfangled "leisure time" to amuse ourselves at the expense of the children. We felt grateful Hannah wasn't on site now, to deliver a big-sisterly talk on how Boy is not an animal.

Ivy ran out of pretzels. She ran inside, returning not with more snacks but with a familiar gray bundle. Ivy introduced Bloody to Boy. Anthony raised his eyebrows.

"Handy that child doesn't speak English," he said.

Boy was enamored. Ivy put the elephant in his arms. Boy hugged. Ivy took Bloody away and took two steps upstairs. Boy followed. Ivy gave Bloody to Boy. This went on for a minute or two before Ivy sounded the alarm: "Mommy! Daddy! Look! He isn't afraid! I think he's starting to like me!"

Harry now walked to school every morning in a cloud of tiny butterflies. He had found a woodsy shortcut from the main road and liked to arrive early to play soccer. I often joined him for the walk. Along the path, we picked the Blue Maria berries that turned our teeth and tongues black. I thought back two months. Morning routine: tearing to Tully's to get in a car to cross the bridge to get to Redmond to go to a meeting. I liked my black-teeth habit better.

Soon Ivy realized that going with Harry equaled less competition for the swings with the view to the Gulf, and more time with Courtney.

If Ivy was Tinkerbell, Courtney was Wendy. Courtney's sturdy little body and straight, brown hair appeared even more sensible next to string-bean Ivy's flying yellow curls. Courtney was all earnest solemnity to Ivy's impetuousness.

"That doesn't seem like a very safe idea, Ivy," said Courtney, frequently.

Once I heard Ivy say, "Let's tickle Hannah!" to which Courtney, honestly confused, replied, "Why?"

Differences in temperament notwithstanding, Ivy and Courtney were perfectly matched in swinging, stubbornness, life goal of becoming a Disney princess, and their mutual love of speaking English.

Every morning, Ivy checked out the hummingbird bush outside the *prepa* classroom. She usually clocked between three and seven. The day she reported twelve, I suspected unintentional double counting, but only for a moment. Ivy had the best nature eyes in the family, perhaps in the world. Our first week, we'd taken the guided night walk up at the Monteverde reserve. (The rainforest has a hopping nightlife, with 80% of its animals being nocturnal.) Ivy had been the first to spot the tarantula emerging from its hole on the forest floor. Later, she'd had to point up into the canopy for several minutes before any of us, including the guide, could see the baby sloth. I decided to trust her hummingbird count.

After school, backpacks got hung up and snack eaten. The first week, all Hannah and I ever wanted for any meal were tostadas. I'd throw a torterica (little tortilla—I never saw at Esperanza anything as garish as the foot-wide burrito shells so common at Safeway) in the pan with a little oil, fry both sides, spread with the avocado/salt/lime juice that Hannah had mixed up in the avocado shell while the tortilla was frying.

But we soon began diversifying, snack wise. Or rather, practicing serial monogamy. The second week we ate only Stefan's mom's granola. The secret to her recipe, as to most things, was butter and brown sugar levels that bordered on the absurd. We could probably have cut out the oatmeal entirely.

Most evenings before dinner, Harry walked the kilometer or so to Santa Elena. He could sometimes cajole Hannah into going with, since once they were there they would buy a little snack with which to ruin their appetites and squander their allowance.

"Mom, look!" Harry tore the corner off a little packet and squirted sugary syrup into his mouth. Same principle as Pixi Stix – unadulterated sweet, straight back in the gullet.

A decent bit of grocery-store junk food was 100 *colones*, or about a quarter. A milkshake at the *fábrica* was 1000. The big kids' allowance had been five bucks a week in Seattle, but given the difference in our income—from something to nothing—we'd planned a significant downsizing. On hearing this plan, Hannah presented a short paper entitled "On Allowance." On it, she had written out the conversation from *Fiddler on the Roof* where Tevye apologizes to the beggar, telling him that business was not good lately. And the beggar says, "So you had a bad week—why should I suffer?"

"Very funny," said Anthony, taking a picture of the note to email to the grandparents in case we ever had Internet access. "Eight hundred *colones*. Take it or leave it."

Hannah changed the subject, calmly. "Dad, could you put this scorpion outside?" We knew by now that scorpions in Costa Rica have a nasty sting, but are not deadly.

After dinner, Anthony and I took leisurely walks up the open hillside across the street while the kids got started procrastinating on dishes and homework.

On our rounds, we visited a tree that seemed always to be filled with parrots. These were just as high-strung as the chattering flocks we'd seen from

Marco Tulio's van our first day here. At sunset they hopped from branch to branch, fussing. *The sky is falling!*

On one such walk a few weeks in, Anthony and I were watching the birds and talking about not-much. This was great. Time together to hang out, look at birds, admire the sky. Now that we were settling in, it wouldn't be long before my husband would be telling me stories from his childhood, and saying, "Let's just talk, really talk. Darling, what are your hopes and dreams?"

Back on the hillside, Anthony's actual voice intruded on my reverie of married-people bonding. "I really worry," he was saying, "about the parrots. I just don't think they'll ever understand that sunset is not the apocalypse."

One night as we returned from our walk, Anthony and I were treated to the sight of Harry perched on a rock, bent over his notebook, alone in his alone spot. He watched the water, did some homework, Harry would turn ten next week. He was small in the States and average in Monteverde for a boy his age, but now he looked tiny against the scale of the giant plant life that surrounded him. When he hopped up to wave at us, one hand held up the size-ten jeans he insisted on.

I always want to intervene when my kids look like that—small or in any way vulnerable. On our walks to school, I'd given Harry lots of openings to talk about any homesickness. He'd shown no sign that he was still dreaming of being back in America, but now I wanted go over and strike up a conversation—ensure he knew he was loved and special, brilliant and funny.

My need to parent is so much bigger, sometimes, than my children's need for parenting.

We waved back, and let him be. Twenty minutes later, Hannah looked out the window and saw him hopping around oddly. Maybe he'd been stung? When he came in, Harry said he'd been doing the Macarena.

We were about six weeks in, and everything was going nicely. Our continued failure to get the phone working was problematic: staying in touch with Seattle friends had figured prominently on the poster board. But we were getting to know people here, Hannah was grooving on her independent math curriculum and our language crimes had largely been victimless.

When there's so much new to get a load of in a place, you might not miss what you've left behind. But being occupied all day with the new and interesting doesn't mean that your heart isn't peering around, wondering what happened to the old and comfortable. We didn't notice, but our hearts were slowly becoming aware that all that stuff was gone.

One night at the end of August, the afternoon rains had cleared and a spectacular sunset was brewing. The five of us climbed the hill across from our house, said hi to a libertarian, gate-crashing horse, and listened to the cacophony of the parrot tree as we watched the sun go down.

"It sounds like they're trying to warn us," said Harry.

"Don't worry about it," said Hannah. "Parrots are always crying wolf." She cracked herself up, that one.

But Harry was onto something. *This is the honeymoon,* the parrots had been squawking. *And honeymoons end.*

Burning the candle at no ends takes more energy than you might think. When we toppled into bed around 9:30 each night, Anthony and I asked each other, "How did we fit all that Seattle stuff IN?" We used to hold down actual jobs, with deadlines and meetings and late-night email, at the same time as managing our lives. But now our lives were all we managed, and we were still exhausted.

Life just took longer, as I tried to explain to my sister when I called from the school office. For example: One Thursday in late August, Hannah had an appointment to get her braces tightened. Our visit to the Costa Rica-born, University of Washington-trained Dr. de la Rosa had taken just over forty-eight hours, four buses and a hostel.

"I'm pretty sure this is more of an effort than orthodontia ever required in Seattle," I had said to Anthony on our return.

"But you never actually timed it there, right?" he asked.

At Erin's request, I made a list (Erin gets me) of some of the activities that took the time we used to spend being gainfully employed:

> You probably think we bundle the kids off to school, have a little sex, and then nap and snack the day away. That's kind of how I'd imagined it. Instead, we spend more time than ever on. . .
>
> **Feeding the fam:** This is a much larger operation here; no Trader Joe's, no takeout. Grocery shopping is a daily Anthony-and-Margot togetherness event because we need two backpacks.

Cleaning: We have no dishwasher. Our washing machine holds about two pairs of jeans, four T-shirts, and a smattering of socks and underwear. Plus, sometimes our dryer tries to kill us.

Walking everywhere: No car.

Ivy: Ivy goes to school for only three hours a day. Have you met Ivy? She is not a real, "Oh, I'll just sit here and color" kind of gal.

Learning Spanish: Tutoring, homework, Harry Potter. I appreciate that I get the spells for free: *Expelliarmus!*

Helping at school: Tuesday mornings in Ivy's class, math on Thursday afternoons with Harry's, and other school stuff here and there. Sometimes I substitute teach.

Hiking: Anthony takes himself out for a serious hike at least once a week. There is a lot of nature here.

Yoga: This one-hour class + long walk to and from = about two hours of my day, three times a week: Sometimes I think yoga takes me longer because I hear so slowly in Spanish, but I seem to finish at the same time as everybody else.

Also, today, Ivy, Courtney, and I saw three huge cane toads. I caught one so they could touch it, and it peed on me. So I had to go home and change my clothes, which took some time.

11

Sunsets vs. Social Lives

W as someone. . .*yelping?* I peered through the floor to see Anthony hopping and swearing next to the evil dryer, socks and boxers flung across the cement.

Except for that one unwelcoming appliance, our house behind Johnny's was starting to feel like home. The shower was good for enough hot water to wash my hair, and almost enough to get it rinsed. We had our walks down pat—whether to school, Santa Elena, or Monteverde, it took about twelve minutes.

We no longer ran to the window to see what was the matter when music blared and a disembodied voice began hollering at us in rapid, excited Spanish. It was just the Monteverde equivalent of a billboard. Anyone looking to drum up attendance at something—maybe a musical performance at the Institute or Ladies' Night at the *taberna*—paid the guy with the loudspeaker on his truck to drive around through dinner hour, playing an announcement he'd recorded in a moment of profound exhilaration.

We were getting in a groove when our new friend Hugo asked us, "Hey, what would you think of moving to Canitas?"

About three miles away, Hugo told us, a modest palace sat atop its own hill, facing west. A couple from Tennessee had constructed a remote paradise with an eye to maximum bird watching. They planned to retire to it, but had a year of work left before the day came.

Hugo started to talk about the house; my mind wandered to the idea of retirement. *What must it feel like, to be so close to pure relaxation?*

Then, *Wake up, you mental patient. Look around you.*

The Canitas Option was a three-bedroom, one-and-a-half-story, North-American-style beauty. The Tennesseans had included a bathtub and a sizable hot water heater. The house was not huge, but it was surely—Hugo looked pointedly down at the view through our floor—not rustic.

Hugo had designed and built the house and its furniture. From Central American mahogany, he had crafted dining table and chairs, comfy living room seating and elegant barstools from which you could chat up the chef in your gourmet kitchen. When the birders (Sally and Glen) asked him if he knew of someone—say, some nice family?—who could take care of their house until they arrived, Hugo had thought of us. The rent at Sally and Glen's would be half what we were paying behind Johnny's.

Our current quarters sat just off Cerro Plano's main road, right between downtown Santa Elena and the tourist mecca of the Monteverde Reserve. We tended to hear a lot more trucks and *motos* than we did birds or wind in trees. And our nightly sunset walks up the hill were lovely—but the house itself overlooked the roof of Johnny's Pizzeria.

Canitas was on the other side of Santa Elena, the side that wasn't really on the way to anything. It sat about twenty minutes on foot from downtown, but during those minutes you'd see maybe five vehicles. The birding almost-retirees had chosen this particular hilltop because of all the wings that flapped all around it, all the time. The house had an unimpeded view from meadows to rainforest to foothills to Gulf.

We faced the Monteverde flavor of a classic dilemma: Did we want more house for less money out in the country? Or less house for more money closer in?

I asked Anthony, "Did we really move this far away to live in a house that might have been built in Redmond?"

Anthony asked me "But did we really move to some of the best nature in the world to listen to milk trucks all day?"

What about seeing people? Cerro Plano held so many friends. Of course, we could afford a lot of taxi rides to visit them, with the money we would save on rent.

And houseguests? Would our friends and family want to listen to the birds and watch the sunsets, or be close to town?

The whole housing question boiled down to people, in the end, and the social lives we were trying to create. School asked that the Tico kids practice their English whenever they were around native speakers, but after school they didn't bother. Our current neighborhood was great for my kids' Spanish.

It would turn out that Harry's closest friends that year had been up at the blackboard that first morning of school. They all lived right in Cerro Plano, so close that when their mothers said they needed to be home by 5:00, the boys sprinted from our living room at 4:59.

Dimpling Diego, Stefan, Pedro, and Harry made a perfect, sitcom-ready foursome: The Beauty, The Hood, The Brain, and The Foreigner. I'd never seen a child so lazy about his schoolwork as Diego, yet so confident he could get around it with the flash of a grin.

"Diego, where's your homework?"

The Beauty did his thing. Slow, brilliant smile, huge eyes, cavernous dimples. "Mees Marti, I forget. Could I did it now? Harry can help me."

And famously strict Miss Marti didn't even bother to correct his English. She just shook her head and tried her best to look exasperated as she motioned Diego over to Harry's table.

Diego forgot his lunch all the time. He'd grin, ask kids to share a *leetle beet*. And everyone did. Unlike most Ticos we encountered, who had an initial, cheerful reserve around the expats, Diego had no problem running up to me from the start to ask if he could come over to play. Had anyone ever said no to this child? I know I never did.

Stefan was a year older than most of the class. He was plenty bright, but had started at the CEC just last year; he needed more English before he could join the kids his age. When we worked together, Stefan stayed engaged until he missed a problem—at which point he'd kick the desk, fold his arms over his chest, and stare at the floor. The Hood. In the cheerful and gracious culture in which we'd landed, Stefan was the only person I met all year who actually got sullen.

But Stefan in his element—on the soccer field, or when he suddenly GOT the math—his smile was huge and his words were quick and his laugh was deep.

The unquestioned cool kid of the class, Stefan had tried ripping the sleeves off his school T-shirt, but they just handed him a new one. I wouldn't have been surprised if he'd shown up the next day with a pack of cigs in the sleeve. I felt protective of Stefan. I wasn't sure why.

Pedro was what Stefan might have been, if whatever was going on with Stefan...wasn't. Funny and open, clever but utterly without guile, Pedro was one of those boys you want yours to be around, hoping a little bit of him will rub off. Pedro turned in his schoolwork on time, his printing tidy on unscrunched paper. His jokes were funny but never mean, and when he came to play with Harry he unfailingly asked Ivy if she wanted to join them. *"Quiere jugar, chiquita?"*

Pedro had the polite reserve that Diego lacked, but without Stefan's worldly skepticism. He never stopped wanting to play chess, and gave Harry a run for his money. Unlike Diego, Pedro never needed a reminder that pawns could only move forward, and he never asked whether we had ice cream.

Pedro's parents routinely paid me what was clearly their highest compliment: that Harry was very polite. My kids had long accused me of caring more about manners than anyone else *in the world*, so I basked in this external validation. Pedro's dad often followed up with, *"Y muy intelligente."* (Pedro's parents were unusually perceptive people.) Across significant cultural, economic, and linguistic divides, these compliments made me feel a kinship with Pedro's family—they valued what I valued, which made me feel on familiar ground.

Pedro, Harry, Diego, and Stefan regularly hung out catching tadpoles at the stream, and let an ecstatic Ivy tag along. When rain forced them indoors, the four boys played chess or made slingshots, enthusiastically.

Harry's taste for weaponry was a long-standing issue. Several years back, Anthony's sister had spotted one of the majestic birds that tended to perch on the bridge near our house.

"Look!" Auntie Lisa pointed. "Bald eagle!" And my boy had replied, "That's so cool! Can we shoot it?"

No matter how much bleeding-heart peacenikery Anthony and I brought to the equation, no matter how many squirt *lions* I bought instead of squirt *guns*, we'd never been able to quell Harry's desire to shoot stuff. We felt real bad about it, in Seattle.

Now, Harry and his *compañeros* spent hours in the woods seeking perfect slingshot sticks. But when I mentioned this shyly in a group of parents—Quakers, no less—no one raised an eyebrow. Anthony and I decided we'd just let Harry follow his bliss, this year, and cautioned the four boys never to aim at any living thing.

Hannah had seemed fine that first day at school, but easy friendships weren't coming as fast for her. Twelve is a hard age to be yanked from all your friends and plunged into a whole new set—whose rules you know nothing about. Plus, Hannah hadn't had to reach out socially since the first day of kindergarten, when she and Lucy had found each other and latched on. Lola, the nice lady I hadn't made friends with at *Casa de Arte,* had a daughter Hannah's age. Liliana sometimes came across the street from the two tiny rooms behind the *Casa* that she and Lola shared. Lili and Hannah studied quietly, but hadn't yet negotiated the leap from homework partners to friends.

Most days Hannah said "fine" when asked, but her temper was getting short and she cried awfully easily. There was no point trying to figure out which of these things came from being Hannah, which came from being twelve, and which came from being in Costa Rica.

Her sense of humor about the whole thing was typically Hannah. One night I came home from Esperanza to find her on her bed, headphones on. She unplugged readily to laugh about her day.

"It's hilarious, Mama. They couldn't rub it in harder if they tried. So today was the first day of sex ed, right? And the teacher keeps saying, 'You're getting to an age when your friends are going to mean everything, and your family is going to be less and less central.' And I'm thinking, *fantastic.* Here I am, thousands of miles away from all my *friends*, and the only people who know me at all are my *family*! And of course, this class is in English, so it's not even like I'm spared by not having a clue what's going on."

I applied the "Do you have anyone to eat lunch with?" rule, and she did. Hannah was friendly with three girls: Rebecca, Anjelica, and Liliana, but was pretty taken aback by the amount of gossip and generally obnoxious adolescent girl stuff in the crowd.

She told me she'd asked Liliana on the school bus if it bugged her when everyone talked behind each other's backs, but Lili had just shrugged.

So Hannah thought maybe gossip was cultural, and she should just get over being bothered.

"It's hard to say for sure. Liliana's really quiet."

Liliana was stunningly beautiful, with long black hair, thick-lashed eyes, and the kind of body adolescent girls point to in magazines, sighing that they will *never* look like that. She didn't need the makeup that so many Tica girls at the school piled on. But I could picture the shrug Lili had given in response to Hannah's question—shrugging was practically the only gesture I'd seen her make. Such a contrast to her effervescent, welcoming *mamá.*

Later in the year, Lola would tell me that the divorce had been hard for Lili and that she was only now recovering from the move to this tiny town and the change from their big city life in San José. This insight gave me a lot more tolerance for Liliana.

Ivy's social life was Courtney. That was all.

Anthony and I had mostly been socializing with each other. But that was about to change with my yoga class up in Monteverde. Soon I would be hanging out with all my pretzel-shaped friends, being all "Blah blah blah triangle pose, Namaste, spinal twist, downward dog," and Anthony would not be able to keep up.

With the option to move away from Cerro Plano, I'd started paying better attention to our individual social lives. I was also fascinated by the overall social scene of Monteverde.

Like many transient communities—Washington, DC comes to mind—Monteverde society was a layered ecosystem, its strata based on tenure. The first, foundational layer was the stable forever guard, both Tico and Quaker. The pioneer Quaker families had fruitfully multiplied, and by the time we arrived, the intermarrying between the Ticos who'd founded Santa Elena and the Quaker settlers of Monteverde had been such that there wasn't much sense to any distinction. That was Layer One.

Next came a solid layer of more recent arrivals, people who had lived in the zone a few years or more. Much of Layer Two had, like us, come for a visit—then seen more reasons to stay than go. Hugo had come over from France, then joined Layer Two. The Layer Two family we got to know best had a boy in Harry's class.

Miles was a small, fast-talking blond kid who'd spoken Spanish before English. Miles had lived the first part of his life in the expatriate enclave of San Miguel de Allende, Mexico, where he'd attended a Waldorf school. But when he turned eight and no one had yet taught him the alphabet, his parents decided to kick things up a tiny notch. They found the CEC, decided to try Monteverde, and stayed.

With Pedro's family, the values had felt familiar. In Miles's case, the inside of their house put me at ease. It was a mess. Their kitchen table served, as did mine, as a temporary repository for homework, groceries waiting to be put away, miscellany, and maybe some breakfast dishes. I never saw a Tico home in any state but spotless, and Ezmeralda once told me that she herself swept the floor three times a day. Miles and his family had lived in Latin America for years, but their house was still Gringo.

The third and final layer of residents were the people like us—long term visitors. Here to live, then leave.

Our first Layer Three friends were Kelly and Mike Jensen, a couple from New Mexico, and their four interesting and slightly-hippie children. Their eldest, also a Hannah, was about our Hannah's age. Their youngest, Molly, was a year younger than Ivy, and they had a set of twins in the Harry-ish zone. Kelly had a tattoo over the entire top of her back, with symbols representing each of the kids. We dove together into learning Spanish, and Mike was very keen to teach us to play bridge—really, Hippie Man? Molly and Ivy immediately struck up a friendship of convenience. Ivy wanted to be a princess and Molly wanted to be a boy, but they both spoke English and their parents were friends, so they overlooked their own cultural differences.

"Let's play Snow White!"

"Yeah! I'll be the dwarves!"

They made it work.

In Layer Three, we were as social and as eager as college freshmen. Layer Two, like the Miles family, were also very friendly—as recent graduates themselves, they knew that some of us were bound to join them. And the stable forevers of Layer One were pleasant to us short-timers, but didn't seek us out. Fair enough, I thought, and figured this might be what Hannah had been bumping into. The CEC eighth graders were all from Layer One. They had a whole world, and they knew that Hannah was just passing through it.

Across all levels, the Gringos in Monteverde were more relaxed than the ones I was used to. There were gentle Quakers and a host of new-agey dropouts, as well as the tattooed Jensens and Miles's family. In our Seattle crowd, surrounded as I was by twenty-somethings who planned to make their fortunes by thirty, I had been way down there on the ambition scale. But compared to white people who lived in Monteverde, I felt like a cross between Hillary Clinton and Gordon fucking Gekko.

And then there were the tourists.

All of us in the substrata counted in a way that tourists didn't. Tourists were a necessary inconvenience, frequently smelly.

"¿Por qué los francéses no se bañan?" Diego asked. The boys had just returned from a snack run to Santa Elena and were sitting on the floor, setting up the chessboard.

"¡Pero los alemanes! Por Dios!" Stefan plugged his nose and fell backwards in a faint, letting a bishop roll out of his hand. Then he was back up on his elbows, and he and Diego both looked at Harry expectantly. The white kid would know why the French and German tourists never seemed to shower. Harry shrugged and laughed. Where he came from, you pretended you didn't notice stuff like that.

We locals would help tourists with a map and let them spend their money, but mostly we enjoyed feeling smugly not-that. Hannah loved saying *"Perdón"* instead of "Excuse me" as she squeezed through clumps of tourists in town, making sure they could see her school uniform.

Many places had a published price for tourists, and a secret price—usually half or less—for locals. At the nearby *Finca Ecologica,* tourists would pay seven dollars a day to explore miles and miles of rainforest trails. On our first visit, Alvin, the owner, recognized Anthony as the weird Gringo who was always picking up cans, and charged us seven bucks for a family membership—for the year.

"You're neighbors now," Alvin told us. Aw.

We were getting the hang of the larger community, and our own micro version of it, when the option to switch houses came up.

Harry had just been invited to try out for a soccer team. He was thrilled and chatty in the week beforehand: "I know I'm small, but I'm so fast I bet they'll put me on defense." The team practiced near Canitas.

Then we learned that Kelly and Mike were going to move their brood out to Canitas, too. Monteverde was beautiful but, they felt, too white.

Our lease behind Johnny's was up in just over a month. In two weeks, Sally and Glen would come to town to find some renters. We started thinking.

12

Stressed Behind Johnny's

W e were considering our future when things began to fall apart within our present. The parrots had tried to warn us. My dad got to watch. The rain drilled sideways into the windowpanes behind Johnny's and there was no escape.

I hadn't been so naïve as to think we wouldn't have hard times, but culture shock didn't strike the way I thought it would. Culture shock sounds impressive, like an actual condition. We were just really cranky.

We'd moved our bodies to an exciting and colorful new world, but our human faults and petty grievances had slipped down to Costa Rica with us. All the newness removed our armor against them, so that we were our absolute worst selves. Our armor wore off in September, just as our first visitor—my father—got to town.

My worst self can be a tiny bit driven. From the moment we arrived, I felt like everyone had to learn as much Spanish as possible, as fast as possible. I instituted a rule that, every other night at dinner, we spoke only Spanish. Fun for everyone! The first night on our new program, I eked out a request. I'd learned "butter" from Dora the Explorer.

"La mantequilla, por favor?"

Ivy answered, "STOP IT, MOMMY! YOU KNOW YOU CAN REACH THE BUTTER."

"Ivy, shut UP! You don't have to be such a brat about it!" Harry's worst self was often on my side, which made it not nearly so bad. This would end.

On Butter Night, Hannah had been trying to hold it together for the good of the collective, but she was done. She burst into tears. "I can't stand it! Everyone is snapping at each other! It was so quiet the first week, before you all got here!" She ran from the room.

Anthony stayed completely silent, the entire meal and after (worst self? check). Harry and I went ten rounds on Why You Need To Clear Your Dish, while Anthony cleared around us and filled the sink. My dad took Hannah's cue and disappeared.

Hannah was right—it was quiet before we got here. But here we all were. In a space smaller than we were used to, in a world unfamiliar. In this peaceful, magical, *National Geographic* cover photo of a place, bickering took over.

It's one thing to be messy and petty in the noisy, tacky USA. Here, the contrast between the scenery and our behavior ratcheted up my stress level, as did my dad's presence. (My dad doesn't really do mess. My dad does wry, and my dad does tidy, and my dad does pathological exercise. Yelling? Mm, *no*.)

Hannah couldn't stand us. Neither, apparently, could my dad. And neither could I.

I had created this amazing adventure for all of us. How could everyone still be so irritating? And not just normal irritating. I couldn't remember us ever before being so consistently rotten to each other.

We were all horrible people for a few weeks, but Harry and I were the loudest about it.

Harry, the one I could depend on to say, "Thanks, Mom!" after every meal. Harry, who never grew tired of hugging and being hugged, who neither held himself apart nor raged against me, and whose bad moods came and went in the space it took to identify them. Harry turned on me. It was an ambush, from the corner where I'd least expected it, and I turned on him right back.

He chose the dumbest battles, and he fought them hard. Didn't do his homework. Didn't help with chores. Got defiant about whether he did or did not have the right to hit Ivy when she clearly deserved it.

He even regressed to an attitude that I thought we had drummed out of him years before.

Of the myriad parenting choices I can and do get wound up about, fairness had never made the cut.

"It's not fair!"

Wait, seriously? You think it should be fair? I reject your premise, little man.

Five years before, when Harry had been going round and round with Hannah on some trivial injustice, I had tossed baby Ivy in the backpack and said to him, "Let's walk up the hill. It's sunset."

"But it's not f..."

"Too bad. Come on."

Seattle's Capitol Hill, on a warm May evening after dinner, provides a pretty stunning view to the west—all Puget Sound and pink mountains.

"Sweetie, look at the sun going down behind the Olympics. Isn't it beautiful?"

We watched together. Harry, usually perpetual motion, could stand still to watch a sunset.

"Harry, you know what I have never done, ever?"

"What?"

"Anything at all to deserve a sunset. Or the mountains, or the Sound. But I get them anyway. All the time, whether I deserve them or not."

I continued. I like to belabor my points. Plus, I was talking to a five-year-old. I had no qualm playing the Morally Superior card with a person who, until recently, bit anyone with whom he disagreed.

"I get sunsets and you guys and desserts. I live in a house with a roof. Sometimes I plant seeds and they grow into something pretty, or edible. How does that even happen?

"You know, I wasn't a better baby than one whose parents had no food. But I got fed all the time anyway. We don't live in a fair world, Harryo. But I don't think I'd better complain. *Life's not fair, and it's not fair in my favor.* I think you want to think about all the ways that's a win for you, and not the little tiny ways it sometimes isn't."

Nice, right?

We'd walked back home hand in hand, in peace. Harry had only needed abbreviated refreshers since then.

"That's not fair!"

"Nope. It's not. And who's the beneficiary of that again?"

"We are."

"Right."

Now, Justice Harry was back with a vengeance, about every little thing. I tried reminding him of how life isn't fair, but it didn't take. The good old days when he didn't yell at me, when I could walk him up the hill and be a good gentle mother with a nice little speech, had vanished.

"You always think you're so right, but you're NOT," Harry told me regularly. "You're SO BOSSY and it's NOT FAIR! The whole world shouldn't have to do what YOU want all the time!"

Everything was a battle with him. It made me more furious every day.

Furious, but also embarrassed and sad. I had wanted to show my dad this new life, this carefree joy I had fashioned after all those years of striving. *Look! I did it! From terrified unwed mother to tightly-wound chess player, all the way to* pura vida *world adventurer. Look!*

But instead of fun family hijinx, I was a shrew and my nine-year-old son was being a *total asshole.*

Hannah learned early the arguments you can't win. Even if righteousness is on your side, isn't it worth just hanging up your jacket to avoid having to listen to mom?

"Here, I'll do it, you guys just SHUT UP!" she said, over and over.

But Harry will argue anything, and does. When Harry fights, he isn't just correct—he's also the only virtuous person in the room.

Hey! Me, too!

Anthony, over and over, cleaned up around the edges—did dishes, made sure there was milk for the morning, read to Ivy, silently fortifying himself against possible charges of not being helpful. I felt like I was parenting by myself, but I couldn't prove it because Anthony kept cleaning up after dinner.

I wanted him to step in, back me up, but I'd have settled for after-the-fact niceness. Something sympathetic, even appreciative, like "I'm sorry you got yelled at, but thanks for making sure Harry got his math done." Nope.

Shortly after Butter Night, in our fully windowed living room just off the main road, in a country where every child I saw respected his parents, Harry and I had a no-holds-barred showdown. It started off about packing.

In Monteverde, shorts were the surest marker of the male outsider. Tico men wore long pants, always. Usually jeans. Harry had been in Central America two months now, and he knew what was what. He was adamant that he'd bring only jeans on our upcoming trip to Nicaragua.

"Harry, Monteverde is up in the *sky,*" I told him. "It's seventy degrees here, but in Nicaragua we'll be at sea level. When rain hits the ground, it will literally steam. You need shorts."

"Mom, you're in Central America—don't you think you should act like it? They use Celsius here. Seventy degrees Fahrenheit is twenty-one in Celsius."

"Dammit Harry, that's not the point! It's not just your business if you're miserable, because you'll make it everyone else's. I don't want to spend the whole week listening to you complain. Just pack one pair!"

"You don't know everything, and you're not the boss of everything. You think you are, but you aren't!"

Five minutes later, we were here:

"I can't believe you're being such a brat! I worked so hard to put all this together. I spent freaking DAYS making sure your school was taken care of, while you were off running in sprinklers. I arranged for our family to travel separately so you could PLAY BASEBALL, and have you noticed that you *are nine years old*? It's not like there were talent scouts on hand. No, we filled out that list of pros and cons and I honored it, honored everything, and now you are being such a little jerk."

I'm not proud of this.

"Oh, so you're calling your son a jerk? That's how you try to make sure everyone has a good time here, by telling your children they're jerks? Great parenting, Mom! Really nice!" Harry had tears of fury streaming down his face; in addition to self-righteousness, the two of us share a tendency to leak when we get emotional.

I left then. It was that or pitch my son through the window, in full view of the road and maybe one of his teachers. It's a bad moment when the threat of an audience is the surest barrier between me and child abuse.

I stomped up the hill in tears. It was supposed to be so perfect. But here I was, being a terrible mother, just like at home. And Anthony was a terrible husband, never stepping in, never being on my side. Where was all that bonding we were supposed to be having, now that we weren't working all the time? And Harry was a terrible little kid, making a gigantic scene about something so easily solvable.

I got to the tree, and the parrots were back. You can't cry when you're looking at a tree full of parrots, mostly because their problems are so much bigger than yours. *Emergency! Emergency!* I watched their hysterics and thought about mine.

Letting kids make their own mistakes had always been important to me. And it's an easy enough philosophy when they're two and their mistakes are adorable.

"Sweetie, I think your feet will be a lot more comfortable if you switch your shoes around," I'd suggest. And Harry'd say NO! and I'd say fine, and then when I turned out to be right we'd bend down and switch the shoes.

The stakes were higher now, but had my philosophy expired? What would happen if Anthony and I stopped playing safety net? If the kids truly owned their own packing and dealt with any fallout themselves?

It would eliminate this particular fight, which sounded good. But bringing only long, heavy pants to a place where both temperatures and humidity were going to be in the nineties? It was a gamble for sure.

I went back, determined to speak calmly. Anthony and the kids were playing keep-away with a mango. I bit back an inquiry about homework.

"Harry, I'm sorry I got so angry. I still think it's a bad idea, but if you want to bring only jeans, go for it." *I am so magnanimous.*

"Seriously?!"

I outlined my every-kid-for-himself plan, and everyone was thrilled. I looked at Anthony, who was nodding. He, too, seemed to be remembering who we were.

"If you end up wanting shorts, you can figure it out. Dad and I will decide whether we think it's safe for you to shop on your own. If we think not, you can wait until it's convenient for one of us to help. If buses or taxis are required, you fund it."

"Okay."

"And you have to suffer in silence," Anthony jumped in for the assist. "We don't want to hear about how hot you are."

Later that night, buoyed by that glimmer of engagement from Anthony, I tried very hard to approach him with curiosity, to have a real conversation. Did we have a difference in parenting philosophy? If so, let's talk about it. If not, why was I the only one hassling Harry about his packing? Or anyone about anything, come to think of it?

"You're *really* good at it," he said.

The day after the jeans battle, Harry bounced out the door to the soccer tryout he'd been preparing for. Two hours later, he drooped back in. I sat beside him on the couch. It still felt new, being home for all the little moments.

I started to get sympathetic, but Harry cut me off.

"I made the team, Mom," he said. "I'm just not gonna do it."

He talked about not wanting to fill his schedule and about not knowing the guys on the team—issues that Seattle Harry would never have even registered. Finally, he got past the red herrings.

"I was playing up front and a guy yelled for me to cross, but I didn't know what he said; I would've known 'cross,' but it was some kinda colloquialism." (*Harry knows the word colloquialism! Focus.*)

"We lost possession." His face was red. "And then he yelled at me." The tears spilled over. "In front of everyone."

Harry had played his first real soccer game at age six. When a high, fast ball headed toward the goal, Anthony and I had flinched in unison as our son, who couldn't yet tie his own cleats, acted on his preposterous, evolutionarily-devastating instinct to jump straight at the ball with his head. Harry's little noggin sent the ball twenty yards up the field while on the sidelines parents gasped and thought about brain damage.

Since that moment, Harry on the soccer field had been high-fived and slapped on the back; he'd outrun boys six inches taller and been praised for his sportsmanship and for his unerring instincts. But not once, until now, had Harry been yelled at. Not once had he felt ashamed.

Harry was off his game.

Culture shock didn't come to us tidily labeled, and it wasn't about missing a favorite brand of toothpaste. It just happened when we'd used all our energy getting through the day—and then still made mistakes at things we'd always been good at. Day in and day out, tasks we once did without thinking were suddenly hard and we still couldn't call home for a familiar voice. No wonder we didn't have the reserves left over to treat each other well.

I was sorry my dad had to be there, but at least, being my dad, he never did mention it.

Then came a trip that would put packing battles and soccer field humiliations into perspective. All the newness had put our family in cardiac fibrillation. Nicaragua was the shock paddles that got us beating again in our old, familiar rhythm.

13

¡Hola, Jerry! ¿Donde está George?

Sunshine had gotten reliable in Monteverde, and so had mist. It came most afternoons, but just as a token, a skin-care strategy. The warm sun zapped it away quickly, leaving a clean, green world. Once again, we took a cue from the improving weather and decided it was time for us to leave.

Year-round schooling works out brilliantly for traveling. The CEC took a month off at Christmas and one in June; the rest of the year, school ran in six-week sessions with a week's break between. We planned to get down the mountain to explore Central America during these intervals.

Our first trip would be to Nicaragua, for a week of intensive language study. My criterion for selection was simple: "the least expensive school in Nicaragua that we can reach by bus in a day." Harry might or might not be bringing shorts; I hadn't checked. Ivy was definitely bringing a tiara.

We'd been in Costa Rica just long enough to get a blast of what many Ticos feel toward Nicaragua and its people: disdain at best, hatred at worst. Ticos we knew seemed to feel that Nicaragua--with its dictators and its lack of infrastructure and its poverty, poverty, poverty--was an embarrassment to all of Central America. They wished Nicaragua would get its shit together. They wished Nicaragua would educate its citizens, brush its collective teeth, and stop being so poor all the time. They despised the Nicaraguan immigrants who, opinion had it, sneaked across the border to steal the crappiest Costa Rican jobs, use Costa Rican social services, and molest Costa Rican women.

Ezmeralda shook a perfectly manicured fingernail at any of us she caught lazily dropping the terminal *s* from words. *"No somos Nica!"* At school, parents delivered lice warnings with a sidelong glance at Nicaraguan children on the playground.

Ticos say "Nica" the way Arizonans say "wetback."

Going into the year, I'd wanted us to learn, learn, learn. Since I wasn't working, I'd have plenty of energy to devote to our curriculum. I'd be so fun that the kids wouldn't even realize how educated they were getting. We would learn the history, current events, and culture of Central America. We would see what needed changing in the world, and we'd be on fire to start fixing it. I didn't want to over-promise, but it did seem possible that our little family would have Central America all fixed up by the end of the year. Nicaragua would be the perfect kickoff.

And so, against the advice of our new Tico friends, we went.

At dawn, we boarded the rickety local bus that would bounce us down the mountain road to the cultural touchpoint that was the Pan-American Highway.

Famous roads come with a mood. I knew when I was young that if I ever made it to Route 66, everything there would be hip and smiling. I'd drive an old convertible, the kind with fins. I'd live on milkshakes and burgers and wear a bra that made my boobs point sharply.

Similarly, I figured that when I someday arrived at the Pan-American highway, I'd feel revolutionary. Che Guevara would be there, and he'd lecture me about how bourgeois I was until I finally got it, *really got it.* I'd leave my parents, become a communist, and automatically know how to tie a bandana on my head so that it wouldn't fall off.

Now I was a parent myself, arriving at Che's highway with a husband and three kids in tow. We climbed, bourgeoisly, off the bus. Anthony had begun experimenting with commie-wear; his bandana looked pretty good.

The Pan-American Highway is actually a series of linked roads that stretch from the very top of Alaska to the very bottom of Argentina. (It takes a hundred-mile break for impassable jungle right where Panama hits Colombia, but runs unperturbed through Costa Rica.)

Two lanes, potholes more visible than the faded yellow line down the middle, heat waves rising from the asphalt. Simple and true and just a road. We arranged ourselves on a backless wooden bench surrounded by cigarette butts. The Nicaragua-bound bus would, we'd been promised, stop there to pick us up. To our right, colorful birds I wished I could identify hopped around in an enormous mango tree that was currently providing shade to an area that was not our bench. Every so often, an overripe mango would thud to the asphalt of the Pan-American Highway. I expected them to sizzle.

The bus came. A private company ran the inter-country buses, which were much fancier than the public ones. I entered its air-conditioned splendor with relief. I would have made a very bad revolutionary.

At the border town of Peñas Blancas, a boy about Harry's age charged fifty cents to help us negotiate the crossing, including changing our Costa Rican *colones* for Nicaraguan *córdobas*.

As soon as our bus got underway on the Nicaragua side, it was clear we were somewhere else. Everything looked hotter. Back among the dusty trees, we could see houses constructed of tarps and scraps of tin. Dogs ate garbage at the side of the road. At a stop, one of them approached the bus just beneath Ivy's window.

"Can I pet him?" Ivy asked. Anthony looked at me. The dog looked exactly the way I'd imagined the one that lurches past Boo Radley's—just before Atticus shoots him, a little to the left of right between the eyes.

"Sorry, sweetie," Anthony improvised. "They won't let us off the bus for a while."

We arrived in Masaya late that afternoon, exiting the air conditioned bus and entering the actual air of southern Nicaragua.

People talk about smothering heat, but when I think smothering, I think pillows. I'm not suggesting that being pillowed would be a *terrific* way to smother, but it would be cool and smooth. Nicaragua's humidity was like smothering in a horrifying myth. The air in Nicaragua put me in mind of poor Prometheus, condemned by the gods to lay for eternity, spread-eagled and chained to a stone. Every day an eagle came and ate his liver. But what if the eagle had instead pulled out Prometheus' entrails and wound them around him? That's how I felt in Nicaragua. Hot, steaming squish surrounded me, and I could neither bat it away nor trick it into leaving me alone.

We found a *taxista,* whose battered Geo strained to get us the final couple of miles to the language school. Even machinery seemed to struggle in the heat. Harry, squished between Anthony and me in the back of the Geo, said, "Hey, family? I just want to thank you ahead of time for not teasing me when I change into shorts the second we get there."

The main school building turned out to be a large wooden house that overlooked *La Laguna de Apoyo,* a creepily warm, pondish kind of thing. A concrete outbuilding would house our family for the week, with bunk beds in a bunker about twelve feet square.

Each morning, we practiced Spanish with individual tutors for four hours—although for Ivy, "tutoring" was mostly *perro* and *gato* and getting piggyback rides around the grounds. In the afternoons, we went on school-sponsored excursions to see artisans and living conditions in the surrounding area. After field trips, we swam in the awkward lake, or visited the sprawling *mercado* in the nearby town. I had an uncomfortable moment when I encountered Danilo, my teacher in the morning, selling Chiclets outside the market in the afternoon.

On our first artisanal field trip, we watched a twelve-year-old girl make a basket out of dried palm fronds in twenty-two minutes. Who knows how long it had taken to gather the fronds—the surrounding area was largely denuded, the trees having been sacrificed to cooking fires. The girl sat on a stool in the family's living room, an area bound by corrugated tin placed sideways and strung between trees. She finished her basket, set it aside, and picked up more fronds, never looking up. Her brother was toddler-sized, but he didn't toddle; he sat quietly at her feet, scratching in the dirt with his hand. A student from our school snapped his picture. He seemed used to it.

Ivy, who never met a small child she didn't want to adopt, moved behind me.

That afternoon in the *mercado,* we saw we could buy a palm-frond basket for less than a dollar.

In the evenings, an almost-cool breeze blew in, and for an hour we'd be almost comfortable. We lay in hammocks and marveled at the bats, swooping black shadows against the darkening sky. We cheered them for eating the mosquitoes.

But then the breeze was done. At bedtime, the five of us tossed and turned stickily in our sweltering bedroom. We stayed on top of the sheets. We tried to think about Popsicles, and the chill of Lake Washington, even in August—not about epic smothering, or the spiders and geckos that would, if we snapped it on, scurry out of our flashlight's beam.

Ivy whimpered all night, her eczema inflamed by the heat. Anyone thinking about what we'd seen that day didn't want to discuss it. Hannah alluded to it, once.

"At least this will end," she spoke in the crawly darkness, "for us." That day we'd visited a man painting decorative pots under the blue, duct-taped tarp that formed his studio and home. We didn't know how to respond. We bought a lot of decorative pots.

Ivy told me in the morning that she'd dreamt last night about feeding people.

After the week of intensive language study, educational field trips, and being aware of sweat pooling in our bodily creases 23½ hours a day, we taxied to Masaya and caught a bus to Nicaragua's tourist gem. The colonial town of Granada, established in 1524, is the oldest European settlement in Nicaragua. The face Granada shows tourists is so darling you almost forget how hot you are. The town is famous for meticulously restored Baroque and Renaissance buildings. Narrow, pre-automobile streets meander toward a central plaza filled with fountains and flowers.

As we got off the bus, Hannah looked over at a wrought-iron lamp post dripping with vibrant, purple flowers, and said, "It's like Nicaragua, but not."

But by the time we got there, the kids were so overheated and exhausted that we couldn't bring ourselves to keep exploring. So instead of hauling them, or ourselves, through the Sandinistas' network of underground tunnels, or learning about Francisco Córdoba, the Spanish conqueror who founded Granada and then later got his name on the currency—we surrendered.

We gave up on history and architecture. Anthony and I led no thoughtful, age-appropriate discussions about privilege and power and how we could justify our lives in the face of all we'd seen. Instead, we hung out at our hostel, a converted Colonial beauty with fountains and courtyards and air conditioning. We played in the pool. The kids shrieked and splashed. Anthony bought pretzels from the snack machine, and we dripped our merry way across the charming courtyard to the blissful cool of our two (!) rooms. We watched *"La Vida de Jerry Seinfeld,"* a weekend-long marathon hosted by the Nicaraguan equivalent of Nick at Nite.

It wasn't bad parenting, though, because for every episode they watched, Harry and Hannah had to write down three Spanish phrases they learned from the episode. (*Estos bocadillos me dan sed!* =These pretzels are making me thirsty! A whole sentence we could apply right here and now!) Ivy failed to see the quirky humor of the most famously self-absorbed people ever, so we gave her snacks as a distraction.

There were bats in Granada, too, and as they began their mosquito-eating swoops outside, the only movement on our walls were the flickering shadows of Jerry and Elaine, George and Kramer. We lay between cool, smooth sheets. It was bliss, yes; but we were, alas, less ignorant.

Wherever we went that year, people were forever asking me about our motivations for moving to Central America. You tend to develop talking points when you get the same question over and over. "I want to show the kids that there are a lot of ways to live a life," kept working for me, but there was another, reason, equally true: I wanted to eliminate some of the lectures.

Lectures are the absolute worst part of parenting. But you have to do them. If you don't, you're sunk and your children become awful.

Hang up your backpack. Manners matter. Here's why we share.

My parental lecture series was rich and varied and had many installments. In moving to Central America, I hoped to dodge a few, living them out instead of yammering on. A strong candidate for this tactic was the talk entitled *You Guys Have No Idea How Lucky We Are.*

Nicaragua did the trick.

Nicaragua was an onslaught. The troubling images and the huge questions were so numerous and so upsetting that my weak, defensive brain ended up blending them into a single desperate muddle. So much so that the only question I could muster was: *How was it that everyone we met there was so clean?*

I never did figure this out. By no means did we get a complete view of the country; much of what we did see was a living, groaning, sweating PBS special on poverty. No running water, unless you count the rivulets through the living rooms when the rains came. Kitchens were outside fire pits or cookstoves, and everything we saw seemed to be coated in children, chickens, dogs, garbage, and flies. Yet our teachers sparkled when they arrived at school each morning. Their jeans dark blue and pressed—never shorts, oh no, no matter how hot, how thick the air—hair still a little damp, shoes perfect and dust-free.

In Seattle, our family was armed with two showers, washer/dryer, and unlimited hot water. Our dirt mostly lived in gardens, parks, and the occasional detergent commercial. Nonetheless, at least one of us was as likely as not to start the day with a crunchy spot on some bit of hair or clothing.

But when we were taken to peer into classrooms at the elementary school near *La Laguna,* not a single child had a smudge. Their uniforms had white shirts, and most of the children had walked a kilometer or two on unpaved roads to get there.

In English I have a decent variety of words at my disposal, but I still can't form any of them into a tactful execution of my vulgar question: *How do you manage to stay so clean when your country is so hot and so dirty, your house has no floor, and there are dogs everywhere?*

In Spanish, I smiled, nodded, and tried to tip very, very well.

By the end of the week at La Laguna, my tutor Danilo and I had covered enough topics in the course of our sessions that I thought I could broach the subject. I shook my head and gave a slight laugh at how trashy many of the tourists, including my family, looked. I wanted Danilo to know I had the sense to be embarrassed.

"When cleanliness is the way you can show your dignity, that you are worthy of respect," Danilo told me, "you pay attention to be clean."

That made sense to me. My family and I had grown up inside a cocoon of self-worth; we didn't need to worry about crunchy spots.

Drying my eyes over and over that week, I wondered whether I would have had a less overwhelmed response to Nicaragua if I'd gotten there when I was young and single. Would I have been able to abstract myself, then? I saw myself drinking beer with a bunch of other earnest nomads, talking into the night about liberation theology and inequitable distribution of resources. Now, I lay next to Ivy in the sticky darkness and tried to devise a way to scratch her back without actually touching her. But for accidents of birth and circumstance, my own children could be living under a tarp. I gave thanks for the lives we had and said a prayer that was not nearly enough for the little boy, for his sister, for all of the children we had seen.

The desperate muddle of Nicaragua reminded me of what I already knew, what we all know: As a country, and even in recession, America is ridiculously wealthy. And Northwesterners are, by and large, ridiculously wealthy even for Americans. And while Seattle does know poverty, my family did not. If Harry needed new cleats, we bought them. We lived less than a mile from a library, but I'd buy books for Ivy four at a time—I had the luxury of supporting local bookstores, and due dates were a hassle.

Seattle, of course, had been packed with the so-legendary-they've-become-tiresome-even-though-many-of-them-are-lovely-people high-tech jillionaires.

Our family lived, quite literally, in their shadow—on the bottom slope of the hill that many of them lived atop. We schooled, soccered, played, and I worked, with perfectly normal people who had amazing resources. Hanging in our circles in Seattle, having a very reasonable amount of money could feel downright poor.

Friends went to Italy and on safaris for their vacations; our family went mostly to the Oregon coast. Our kids loved the weekends they spent at their classmates' ski retreats, but they could never return the favor.

Through the tireless work of many parents (many of them the at-home wives who spent Microsoft millions), our sweet little neighborhood public school had recently become attractive to the many high-high-high-end families in the area.

One spring day, Hannah was invited to play with a new classmate. In our ancient but entirely serviceable Toyota Previa, I drove her up one of the curvy, leafy streets whose homes overlook Lake Washington. Stunning Colonials and Victorians mixed with glassy ultramoderns, but even the diverse architecture came in just one size: *efuckingnormous*. Azaleas bloomed among Japanese maples in the artfully artless front gardens. Hundred-year-old oaks presided in the expansive parking strips. It was the kind of neighborhood you want to drive to, just to take a walk. Birds chirped. Joggers were toned and tanned and wore fabrics that wick moisture.

Hannah had reached the age when I could drop her off, rather than doing the whole mom-chat inside. I double checked the address and drove into the circular driveway.

I leaned over and kissed Hannah on the head. Such a big girl, all of a sudden. "Have a great time, sweetie. I'll come back at six. Be sure to help pick up." I ducked down to see out the passenger window, so I could wave a quick hi/thanks at whoever answered the door.

Hannah didn't move. "Okay but which one?"

"Hmm?"

"Which one do they live in?"

"Honey, it's right in front of you. You're sitting ten feet from the front door."

Hannah's voice took on the edge that meant she was being very, very patient with me. "Yes, but which *apartment* do they live in? I need to know the number, to push the buzzer!"

Oh, right.

I explained that just Maddie's family lived in this house. Hannah looked up and down the street.

"In all of these? No apartments? Every single house on this street has just one family?"

It's one thing when your kids are surprised by that kind of wealth. More insidious, for me, was when they started taking it in stride. Hannah was embarrassed by her mistake that day and would never make it again.

When my children thought they came from a needy family because two of them shared a bedroom, it stopped me short. I'd been proud of the way we'd been able to live; still, in our neighborhood we mostly wore cotton t-shirts to go jogging.

So I might feel middle class in the States, and even in Monteverde, where our growing community of expat friends included many who lived simply yet beautifully and who hadn't worked for years. But I could not avoid the truth in Nicaragua. Nicaragua launched a full-on truth assault until I couldn't take it anymore. I hid away with my kids, from the flies and the dogs and the sadness and the air that you have to do the breaststroke through. Eating pretzels and watching Jerry Seinfeld reruns in an air-conditioned room, I hid from the truth of the poverty in which too many people live. And I hid from the truth of my own, unimaginable wealth.

I think that most of us who never go hungry (unless it's on purpose) do know how fortunate we are. But I forget. Why do I keep having to remember and re-remember this thing I know I know? On the sweaty bus ride back from Nicaragua, I swear to God, I caught myself whining because we wouldn't be able to afford to get to Ecuador at Christmas. Anthony stayed quiet. I heard myself and felt ashamed.

I was confused by issues of having and not having, and didn't know what to do. Our Seattle was a dream world, where wealth was assumed and want was nonexistent. I knew it would be a failure on my part to not expose us all to a bigger reality. But while I wanted my children to be aware of suffering, I didn't want them to become inured to it. What a terrible backfire it would be, to expose the children to so much poverty that they decided it was unavoidable and unaddressable—and so they need never try to address it.

Even Jesus had some class issues. On the one hand, He was clearly very big on feeding the poor, clothing the naked, and so on. On the other, there's that one disturbing story, when Judas gets so snotty about Mary Magdalene—*that slut!*—anointing Jesus with oil. Judas thinks the oil should have been sold and the money given to the poor. Jesus defends the extravagance, saying, "The poor will always be with us." I've always thought that was a fairly dickish statement on His part.

But I understood it better in Nicaragua. Being anointed in oil was the Jesus version of an air-conditioned hostel.

So I let my kids laugh at the television that whole weekend. They'd lived the lecture.

What we saw in Nicaragua would percolate and distill, and become part of each of us. I wanted us to have the will and the energy for baby steps. Sometimes we'd give deeply, and sometimes we'd give ourselves a break. That weekend, I surrendered my plan to learn and grow and be educated citizens of the planet, every minute of the trip. I shut up, and we all ate pretzels.

Returning to Monteverde from Nicaragua, we filled our lungs gratefully with the cool mountain air. When we reached the top, the time had come to confront our privilege in a whole new way. The Tennesseans had come to town. It was time to decide whether we were going to leave the diesel-filled bustle of Cerro Plano and move to their dream house.

Sally loved to cook and had built the kitchen she'd always wanted. Glen had designed the two-story living room windows, which looked all the way down the foothills to the *Golfo de Nicoya*. These dream-come-true landlords wanted to check us out, which seemed fair enough. Less comprehensible was that when they met us, all five of us, they still wanted us to move in.

It was a beautiful house. We were leaning toward taking it. And yet.

I felt conflicted and weird all over again. Would it be somehow inauthentic, to move to Costa Rica and live in this house?

Though modestly sized, Glen and Sally's home was more carefully designed and more beautiful than any I had ever lived in. And I was plenty shallow enough to worry about what our friends would think. When visitors saw our how our mahogany furniture created the perfect complement to the light airiness of the architecture, would we lose our adventurer cred?

In Seattle I'd envied people who had enough money to buy the life I wanted. Now here I was, uncomfortable with the life I could have. I could hear myself already, explaining to anyone I could trap into listening that this lovely house was *also* the economical choice, half the price in fact, and plus we would have duties to fulfill!

For crying out loud. Did I have too little or too much, and would I never make up my mind?

And then I saw the wood stove.

It was one of the great regrets of my childhood that I had to grow up in a 1920s bungalow on Seattle's Phinney Ridge rather than in a cozy dugout near Plum Creek, safe from the harsh prairie winters. I knew I could be Laura Ingalls and longed for someone to give me a chance. I'd sweep the dirt floors every morning and in the afternoons run wild in the meadows. I'd let my bonnet hang by its strings and get scolded for letting myself get brown as an Indian. I dreamed of Erin getting scarlet fever, going blind, and starting to be nice to me.

Years passed, and I reconciled myself to the cruel realities of central heating and childhood immunizations. But as I looked at the woodstove in Glen and Sally's living room, I realized: *I could still be Ma.* I pictured us on a 56-degree morning in the rainy season, the cold no less bitter for its being highly occasional. We'd cluster together around the stove, twisting banana leaves into fuel to feed its hungry maw. "Quickly, children! The baby's getting cold!" We'd obviously have to have another baby. I wondered whether it might be possible to get Anthony a fiddle.

I looked at the stove, then at Anthony, and tried not to look too much like a hopeful puppy. Anthony rolled his eyes only the tiniest bit.

As Glen, Sally, Anthony, and I were wrapping up the interview and shaking hands to seal the deal, we came to the question of hired help. We'd reviewed the various caretaking tasks—tending the tiny avocado seedlings Glen had planted, minding the spring and reservoir, putting coats of preservative on the deck every three months. The teak floors were beautiful and would need to be polished.

I had worked my whole adult life, as had Anthony. Together, we kept our house reasonably clean if you didn't inspect weird areas, like the top of the fridge. I'd always gardened. Anthony and I were both competent and willing. We would happily perform all the maintenance items on their list. Not a problem at all.

Glen was gentle, "Are you sure you wouldn't like to hire Luis to do the outdoor work?"

I persisted in not getting it. It was just so far out of my mindset to hire a— what would you call him, a gardener? I was basically idle and loved to garden. We were trying to live on $800 a month. Our family would be a family that had a *gardener*?

Meanwhile, my frugal husband was sitting beside me, undergoing a dramatic personality change. Or perhaps he was under a spell (*hechizo*) of some kind.

"Oh, that's a great idea," he said. "We'd love the help. When can we meet Luis?"

I blinked. Was this the same fiscal conservative who would spend an entire weekend with greasy fingers, his bike in pieces all over the yard, rather than pay someone who could fix it in ten minutes?

Sally helped me out:

"Luis's family has been very good to us. Luis helped carry most of the construction materials up here; we couldn't have built the house without him. Now that it's complete, I know he'd appreciate some continued work."

Ah. The question wasn't whether or not we could do it. The question was whether my feelings of competence and independence were more important than Luis's ability to make a living.

Anthony had seen this immediately and had been comfortable with it immediately. As we continued the conversation, Sally was able to be very frank with me, for which I was grateful. She told me, always gently, how much she and Glen were looking forward to participating in the community *in any way they could*. This didn't just mean going to concerts at the Friends School. Glen and Sally could, and would, assume a role in the Monteverde zone's economy. They could, and would, become employers.

In addition to Luis's help with the grounds, Sally also knew of a local woman, Magda, who apparently did a fine job cleaning houses. Sally could get me her number if I wanted.

I grew up in a bootstraps kind of family. Hiring someone to do housework was for pretentious society ladies. But pretentious comes in many guises, I realized. Would I really pretend that my image of *how we should be* was more important than my neighbors' ability to feed their kids?

I didn't consider us the rich people, *really*, not even after Nicaragua. Which is pretty funny, because although I signed the lease wearing crappy sandals and an old T-shirt, I also felt quite at home doing so sitting on an artisan-made mahogany chair, behind a plate-glass window, and in front of Sally's $2,000 stove.

Of course we would hire Magda as well. I nodded to Glen and became, like Vanessa Redgrave in *Camelot*, noblessely obliged.

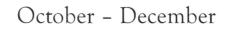

October – December

14

Seep of Faith

Every Sunday at the Mass we could not understand, the five of us acknowledged our guilt. *"Por mi culpa, por mi culpa, por mi grandissima culpa,"* we said in unison, smacking ourselves in the chest. I was pretty sure this meant "It's my fault, it's my fault, it's *really* my fault," and I took a lot of pleasure watching my own personal children go through this litany.

Today I had the tiniest bit of confessing to do my ownself. On the walk to church, I'd asked Anthony, "Do you think someone's going to walk up to you and say 'Would you like me to install a phone line?' Or do you think maybe you should *keep working on this problem until the children can send a fucking email?"*

Over the kids' heads, Anthony glanced from me to the church, then made his eyebrows go all smirky. "Jesus just loves it when you talk like that," they said.

Point taken, but it was still Anthony's fault that we had no internet. Plenty of *culpa* to go around.

We were going Catholic now. This was new to me, and I was only the tiniest bit disappointed that my new spiritual home wasn't more ornate; I had thought the Catholics were all about the flying buttresses and the big rose windows.

(When it comes to understanding Catholicism, I am deeply indebted to the novels of Dan Brown.)

But the Santa Elena church had no stained glass, no ancient crypts, and no murderous albino (*that I could see*). Just a low yellow building with a simple cross out front, and a sign: *Iglesia Católica*. Families trooped in together. Men and boys wore their darkest blue jeans; women and girls teetered, precarious in their high-heeled sandals, but the babies they carried did not seem nervous.

Although I loved *por mi culpa*, my favorite part of Mass was when the children lined up to get blessed. Each Sunday after the sermon, the younger kids got to stop squirming on their big sisters' laps and hightail it to the side aisles. Two lines bloomed up the edges of the wooden pews and headed to the front, where the priest sat in his throne (possibly not the Catholic term) like a jolly, slightly-more-formal Buddha. Progress was slow. Some of the boys passed the time by picking at the paint that peeled from the walls, then throwing the little chips at each other.

"La paz, la paz, la paz," said the merry fat priest from his perch. He rested his hand for a moment atop each shiny head, blessing the child beneath. *Peace.* Little boys stopped chucking things and returned to their seats looking transformed and holy; the girls had looked pretty beatified from the beginning, but they seemed to glow even brighter on the return trip.

For a few weeks now, Hannah and Harry had been urging Ivy to line up with the little ones and get herself blessed. I had been staunchly against this plan. What if her participation was seen as some kind of cultural insult? What if you had to be Catholic? Or what if she headed up under cover of *la paz,* then did some other nutty thing?

This fear was not far-fetched. Ivy was three when she broke free during Christmas Eve service at our own church and strode up to the manger to see whether the role of Jesus was being played by a real baby (yes), and if so, could she hold him (not right now, sweetie). But that was home. They knew us there. Plus, our Seattle church is United Church of Christ, about as lefty-liberal as you can get while still keeping Jesus around. At Plymouth, we mostly try to make sure the kids know they are loved; we don't worry too much about protocol. This didn't sound very much like what Dan had told me about the Catholics.

But we wouldn't get to *la paz* until after the sermon, so I didn't need to worry yet.

My Spanish mania had made me an unusually attentive churchgoer. I'd found lyrics to the songs that came up most frequently—folky ones about putting my *mano* in your *mano*, and then holding the *mano* of God—and printed them in a tiny font along with the Lord's Prayer and Nicene Creed. I made *iglesia* cheat-sheets for us all, so that we could kinda-sorta participate in the Mass. But I still tended to drift during the sermon. (I might have done better had the priest borrowed more heavily from pop lyrics.)

The day was hot, and a scraggly yellow dog had found a nice place to nap in the center aisle. I was considering the consequences of laying my own hot cheek on the cool tiles when I heard a familiar word, and my ears perked up.

¡Quetzal!

You can't go to Central America without hearing from everyone—guidebooks, locals, a well-meaning couple who served in the Peace Corps forty years ago—*you must see a quetzal.* This lovely little bird, all colors and long tail and darling rounded head, is elusive but worth it. Named by the Aztecs, the quetzal symbolizes goodness and light. Quetzals are showy as all giddyup, and people who have seen one never forget it. They tell and retell their story, polishing it like a precious metal until every detail dazzles, every adjective shines.

Knowing all about the quetzal already, I felt sure I was going to be able to follow the sermon today. I prepared to tip my head to the side and nod thoughtfully along.

The priest was talking about those who have seen *Señor Quetzal* and those who have not. He said the latter bunch believes in the splendor and goodness of *Señor Quetzal* even without ever seeing him. He made extra-sure we all got the metaphor, going on (I'm pretty sure) about how faith should not require proof.

I was crushed—I already knew this one!

I am a bubbling cauldron of petty sin, one misdemeanor after another. And I surely have some spiritual felonies in my burbling stew. But *faith in things unseen* is the one spiritual practice I was born good at. I cannot explain this and take no credit; but there it is. I stopped listening to the sermon and let my mind wander to events that showed I didn't need to.

For anyone looking, ironically or not, for proof of my good faith, I could submit several significant displays of aptitude. I started with the biggie—belief itself, in God, in Jesus, in the preposterous Resurrection.

Walker Percy spoke right to me, which was thoughtful, in his great novel *Love in the Ruins:*

"I believe in God and the whole business but I love women best, music and science next, whiskey next, God fourth, and my fellowman hardly at all.

Generally I do as I please. A man, wrote John, who says he believes in God and does not keep his commandments is a liar. If John is right, then I am a liar. Nevertheless, I believe."

Exactly. Misdemeanors all over the place. And yet: Faith.

But that's just the beginning.

Most people of faith, no matter which formal religion provides the structure for it, tend to share a belief in our own limitations. It's the pinnacle of expectations management, and I find it highly comforting. My philosophy of my own limitedness goes like this: *I'm human, what did you expect? You say religion is a crutch? Um,* duh. *Did you not notice my limp?*

It's a given for the faithful—I guess you'd call it an article of faith—that in our limitation, we don't always see the big picture. It's axiomatic, then, that a thing can be right even if it's looking awfully wrong, or scary, or too much. Thirteen years before, staring bewildered at those two blue lines, my brain got all staticky and fuzzed over. Its signals couldn't quite get through. My skin sat wrong on top of my muscles, as if it was no longer quite up to the job of holding me together.

Everything felt raw and shocking and exorbitant. And yet, against all reason, I believed in my pregnancy's goodness. I believed in its light. I believed that God did, too, and in prayer and terror I picked my way across to I-knew-not-where, finding one stepping stone and then the next. And then I leapt—into motherhood, into Anthony, into an adulthood for which I was sure I was not ready.

Nearly thirteen years later, not knowing exactly what it would do to us, I knew we should pack up our lives and bring them here. I didn't know what "here" would look like, but I believed.

When it comes to accepting the big unknowns, I am all hooked up. I hardly needed a priest belaboring a metaphor about a gaudy little bird.

But the other congregants probably had much to learn, so I resolved to be patient. It was such a comfort, being able to understand the sermon well enough that I could tell I didn't need it.

The priest had stopped talking, and up came the little ones, and oh good heavens, Ivy. How had that happened? While I'd been reviewing my leap-of-faith Greatest Hits, I'd relaxed my constant vigilance. Harry craned his neck to follow her progress, while I broke out in hives. I nearly spat at Anthony, but settled for hissing:

"I can't believe you let her go up there! She doesn't know what to do! What if she starts throwing paint chips? She hasn't had her first communion, or whatever you're supposed to do...dammit! What if she tries to talk to the priest? Jesus, this is a disaster."

At the front, *Señor* was placing his hand on each dark bowl-cut or set of shiny black plaits. The blond curls moved closer.

"*La paz, la paz, la paz . . .*"

Blessed, the children returned in a single line up the center aisle, daintily sidestepping the dozing doggie. I saw only that single head, moving inexorably toward the front. So far she wasn't throwing anything.

At her turn, Ivy bowed her head like a pro. "*La paz.*"

She raised her head and beamed. Beatific. Harry pumped one arm, and with the other gave Hannah the sideways, no-looking fist bump they had been perfecting at the bus stop.

But on her way back to us, Ivy went off road. *I knew it.* I clenched my teeth as she stopped in the center aisle, holding up the line. She dropped suddenly to a squat, the way you can when you're five and close to the ground already. Reaching out, she gently patted the head of the only other creature in the room whose hair was the same color as hers.

"*La paz,*" she told him.

The stray, still sleeping, thumped his stubby tail.

"*Que preciosa,*" murmured the women all around, and pointed, and poked their husbands.

When Ivy stood up, she looked around and seemed unsure where to go. A bigger girl, maybe eight, came up from farther back in line. She wrapped a protective arm around Ivy's little shoulder and walked her back to us.

Give me some high stakes, and I could trustingly, faithfully, feel my way to a solution.

But what about between all the watershed moments? The most-of-the-time times, when life just kind of creeps along? My world presented me infinite small opportunities to believe, to move from one moment to the next with faith in the people around me—yet so often I chose doubt.

How was it that I could swallow hard and accept whatever an unplanned pregnancy might bring, yet fear disaster if Harry didn't pack shorts for a one-week vacation? Faith-wise, moving to Costa Rica had been quite the *grand jeté*. Once here, could I not trust that the people around me, who had tiptoed politely up the aisle so as not to disturb the *dog,* would behave gracefully if a foreign five-year-old dared to get in their line?

We gave the quetzal a year to show himself but the little bastard stayed hidden. No matter. I had no problem believing in an invisible bird with a three-foot tail and a fluffy little head. But believing that Anthony might ever get the Internet hooked up without me having a tantrum about it?

I considered the possibility that I might have some faith issues.

15

A Lot of Places Can Feel Like Home

We set out to move again, this time to Canitas and the house up on the hill.

Back behind Johnny's Pizzeria, I'd wiggled my thumbtacks out of the wall. Now, I held them in my teeth and stood on a mahogany armchair to hang Vic's little painting. A movement caught my peripheral vision. I shifted my attention out our enormous front windows and into a scene from the Discovery Channel.

The rainforest grew tall on the hills here, but our house stood in the middle of a clearing at least a hundred meters across. During any hour of the day, natural light poured in through the house's many windows. Now, outside one of them, a *sopilote* was testing its wings in the cow pasture that shared our meadow.

"You can do it," I told the giant bird through my thumbtacks.

In flight, *sopilotes*—buzzards—vultures—generally stick to the higher altitudes, much farther up than toucans or parrots. Being from the Pacific Northwest, Anthony and I had reached the same, surprised conclusion the first time we saw one of these huge, primal birds way up there: "Bald eagle!" But after squinting at the sky for a moment, looking for the snowy white head, Anthony said, "Um, the eagle is wobbling."

Sopilotes tip from side to side in the air, looking like they can't quite get their balance. They're awkward and jittery, which is bad enough, but my heart really went out to the *sopilote* the first time I saw one up at the school. Stefan and I sat on the covered porch outside the math classroom, doing some long division, when I saw a huge, ugly bird crouching on a fence post in the meadow, wings half spread. There was something off. The poor thing seemed to be trying to look simultaneously less noticeable and more adorable.

"Stefan, what's the deal with that bird?" I asked. Stefan liked slangy English.

"*Sopilotes* are so lame," Stefan told me. "He seets in the sun to dry."

Sopilote feathers don't have that special quality, that whatever it is, that lets water just roll off their backs. Ducks have it for sure, or we wouldn't have the saying. When *sopilotes* get wet, which you have to imagine they do when they live in the rain forest, they have to hang themselves out to dry. We'd see them on fence posts around the larger fields, as far as they could get from any shadow-casting trees. Soaking up all possible sunlight. They spread their wings a little, so the sun could get in between the feathers.

Now, outside my picture window, the *sopilote* was trying a little takeoff test. I stood spellbound on my chair, rooting for him. Things looked dicey for a moment, but he pulled himself together and teetered into the sky. The *sopilote* wasn't quite designed for this place, but here he was, figuring it out.

Our house was built by people who liked each other, who wanted to be able to chat no matter what they were up to. Kitchen, living, and dining rooms were all one space. On three sides, sliding doors to the wraparound deck opened wide, erasing the distinction between inside and out. It was a little like living in a sidewalk café.

Even the stairway to the partial loft was freestanding and minimal. Stairs descended airily to the giant downstairs. Graceful railings ensured that you didn't pitch yourself down into the kitchen in your eagerness to be part of everything. And all the luxury of the house, the bedrooms weren't large. Although the master bedroom had the only soaking tub and walk-in closet I saw all year, it was clear that the bedrooms here were for sleeping. The priority of this house was for being together within it.

And we had better like togetherness. Because our home's comforts weren't the only reason that, once we got there, we didn't want to leave.

I had never thought much about how the geography of our daily lives shaped our activities and our relationships. Until now, when the umbilicus that joined us to the outside world was nearly a kilometer long.

Starting from the road through Canitas, the first three hundred meters of our driveway were easy. We were still in civilization here. To the right lived Luis, Paula, children, dogs, and chickens; on the left marched the perfect, glossy rows of the Santamaria coffee plantation. A left turn about a hundred meters in marked the corner of the coffee field.

The first few times we walked our driveway, our eyes couldn't get enough of the landscape, and our brains could barely process our great good luck. Here we were, walking home from the grocery store, where we had just bought six avocados for about fifty cents. We're walking along a row of coffee, close enough to see the red cherries whose pits—soon to be coffee beans—will caffeinate our mountaintop mornings. There's a cow in the road, and we're on the way up to our designer kitchen from whose windows we can look all the way down to the sea.

It took maybe three climbs to take it all for granted. Ho hum. The walk home was no longer a series of miracles unfolding with every step; it was just transportation. Everyone knows you need to find something to while away the time on a long trip, so we started playing *What Do You Like Better?*

The rules got elaborate. Naturally.

- You got one free pass a day, when you could simply refuse to choose.
- Any choice you posed, you had to be able to answer. Or use your free pass.
- No people. This was my single, critical contribution to the rules. The slope is too slippery between The guy at the bakery or the ice cream lady at the grocery store? and Mommy or Daddy? No way.

Hannah spun entire scenes. "What do you like better: warm day, hammock, book and perfect mangoes, no chores, OR, snow day in Seattle! No school, you've just been sledding in the street, and you're inside having cocoa?"

Ivy's were meticulously tailored to her audience. "Okay, Mommy, you have Irish Breakfast tea and then all your kids help you in the garden and no whining, OR, at every dinner for one week, nobody argues and everyone speaks Spanish?"

Harry's pairings were simple and always had a right answer. "Invisibility cloak or the ability to turn anything into gold?"

Ivy: "Gold!"

"Nope. Invisibility cloak. Because whenever you need gold, put on your cloak and steal some!"

Walking the flat section of our driveway that year, I learned that Ivy, when pressed, preferred a world without flowers to a world without butterflies, and that Anthony, given the Sophie's Choice of s'mores or Milk Duds, would choose the Duds. (Me, too! But not the kids. They're so unrefined.)

In this first part of the driveway, across from the coffee, grew a flowery tangle of pinks and lavenders and whites. It started at our feet and extended overhead, lasting the length of what would be a city block if there were a city anywhere. The primary backdrop of Monteverde is a thousand shades of green, dotted with the occasional eye-popping tropical color of a butterfly or flower. But this was a cottage garden gone mad.

The story I heard was that some years ago, the coffee farmer's wife got her hands on some seeds from the States and planted a tidy little patch of impatiens and cosmos, to see if they would grow here. But when impatiens-the-annuals met Monteverde-the-temperate-rainforest—*ka-blam*. These plants were four, five feet high, with buds as big as ping pong balls. If you gave them a gentle pinch, the buds went *POP!* in a highly satisfying manner.

From the forest behind the flowers, we could hear the orange-bellied trogon that is a close cousin to the quetzal, but not as coy. In front, we saw butterflies in every color.

Past the poppers, the road veered right, plunged, and got rockier as it descended into the shade. Fist-sized stones stubbed your sandaled toes. Down, down, down we climbed. It felt good in the moment, but we knew it just made life harder, the ascent steeper, on the other side of the stream.

The air cooled as the shade deepened. The forest canopy closed above as the driveway wended down to a waterfall and a nurse log that was taller than Ivy. This shady stretch of driveway was blue morpho country; they chased each other down to the burbling water, or back up to the playful sunshine.

The blue morpho butterfly at rest is nothing, an everybug. Held together, the undersides of its wings are brown—just another big leaf. And its body? Tubby is a strange word for a butterfly, but there you go. The resting morpho looks to have been engineered for lumbering up twigs and taking a nap.

But somehow, the blue morpho takes to the air.

Wings spread, the morpho becomes the electric, shimmery blue of a tropical fish. A contrasting black band outlines the wings, which from one tip to the other span a space as big as an adult's splayed hand.

In the two weeks a blue morpho lives, its only task is to find a mate, ensuring the regeneration of its species. This is typically taken care of in the first day or two; the rest is play. The morpho makes merry easily and constantly, with humans and fellow butterflies alike.

Cows, coffee, and impossibly sized flowers might become old hat, but the morpho never stopped taking our breath away. And they didn't play coy, unlike a fancy pants bird I could name. They burst up from their drab brownness to float bluely along beside us, keeping us company.

"It's like the Harry of insects," observed Anthony, as a morpho floated circles around his head, zigging and zagging, as cheerful and random as a child's first sparkler.

The sounds changed, as we and our butterfly buddies went down to the creek. Vague hummings and warm-weather noises gave way to closer, clearer sounds. The creek burbled. The bellbird chimed. The trunks of the kapok trees creaked as they adjusted to mysteries far above. Everything had moss on it, or vines hanging from it. It smelled shady.

Logs crossed the gurgling water, the continuation of the spring that put water in the tap up at our house. The driveway veered and began its ascent.

Three hundred uphill meters left. We'd emerge from the forest to the steep, pastured hillside. There was no protection here from the blazing sun. Bend forward. Concentrate. This last stretch was the hardest, and we were always puffing by the time we saw the house.

In Seattle, the world of not-our-family activities and people was right next to us. Our house sat ten feet from the neighbors on each side. We had bikes, feet, buses, and the closeness of city geography; once you added Anthony, Margot, and two cars, the world was at our fingertips—right there, where they hit the steering wheel.

In Canitas, it took work to separate. To leave our cozy mountaintop on a rainy day was hard work, but even perfect weather involved a new calculus: *How much do I want to go hang out with Pedro? Enough to walk the whole driveway—twice?   What about a taxi—do I have 1000* colones?

I began to see how geography encouraged a certain family-centeredness. No lecture required.

But even as our location bred togetherness, Hannah started separating out.

She turned thirteen, far from her closest friends. We'd invited Liliana and a couple of other girls up to the new house to celebrate; Hannah looked relieved when they left. Lola had made her a beautiful painting. *Hannah en Azul,* it was titled. Lola had painted Hannah in the jeans she wore almost every day, embroidered at the bottoms with flowers and vines. Her ponytail flew above her head and her arms reached into a sky as blue as her eyes, filled with stars and birds and moons. It had been a long time, I realized, since I'd seen my daughter that exuberant. I said as much to Lola.

"What *you* see doesn't matter," Lola replied, smiling and patting my hand. "Hannah has a soul that reaches." My throat ached with wishing that Hannah's peers would love her as much as adults did.

The bedroom situation in the new house had worked out perfectly. Anthony and I pulled rank, of course, and took the master suite with its miraculous bathtub. Ivy needed to be close to us and Harry was always happiest in a pack, so the two of them took the other room downstairs. The single upstairs bedroom was its own little world, complete with tiny bathroom. It captivated Hannah. She had her own windows from which to gaze at the sweeping view. This private upstairs retreat suited not just her adolescent timeline, but the disposition she had had since she lay in her crib.

At three months, Hannah would wake up from naps and nighttime and begin chatting to herself in the mirror. When Anthony and I heard her through the baby monitor, we'd sprint to her room, so she wouldn't ever have to cry. We'd wait outside the door, then wait some more. We could hear her burbling along in there, completely satisfied with her own company. *Isn't the baby going to fuss and want us to come in and pick her up? Ever?*

Now Hannah claimed her garret in wonder saying, "How can I know this is what I always wanted, when I'd never seen it until now?"

The space was a perfect match for the other thing Hannah had always wanted.

"I can read *anything*. I have oceans of time, and the Friends library has all these classic books, and school isn't loading me up with a bunch of busy work."

Hannah made her bedroom, this lovely top-floor viewpoint from which you could see the world, into an escape from it. In this house that was designed around being together, Hannah found a way to be apart. Thirteen is a private age anyway, but Hannah moved into this solitude as if it had been waiting for her, and her for it, all along.

She curled up in her garret, with Salinger or Austen or Allende. We missed her.

"Hannah, do you want to play . . ." Harry or Ivy would begin.

Their sister was polite, always.

"No thanks," Hannah said over and over, as she slipped upstairs after school, after dinner, after anything, just when we thought we might keep her for a while. "You guys go ahead without me."

The mists that rose from the lowlands provided the ultimate now you see it/now you don't. Guava tree, cows, pasture, forest, hills, gulf spread out before us—we had grown to love them. And then, several days a week, they vanished. The view from upstairs was the best.

I imagined the mists enveloping my daughter. I didn't know how to keep them from coming and, once they were here, I didn't know how I would find her again. I worried that one day as they retreated down the mountain, the mists would take Hannah, too.

Even with Hannah's new disappearing act and our remote location, our new togetherness-house would be, in one way, more crowded than behind Johnny's. Yes, birds and trees and hillside were our only close neighbors, but our lives now involved two additional people on a near-daily basis: Luis to take care of the yard, and Magda, the house. I was uneasy at first. I didn't know how to be, in relation to people I paid to do tasks that I knew I could be doing.

I reminded myself of the *sopilote:* If that big, awkward bird can adapt, so can I. Surely I'm as clever as a *buzzard.*

16

We Got Served

Our gardener, Luis, had more negative space than we were used to. His empty spots bore out the only design principle I ever managed to remember from the high school yearbook staff: *Don't fill every space. There's power in what isn't there.* When Luis raised his hand to wave as we passed on the driveway, his 2.5 missing fingers and five or six missing teeth had a bigger impact on me than the ones that remained.

Luis's weathered-leathered face was starting to crease around the eyes, but I always got the feeling that he was much younger than he looked. He had the gravelly voice of someone who'd been smoking for decades. Luis always wore jeans, a belt, a white T-shirt--very Bruce Springsteen. I found his incredibly thick, wavy black hair to be out-of-whack sexy compared to the rest of his presentation. He moved slowly, cigarette dangling. Luis seemed to have no need to hurry. *Pura vida.*

Luis had two goofy animal sidekicks, and I felt he would make a radical and outstanding choice for a Disney hero. (Also, Luis never went anywhere without a machete, and he swore a lot. I'd watch that movie.)

His dogs, Capitán and Tonto (Spanish for "Stupid"), ran around Luis wherever he was working. They were always goofing off and bumping into things, pricking up their ears whenever Luis let loose a string of profanity in their direction. Capitán and Tonto had been designed for maximum hilarity:

Capitán was a skinny, shepherdy kind of thing with oversized ears, and Tonto was a squat, orange-and-white mutt with legs too short for his long body. Tonto looked like a toughed-up *campesino* corgi, although such a snooty breed seemed unlikely here. (I never saw a Tico with a labradoodle, for example, or a Portuguese water dog.)

I believe that Luis liked us. He was the only person who called Anthony "Antonio"—which was how Anthony typically introduced himself but which fooled no one. Luis called me *Señora,* always.

In addition to amorphous, middle-class discomfort, I was afraid of what having a housekeeper three days a week (!) would do to us. Our kids were bad enough keeping their stuff organized and put away—what would happen when someone showed up to tidy their bedrooms regularly? I feared we would become impossibly lazy and entitled.

Sally had told me to expect Magda, our housekeeper, the first week. One hot morning, I was just about to put down my book *(¡Hermione! ¡Cuidado!)* and go get Ivy when a beautiful young woman appeared at the top of our driveway, sweat shining on her high cheekbones. She was maybe in her early twenties, wearing a tank top and skin-tight Levis—which was exactly what I would wear if I had her body.

When I went to the door to say hello, she took a breath and said, in Spanish, *"Por Dios!* Only very silly Gringos would build a house up here!"

Magda could be tricky to get along with. Very quickly I realized this had nothing to do with her sweeping my floors and much to do with the fact that she could be kind of a bitch. Magda had strong thoughts about the ways Gringos fell short. We didn't take care of our children, for one thing. (Magda's own daughter was five and lived with Magda's parents a couple of hours away.) Gringos just let *niños* eat Rice Krispies for breakfast. Magda spat out the word, with a sneer, and a very adamant first syllable: *krreespiece,* in the tone most of us reserve for the woman who slept with our best friend's husband. The way to take care of children, Magda lectured, in the fist-on-hip stance she adopted whenever she was setting me straight, is to give them a hot breakfast in the morning, *gallo pinto* or *por lo menos, café!* ("At least, coffee!")

We knew from *prepa* that Magda was right about this. One day when Anthony was helping out, the *pregunta del día* at circle time was, "What did you have for breakfast today?" Of the fifteen children, two answered "mango" (Ivy and Courtney), two *"pinto, que rico",* and eleven giant smiles of *"tomé café!"* ("I drank coffee!"). I began to understand the twitching nature of our daily circle.

Having a housekeeper? It took me about a week to ditch my squirmy discomfort. No one forgot how to pick up their stuff. When Magda took two weeks off to go see her family, we just started doing it again—at least to the extent we ever had before. And when Magda was around, she inspired a tidiness in all of us that we'd never approached. When clean clothing is as crisp and well-folded as Magda made it, its shoddy, post-worn state is just embarrassing—we got it in the hamper as fast as we could.

Magda was nothing if not frank. Our friend Nia visited from the States and had a terrible allergic reaction. To what, we never knew—possibly to Magda? Strong personalities do tend to collide. Magda took one look at Nia's swollen, miserable face and said, "Yes, probably you will die."

Magda also cleaned house for my friend Kelly, and the two had an ongoing battle about the placement of living-room furniture. The Jensens had moved from Monteverde to Canitas a couple of weeks after we had, to a house about two hundred yards from the foot of our driveway, and Magda often came to our houses on the same day. When the furniture wars began, I received bulletins from the front lines of both sides:

- Kelly hadn't liked the *feng shui* of their furnished rental and had moved things around.
- Magda, who had cleaned for the previous occupants, disapproved.
- Every time she came, Magda moved chairs, tables, and rugs back to their original locations,
- and every time she left, Kelly moved them back.

After a couple weeks of this, Kelly had had enough. Armed with some sentences she and I had worked on together, Kelly told Magda firmly that from here on out, the furniture needed to stay where it was.

"Okay," responded Magda. "But your way looks very stupid. You might not want to have anyone visit you until you have seen that I am right."

Magda often accompanied her truths with an impatient shake of her head, as if she couldn't quite believe she had to tell someone this. When she asked a question, it was a challenge. "*MargGOTE*, where's the broom?" carried the implicit, "I've told you where it goes. Why is this so difficult for you? Also, why were you sweeping at all, when you and I both know you do such a piss-poor job? Why can't white people just leave it to the professionals?"

Like Luis, Magda seemed to like us personally. She just thought Americans were, on the whole, completely bassackwards.

Although none of the expat mamas wanted to say it, the problem with Magda wasn't just her attitude; the other thing that made the white ladies uneasy was Magda's extreme hotness.

"Keep an eye out," advised Kelly, when she learned Anthony was often home when Magda came to clean. "You know she'd just love to catch herself a rich American sugar daddy."

Actually, it hadn't occurred to me. And it was such an incongruous statement coming from Kelly, with all her tattoos and her liberal "I can't live in the States while Bush is president" persona. I chalked it up to the furniture wars. I never got a husband-stealing vibe from Magda, so it didn't worry me. Magda was young and totally hot and she was cleaning my house within an inch of its life—go, Magda.

I practiced getting used to it. I was the *Señora* and Magda was my housekeeper, and I was going to have to deal. It felt like progress when one day I stayed at the table, translating a squabble between Ron and Hermione, and did not blush while Magda swept under my feet. *("Señora, levante los pies.")*

I let Magda lecture me not because I felt guilty, or because I had so much to learn from this noble, simple Tica, but because I needed Spanish practice and Magda had things to say. Sometimes I argued with her and sometimes I wasn't up for it, but keeping up with her rapid-fire opinions was challenge enough. I appreciated her in-my-faceness; reverence or solicitude would have freaked me out completely. And there was nothing to worry about on the Anthony front—Magda terrified him.

I knew Magda had been fired from other homes for her attitude, but it didn't bother me. She had to climb a giant hill of rocks to get to our house, and once there she charged us a dollar an hour. A little attitude seemed fair enough.

17

Risks & Litigations

The first way we did not quite kill ourselves in Costa Rica was called *jupo*, only really it wasn't.

Luis had brought his son to meet us. We adults exchanged pleasantries while Harry and Adolfo got fidgety in the way of children of all cultures who feel they've paid sufficient dues to the chattering-nattering grownups. Adolfo whispered, *"Venga, venga! Jupo! Vamos!"*

Come on! *Jupo!* Let's go!

Adolfo wanted to show my kids a lawsuit waiting to happen. Only not really, because this was Costa Rica.

In the land of my birth and citizenship, by law I must wear a seatbelt in my car and a helmet on my bicycle. My Cuisinart is equipped with a safety mechanisms so intricate it's usually less hassle just to chop the carrots myself. It's possible everyone cares about my safety, but I think they're more concerned about owing me money.

In a less litigious society, people are free to put themselves in all kinds of danger.

Luis had taken off and Anthony and I were finishing the last of the unpacking when Hannah and Harry burst into the living room fifteen minutes after Adolfo had led them down the hill.

"You HAVE to try it! Mom! Dad! Seriously, there is nothing you could possibly be doing right now that is more important than this. Come." Hannah had not been this visibly excited since she discovered *rompope* in a juice box. Maybe I could stop worrying about the mists.

Anthony looked at me hopefully, in that way that made me want to shake him and say *Do you really not get that you are one of the grownups?*

"Show me!" I said. The kids took off down the hill, Ivy on Harry's back.

Jupo was freedom. *Jupo* was everything your mother doesn't want you to do. *Jupo* was desperately in need of some governmental regulation.

Jupo was, fundamentally, simply swinging on a vine. *Jupo* was two inches in diameter, three in some places, and while it was supple, as a vine should certainly be, it was woody and tough, too. *Jupo* was a vine you could trust. Where it attached, way up in the canopy, nobody knew; *jupo* disappeared into the high green muddle, too far up to tell.

From its origin somewhere in the dappled sky, *jupo* had grown earthward over the ravine that held our creek. It bent jauntily every so often, as if it had been momentarily distracted on its way down to meet us. The vine had a particularly loopy bend in it right where a person could wedge her feet.

You climbed a tree stump that was taller than Anthony and crazy with orchids, growing on the edge of the ravine. Someone handed you the vine, and you stuffed your feet in the loopy place and held on tight and jumped, and as you began your flight through the leafy tranquility of the rain forest, you filled it with your own raucous merriment because on *jupo*, you cannot be contained.

Jupo was super fun, in the way extreme things are right up until they kill you dead.

The pendulum of *jupo*, one of my children the deadweight at its bottom, arced maybe twenty meters from the giant stump, through the air and over the creek.

Sometimes we did a twofer, two people clinging, feet wedged, facing each other. I tried really hard to trust the whole situation but in the end, whether watching or swinging, my jaw clenched. Adolfo assured me, *"Es seguro! Muy seguro!"*

"If you jump really hard off the stump," Hannah (Hannah!) advised, "you can twist a little at the same time, and your momentum keeps you twisting so you can hit the trees on the other side with your butt and your back, which is less scary than with your face."

Shouldn't someone have cut this thing down? Put barbed wire around it, posted a sternly-worded warning?

With no one mandating our personal safety, staying out of danger became a set of choices rather than a set of rules. Like toddlers, teenagers, and college freshmen who'd left very strict parents back home, we tested our boundaries.

We decided, after a round of semi-cautious testing, to trust *jupo*. I went over and over. It scared me every time.

Ivy hopped and pleaded until we hit upon a system that felt almost safe. She wrapped herself around Anthony like a little front pack—she always was a good clinger—and he used his prodigious upper body strength to hang for the two of them. They swung and they swung, long enough to leave Ivy howling and me unable to move my jaw.

Up the hill, I kept Dr. Doogie's number near the telephone.

Jupo was the first in a line of activities that were fun in a breathless, *can you even believe we get to do this?* kind of way. *Jupo* emboldened us until we began falling off things that, one could argue, we should never have been on in the first place.

18

Friendly Takeover

I wasn't in the mood for people. Today in math groups, Stefan had missed a problem early on and spent the rest of the session slouched in his chair. He folded his arms and scowled, while hummingbirds darted back and forth behind his head and I felt foreign and ineffective.

Now I was stewing along the flat part of the driveway. I passed the spot where even Ivy had recently proven herself better at Costa Rica than I was. Walking back from the bus, we'd found our path partially blocked by a large, black cow eating impatiens poppers. Always on the lookout for opportunities to shovel more Spanish into her. I pointed and identified the animal by color: *"vaca negro."*

"Vaca negrA," she corrected my grammar. "And don't talk in Spanish to me."

The cow stared at us with obsidian eyes, bit off some mutant impatiens, and chewed. Ivy patted its flank absently as we passed. Cow in driveway—sure. Old hat.

Everyone was more at home here than I was.

I was psyching myself up for the ascent when Luis's enormous wife, Paula (POW-la) came bundling out of their house, followed by another woman. In less than a minute, I had a gaggle of smiling strangers on my hands. They just kind of came spilling out, of a house I would not have imagined could hold more than four people and a table. Now here we all were, heading up the hill. Some of us seemed pretty excited.

The women talked and laughed with great animation. The children ran up the sides of the dirt road, plucking oversized pods out of the rainforest and throwing them at each other.

I felt my funk lift a little, replaced by curiosity. Did Paula want to show her friends my house? Was she coming to inspect my housekeeping? Oh hell, were they coming to *clean?* Or perhaps I had somehow extended an invitation without realizing it. Sometimes, when I got tired of not understanding, I'd just smile and say, *"Si, claro."*

Maybe it had happened the other day, when I'd bumped into Isabella, Ivy's teacher, in town. She spoke to me quickly, which I took as a compliment. Not wanting to disappoint good, kind Isa, I'd nodded along. Maybe she'd been saying, "Hey, how about if I send my friend Paula and her pals and their kids over to your house next Friday, and you can give them all an English lesson, maybe make them some lunch?"

"Si, si, claro." Sure! Big Gringa smile.

I shook my head and brought myself back to the moment at hand. I could do small talk; I knew weather words and children words and could configure simple sentences without setting them up in English first. Paula and I chitchatted up the hill. In my head, I ran through the contents of our kitchen. I'd made a pot of beans yesterday, so that was good. Was I supposed to be ready to have seven people over for lunch at any given moment? I hadn't been stocking for that. Rookie.

We arrived, sweating and panting. I busied myself getting glasses of water for everyone and waiting for our purpose to be made clear. Paula and her friends looked at Sally's fancy stove and shook their heads. They seemed pleased, though, when one of them, rooting through the cupboards, produced a very nice sauté pan.

The pan was one of those magical ones with a truly nonstick coating and a heavy bottom made of heat-conducting metal. It was a pan you register for separately when you're getting married, and maybe a couple of friends who really like you go in on it together. A $200 sauté pan seemed to be just what Paula needed.

Well, don't we all.

I realized then that it was entirely likely that, while I'd been ruminating up the driveway about Stefan and *vacas negros*, Paula was probably explaining the situation. My Spanish wasn't good enough for half attention. I'd heard of this practice called "staying in the moment," but it had always seemed a little sketchy to me. A kind of self-satisfied rationalization trotted out by people who, I suspected, didn't get much done.

Never mind. The sun blazed alone in a perfect blue sky. Harry and Hannah appeared at the top of the hill, dumped their backpacks and chugged big glasses of water. Paula gasped at the sight of Harry. Apparently she'd heard there was a redhead:

"Ah! El pelirojo!"

Harry let her ruffle his hair. The two of them had a conversation in Spanish that I couldn't track – when it came to the language, Harry and Hannah had left me in the *polvo.* I caught *"divertido"* and saw Harry nod his head in my direction. Fun? Funny? Probably he was telling the nice lady what a fun mother I was!

Paula laughed and nodded and got her hands in his hair again, then dismissed him with a pat on his shoulder and a smile that seemed to know a secret. Harry grabbed a soccer ball and headed outside to join the kids with normal hair who never got detained.

Well, I was all in now. Was I being cheerfully, chattily burgled? Surely not in front of the children.

It'll be months before I have to replace that pan, I figured. *Let us see what happens next.*

What happened was that two of the women started a cooking fire. Despite my woodstove-worship and being embarrassingly well supplied—kindling in a Sally-adorable basket in the living room, and a giant woodpile created by Luis—I'd had no success with the stove so far.

It liked these women better. They understood it. My new friends showed me how to open the flue, how long to leave the door open to ensure everything was crackling merrily, and when to shut the door so the wood would burn slow and constant.

Someone produced a bag of *masa rica,* the corn flour used to make tortillas and tamales, and stirred in water to make a stiff dough. A conga line formed along the big mahogany table. Experienced hands rolled two-inch balls and passed them down to the woman with the tortilla press at the end.

Tortillas! We were making tortillas! O happy day! I had never made a tortilla before.

Paula smiled and pitched a wad of dough at my chest. I didn't know the word she said, but it clearly came with an exclamation point. I took her to mean "Roll!" I did my best and tossed it back. Paula held my little ball up and turned it this way and that, faking an intense inspection. Finally she raised her eyebrows, nodded slowly, and made a circle with her thumb and forefinger. Mock cheers went up from the women at the table. *"Bien hecho!"*—well done!

Paula handed my ball down the line to the press. I watched with pride as it came out, a smooth disk. Look what I made.

We kept rolling. Once I got the rhythm, I took a moment to glance outside at the children in the yard.

Harry was playing soccer with the younger ones. Hannah lay in a hammock with a book and a halved avocado, which she was eating out of its shell with a spoon. When the ball bounced into her domain, she tossed it out again, not looking up. Three hummingbirds fed at the butterfly bush.

Back at the wood stove, Paula was wielding our excellent pan.

She showed me how to flick water in to determine when the pan was hot enough. If the water didn't sizzle immediately, we needed more heat. If it hit and evaporated right away, she moved the pan to a less-intense corner of her friend the stove. Just right was when the droplets hit the pan, sizzled for a moment, and were gone. The two of us took turns cooking the tortillas on each side. Paula noticed me looking from my pile, which leaned, to hers, which did not. She patted my arm and made the okay sign again.

Soon, she left me to it. When Paula found my pot of beans and put it on the wood stove to begin heating, I felt like a real contributor.

When there was no more *masa rica,* but two stacks of tortillas, Paula wrapped these in a towel and put the bundle at the corner of the wood stove to keep warm. I was startled to notice that, while I had been focusing on piling tortillas in a precise and non-tippy manner, the ladies had already cleaned everything, including the floury mess on the counters and Hannah's avocado knife. The beans were simmering. Paula squinted into the fridge, producing five raw eggs. She stunned me by chucking them whole into the pot of beans. Goodness!

Then, suddenly, children were gathered and everyone was saying goodbye. *What?! We weren't going to eat? Wait!* Paula kissed me on each cheek.

"Los huevos—cuatro minutos, no mas. M'entiende?" Yes, I understood. I'd cook the eggs for just four minutes. But, but...

Paula made the okay sign one last time.

As everyone filed out, each took two fresh tortillas to eat on the way down the driveway. I watched the mothers watching their children, ensuring the limit was strictly enforced. The ladies all hugged me and kissed my cheek. As they disappeared down the hill amid a final chorus of *Adios!*, they called me *MarGOTE*, not *Señora*.

Yes, I am foreign, I thought. *But that's not a good thing or a bad thing. It's just a fact. Paula told me and told me, with her thumb and her finger, that it is okay.*

We ate our tortillas that night with beans I heated on the woodstove and a peeled, boiled egg for each of us. And slices of avocado, which I'd found daintily arranged on two plates in the fridge. We poured delicious *Salsa Lizano* on top, from a fresh bottle Hannah had discovered on the spotless table, just after everyone disappeared down the hill.

Later that night, I remembered to ask Harry, "Hey, what did you and Paula talk about when you first got home today?"

"She asked me if you were okay with the tortilla thing," he said. "She said she tried to ask you, but she wasn't sure you really got it. She asked me to translate, to ask you if it was okay."

"But...?"

"I told her I thought it would be a lot more fun if they just let you figure it out."

19

I Can't Do Art

Anthony was getting smaller.

He hadn't found it difficult, when we were leaving Seattle, to fit his world into a single trunk. Here, he'd whittled even further. When Anthony's sandal broke, he didn't look for a new pair—just switched to sneakers. He spoke in either language only when necessary, and when he cooked there were no leftovers.

The wordlessness was the hardest. He didn't seem angry; it was just his regular stillness, supersized. I remembered: That ten-day bike ride, the last time Anthony and I were around each other 24/7? We'd emerged from that trip cheerfully certain that our differences in temperament were probably dealbreakers.

How had I forgotten? It wasn't scheduling that kept my husband from having soulful conversations with me. *It was his personality!*

And it wasn't just the deep stuff. Anthony was also useless at conjecture gossip, my favorite kind. When I invited him to muse with me on whether Miles's parents were happy, or what had made Mike quickly sell his business and leave the States, Anthony said "Sure," or "I guess we'd have to ask Mike." I'd never thought husbands and wives should be everything to each other, but this was ridiculous.

Harry, Hannah, and Ivy were all plugged in with friends and school. I didn't have Lizzie and I didn't have Vic, and no amount of free time was going to turn my husband into my best slumber-party buddy ever.

I needed some friends. I knew exactly who I wanted, and hoped I hadn't already blown it.

I can't do art. I can't do art any better than anyone I've ever met who claims they can't do art. And I'm pretty committed—I have been Can't Doing Art for as long as I can remember. I follow the proud tradition of people who really like to be good at stuff: When I come up against something I'm bad at, I pick myself up, dust myself off, and refuse to do it at all.

Nonetheless, I had set my sights on the *Casa de Arte*. I was going help the people there do art, and see if they would be my friends. The good pixie Lola never seemed to hold it against me that I hadn't come in for coffee that first day, but neither did she try again.

"Todos los dias!" Lola had said. Ivy and I had complied, but for months we had stopped at the magical swing. The first time the two of us ventured inside the spacious front room of the *Casa* itself, I thought we'd come in the wrong door, entered the secret staging area.

Natural light spilled over tall shelves crammed with all manner of artistic paraphernalia. Canvases of cloth, wood, and paper spread themselves on every surface. A paint-splattered picnic table sported several square meters of bubble wrap and some wine bottles that appeared to be participating in a papier mâché experiment. I finally spotted an arched, interior doorway and a sign pointing to the gallery beyond, and realized: We we were right where they wanted us. We hadn't gotten it wrong at all.

With its very layout, the *Casa de Arte* told its guests that creation was at least as important as result. In the chaos of that front chamber, the unhidden was cheerful and beckoning. *See? Art is not so mysterious!* the room assured me. *We have no secrets here!*

I was hooked. Over several weeks, I cased the joint, occasionally buying a little something so I didn't seem creepy.

The house of art really had been a house, and the people who converted it had had the great good sense not to knock down any walls. Walking through, I was forever coming across new themes and brilliant surprises in tiny rooms and nooks.

I learned that Lola had a co-owner, Beatriz. The two of them worked in the front-room studio. They sold their own art in the gallery, but they also carried the work of several Costa Rican artists. I pumped Hannah for information and learned that that Lola and Beatriz were best friends. And that they both spoke only Spanish, which I thought showed a certain level of refreshing up-yours in such a tourist town.

Even I could tell that both women were gifted artists; I scoped the gallery for signatures, and saw that Lola's work was crazy and daring and beautiful. Her paintings vibrated with color. Cows were green and blue, with yellow spots on purple udders. Beatriz's work was calming and detailed and beautiful.

I learned that Lola and Beatriz sometimes taught their techniques to artistic strays who wandered up their path. In return, the strays contributed to the gallery the way a sous chef supports a kitchen—preparing canvases and painting undercoats. Doing your basic chopping and slicing so the real chefs could come along and make Art.

I envied and admired the strays. On my visits, I paid attention. *I could probably do that,* I thought, watching a college-age student slap wet, floury newspaper onto a wine bottle.

And then: *I want to sit at that table and try things.*

And: *Wow. All Spanish, All the Time.*

And then, finally: *I need some friends.*

I decided to start a mini-career as a sous artist to Lola and Beatriz. Beatriz and her husband had raised four children in Monteverde and had deep, Layer One roots. Lola was Layer Two, having left San Jose and her marriage a few years ago, bringing Liliana and hopes for a fresh start. It felt pretty ballsy for my short-termer self to shop for pals among this crew.

Lola and I had chatted about our daughters on my gallery visits, but for anything more than that, it was clearly my serve.

On a misty day in October, I headed up the lush rainforest path and past the swing. I strode into the studio, smiled and said *hóla,* and...my feet kept moving. I spent the next ten minutes wandering through the gallery rooms, losing my nerve. These ladies might be very nice and all, but why would they bother with my talentless, temporary self? What could I possibly bring to the equation?

I reminded myself that I'd recently sat in church and resolved to trust the people around me a little bit more. Sure, we might not be instant best friends. But Lola and Beatriz and I had spoken a few times by now. They wouldn't *laugh.*

Besides, if I didn't try to make friends, I definitely wouldn't. This is elementary. This is what you tell your third-grader.

I wandered back through the gallery rooms and into the studio. Haltingly, half in Spanish and half in gestures, trying to make clear with waving hands and goofy eye rolls that I possessed no artistic ability at all, I offered myself.

I started spending three mornings a week in a world of art supplies and Spanish, trying my best at both.

In my artistic infancy, Lola was patient. She drew shapes on thick paper and set me to work filling them in with acrylics, learning the paints. One day, I graduated to shapes that looked like Monteverde things—armadillos, anteaters, butterflies. *"Ay, MarGOTE,"* Lola would say. *"Claro que si puede!"* Of course you can! And then she'd have me do the same thing, all over again—proof that I couldn't, quite. I looked at Beatriz, who smiled and nodded. Occasionally, Beatriz would come over, adjust my grip on my paintbrush, and murmur, *"Perfecto."*

After a few weeks, I became more than just a waste of art supplies. At the big table, on top of years' worth of spatters of paint and glue and wax, I was proudly painting actual cards that would, after Artistic treatment, sell for 800 *colones.*

I worked alongside another volunteer. (Had I known that the other strays were straying from art school, I would never have dared approach. My coworkers were young, hip, hot, and *talented.*) Adriana came from Holland, and was so blond and healthy, so rosy-cheeked, that I suspected she was on sabbatical from her regular career as a milkmaid. Adriana was a gifted artist and unfailingly nice. She couldn't help it if she was good and I was me. I will say this for me: I am not the jealous type. I really was delighted to see Adriana's hummingbirds looking as if they were actually humming.

Adriana spoke very little Spanish, and liked to be at the *Casa* when I was so she could practice her English on me.

"That is very nice, the thing that you are painting," Adriana said to me, speaking slowly. "What do you call it?"

"It's a flower," I said.

Adriana squinted and finally said, "Okay."

Clearly, her English was pretty bad, too.

"Tomamos un café?" we heard Beatriz's voice from the other side of the tall shelves. She had been dripping wax onto rice paper, creating the initial layers of a batik-like project that would eventually be a quetzal floating in dappled green. Lola turned off a painty blow dryer, which she'd been aiming at some papier-mâché not-yet-cows.

Every morning around ten o'clock, Lola or Beatriz would look up from whatever beautiful, exciting thing they were creating.

"Tomamos un café?" one would ask, and the other would take the cue to put coffee and water into the ancient electric percolator and plug its fraying cord into the wall. Whoever had something to eat would produce it—maybe cheese and bread, sometimes sausages left over from someone's dinner last night. If no food appeared, Lola would rummage in her tiny kitchen at the back of the house.

At the big table, we moved projects aside just far enough that the four or five of us could all sit down. We spread napkins on top of the splatters, picked our snack from the communal offering, and talked.

Evolution is on the side of women's friendships. We have a lot to cover, and Anthony was hardly the first of our brethren who couldn't keep up with the word count. In Seattle I'd make a date with Lizzie or Erin. We'd walk or drink coffee, cover everyone's love life, kids, job. Then I'd go back to my chess game.

One day in late October, I wanted to tell my *Casa* friends about Anthony. About his creeping minimalism and how he'd been paring down so completely that I wasn't always sure which pile I was going to end up in—Keep? Store? Toss? I didn't have the right Spanish, of course.

"Anthony no necessita nada," I said to Lola, Beatriz, and Adriana. *"El no habla nunca conmigo."*

"Nunca?" questioned Beatriz.

Okay, fair. Never was an exaggeration. But he didn't talk to me as much as I wanted him to. And there was never an emotional component. Beatriz who had been married for thirty years, told me that sometimes men needed to need nothing, to not talk.

Was Anthony unkind? Did we still get along?

No, never, I told her. And yes, fine. But it was lonely, him over there being an island and me over here with much to discuss. Beatriz patted my hand.

"You came to Monteverde for a year away, right?" she asked in Spanish. "Why not let him have a year away?"

Um, away is kind of his regular personality, I tried to clarify.

"Not a year away from being quiet." There she was with that sly little smile. "A year away from you asking him to be noisy."

And then we changed the subject to Liliana, whose birthday was coming up.

Tomamos un café? Shall we drink coffee? Time with my friends wasn't an appointment now. It was part of the fabric of every day. We didn't have to solve everyone's everything in a marathon conversation, ticking through a list. We'd all be here tomorrow.

20

Super Pollo

After three months of essentially camping behind Johnny's, our move to Glen and Sally's had produced a kitchenware extravaganza so extreme it almost hurt to look at it. My round wedding cake pan would fit in my brushed-steel oven, but of course I had Sally's cookie sheets now. Nice ones, carried lovingly to my mountaintop direct from Williams-Sonoma. Now that the wood stove and I were pals, I was happier than ever with my rustic pot. It looked so at home, bubbling with beans. I wouldn't have felt right putting Sally's Calphalon there.

I loved making *gallo pinto* for my family and for the stream of houseguests that began in earnest in October. Magda taught me how to cut a Gungo chicken into big chunks, bones and all, and make *arroz con pollo.* Its color came from *achiote,* a Latin American spice that stained everything, especially my cuticles, bright yellow. I introduced our houseguests to the Costa Rican foods we loved and the ones we had invented. At home we'd make tortillas, *gallo pinto,* yucca latkes, and chicken-chayote soup for dinner. For dessert, banana something, *arroz con leche,* or molten chocolate cakes with mango.

But we didn't eat just at home, and eating out didn't necessarily mean *muy tipica* Costa Rican fare. On the road to Monteverde, Elizabeth, a woman from one of the five original Quaker families sometimes sold donuts in a tiny outdoor setup. Vases of flowers sat atop lace doilies on the wooden tables, and chickens wandered beneath, pecking crumbs. We kept our eyes peeled whenever we walked to the library. If we were lucky, the hand-painted (in English!) wooden sign would be hanging on its tree by the side of the road— "Fresh Dough Nuts." We walked the winding path, passing trees sprinkled with orchids, to eat fresh old-fashioned donuts sprinkled with cinnamon sugar. Anthony, who'd become extra thin and wiry on mangos, *gallo pinto*, and walking everywhere, made exceptions to his burgeoning asceticism when it came to sweets. Once, when we arrived at the library ten minutes after stopping for donuts, Anthony headed down to *la fabrica* to get a milkshake.

"Dad, are you serious? You just ate *five* donuts!"

"I know! They made me really thirsty!"

At 1000 *colónes,* a milkshake was out of reach as a snack food for many of the families our kids played with. But Hannah and Harry had savings from babysitting and odd jobs back in the States, and an ongoing allowance. A two-buck milkshake was an extravagance for them, but not an unreachable one. It made Harry happy to take Pedro and Diego for milkshakes, and so sometimes he did. I asked Harry if that was weird.

"At first I thought maybe it would be," he told me. "But sometimes a brother wants a milkshake, only not if your *compañeros* can't. If I have the money and Diego doesn't, *no importa.* I can just buy for us both. Miles and I kind of trade off offering. 'S'all good, *Mamacita.*"

I parsed the Spanglish slang (Slanglish?). Then Harry spoke again.

"Sometimes I want to go for a shake but I don't, because I don't want my homies to feel like they have to have money to hang out."

I flashed back to Seattle, to Carl and Tammy's Xbox and trampoline. "We are totally poor compared to these guys!" Harry had said.

Harry never wanted to discuss all that we saw in Nicaragua, and he also never mentioned how much we had or didn't have compared to friends in Monteverde. I bit back my desire to pontificate and watched him feel his way.

At restaurants we ate *bistec* (kind of a steak/tire fusion) and pig cooked all ways, *gallo pinto* that was still better than mine, and *tamarindo,* a drink made of boiled seed pods that makes you want to cry, it's so good. But the single food I made every one of our visitors try was Super Pollo.

How on earth did the best fried chicken on the planet get to Costa Rica?

Fried chicken was invented in a few places, apparently, none of which is the Central American isthmus. People have been deep frying chicken in Vietnam, Italy, and West Africa for centuries. The fried chicken we think of, the Colonel

Sandersy kind, is thought to have originated in Scotland and been brought over by immigrants. The recipe underwent improvements in the Southern US, as slaves unblandified it in Southern kitchens with the addition of spices and seasonings the Scots knew not of.

I guessed the Alabaman Quakers must have brought the idea down. But they were too tasteful to do something as tacky as open a fried chicken restaurant in Central America. Then a Tico tried a home-fried chicken, went HOLY FUCK THAT IS SO FAR BEYOND DELICIOUS, I CAN BARELY SEE DELICIOUS FROM HERE, and insisted the Quakers teach him how to do it. Then he made it for his kids, and one of them grew up and made a business of it, improving it in a way that will forever remain a mystery. Probably magic. And that was how Super Pollo was born. I'm guessing.

I can't tell you how Alejandro made his chicken. No one can. I can tell you this:

Super Pollo was so delicious that on two separate occasions, Hannah, who had been a vegetarian since she learned to pronounce the word at age four, fell off that wagon to eat a thigh.

When Vic visited with Max, her understated Austrian husband, we took them to Super Pollo. We ordered at the tiny counter and sat down at a Formica table to wait. I tried not to oversell, but I was pretty excited. Harry went to the video game in the corner and shot things.

Was I suddenly okay with video games, just because it was Central America? Naw. It was the noise in my house I rejected, and the inevitable battles about time limits. But games that ate quarters? Self-limiting, which pleased me. Ivy stood at his elbow, studying. He mostly ignored her helpful suggestions but did not bat her away.

Our chicken was ready in about seven minutes. Vic took her first few bites into the perfectly crisp outside, perfectly moist inside and, as was appropriate, had an orgasm right on the spot.

"Jesus," she said, recovering, wiping her bangs out of her face. "What did they do to that chicken?"

Max ate his chicken in silence. I refused to ask him how he liked it. I knew how good it was. He could come to me, for once.

But Max said nothing. Just as he had on the amazing pendulum of *jupo,* while Vic whooped it up breathlessly.

After Super Pollo, we hiked up to the school to show off the 720-degree view of perfection (I liked to turn around twice) that was our children's educational experience. We played on the slide a little, with no kids there to be embarrassed for us. Finally I couldn't take it anymore.

"Max, what did you think of your Super Pollo?"

"Well," he said, "It was pretty good." Only he pronounced it with an umlaut, of course. God he's pretentious.

Vic pounced. "WHAT THE HELL?! Be a little more specific, please. WHAT DOES THAT MEAN, PRETTY GOOD?"

"Well," he said again. "I guess it was the best chicken I ever had."

Would it have been so hard to say that, right out? Vic and I thought not.

Anthony defended Max. "It's okay for him to just sit there and quietly enjoy his chicken," Anthony said. "He doesn't need to issue a press release about it. What's the problem?"

I turned to Vic. "Men are so withholding," I said.

"I hate them all. Let's go get more chicken and not invite them."

For years afterward, Vic and I would repeat "It was pretty good," and die laughing. We didn't just reserve it for fantastically delicious food. We'd say it at a sunset, at a perfect movie. At the end of our friends' Rico and David's wedding, when, at long last, the groom kissed the groom.

21

Rhythms

W
e were all settled in (again). School provided the twin comforts of structure and routine. October brought an end to the exhilaration and exhaustion that come with constant change; we could finally establish some rhythms.

I was now volunteering several times a week at the *Casa*. Beatriz and Lola assured me I was very helpful. Adriana the dairymaid was also supportive. One day when the break signal sounded—*"Tomamos un café?"*—Adriana had stretched her neck and peered over to my side of the table.

Earlier, I had admired her advanced anteater work. Now, Adriana inspected what I'd been creating with such absorbed focus. With all sincerity and in her very best Dutch-tinged English, Adriana said, "Margot, you are getting very good at coloring inside the lines!"

In addition to my sous-painter tasks, Lola and Beatriz had decided over our coffee one day that the time had come for me to create my own body of work. Lola sent me outside to look at giant leaves, then handed me tubes of bold acrylics. Beatriz set out watercolors, and told me that every time I went outside, I must pay careful attention to the sky.

Lola continued to assure me that Hannah would come into her own, but what could Lola know? Her gorgeous daughter was the focus of every crowd. Liliana's breasts and vocabulary were appropriate for a thirteen-year-old, while Hannah had none of the former and too much of the latter. (Hannah's vocabulary issues had recently gotten more entertaining. She'd long been mispronouncing words because she read them before she heard them spoken, but her mistakes had taken on a bilingual flair. Shortly after she'd found *Pride and Prejudice* at the book exchange, Hannah materialized from her loft at dinnertime announcing, "I don't think Mr. Wickham has very good scroop-lace!"– pronouncing "scruples" as if it were Spanish.) Hannah seemed happy enough with her books and her solitude, but I kept wondering: Did she embrace solitude as a defensive measure? Was she truly happy, up there in her garret?

I made the radical choice to just let her be. I succeeded, sometimes.

Back at our house, I dove into a new set of chores.

In my previous life, chores had been a necessary obstacle between how a thing was and how I wanted it to be. Now, with my oceans of unscheduled time, I wouldn't say I got *intentional* about everyday tasks...but I did kind of dig them. It's not hard to take pleasure in the everyday when the everyday is so good looking.

Anthony was already there, chore-wise. He had become a kitchen-cleaning hawk, and had the kids rotating through the usual disciplines—clearing, scraping, washing, drying, sweeping the floor, putting away. He was a cheerfully ruthless enforcer.

"Daddy, I'm so tired. Please can I just go to bed? I'll do extra tomorrow!"

"Nope! You're part of this family. You get its benefits, and you're part of making it work." I could learn from this. In keeping with his other no-frills behaviors, Anthony employed no guilt, no outrage that they even had the gall to ask—and no mercy.

I, meanwhile, was getting into laundry. (Anthony was off this one for a while; the electroshock aversion therapy behind Johnny's had been highly effective.)

At the new house, just like on the prairie, our laundry hung outside to dry. Standing at our laundry line, I could see past the guava tree, over the foothills and down, down, to the thin blue band of the Gulf, its line about as wide as the line in front of my nose.

I played games, challenging myself not to let anything touch the ground. Our thirty-foot clothesline threaded through a wooden post at the middle, and I balanced the two sections carefully. If a top sheet went up on one side, I hung its fitted partner on the other. I learned from Magda to clip clothespins on the bottom of my shirt before I started. Thus spared any extraneous movement, I could concentrate on the physics of the thing. I organized as I went, big stuff on down to tiny Ivy anklets. I walked back and forth. I remembered to look at the sky.

To my left, the grass grew tall past the boundary of Luis's machete work. Behind me, the rainforest rose up. Within it, bellbirds chimed. If the morning had been wet, I worked in solidarity with the *sopilotes* on the fence posts, who were also hanging out to dry.

I watched the trees instead of television, but there was still high drama. Flocks of parrots passed overhead, racing to their next emergency. Once, a pair of hummingbirds got confused by the flowers on Ivy's dress as it moved in the breeze. I unpinned the decoy and held it behind my back. "Over there, guys!" I told the birds. They got it, and removed themselves to the purple spikes of the butterfly bush.

On very windy days our clothes could be dry in twenty minutes, but those same winds also blew rainclouds up the mountain. Left on the line, our shirts could be dripping again by minute twenty-one. I loved taking the laundry off the line already organized, thanks to my earlier efforts. It was different from the random warm jumble of a load from the dryer, and just as comforting. Certainly my enjoyment of laundry was aided by the fact that I now had a housekeeper doing some of it.

I've never been in the armed forces, but I know a lot about what it's like because I've seen *An Officer and a Gentleman*. Nothing disorderly was permitted when Magda got going, but the most aggressive form of her work was the folding of the laundry.

Magda's folding was precise and unyielding, like that mean Sergeant Foley. Out of our underwear, Magda created little origami bullets, so compact and balanced you could create a perfect pyramid with them. And, on a shelf in our walk-in closet, Magda did.

One afternoon after she left, I sat on the bed with a stack of Magda-folded missiles and tried to reverse-engineer her technique. Magda folded like Black Undergarment Down, Operation Desert Shorts. I surveyed my teetering pile. Just panties. I asked no further questions.

In addition to my dreamy moments at the laundry line, I was also cleaning the floors with some regularity. Since I liked to leave our doors open in order to reduce the difference between inside and out, sometimes our hens would wander in. Eventually, one of them would figure out that something was amiss. She'd panic and try to run out, and her sisters would follow. But a full-on chicken stampede on hardwood floors is not practical. It amused me to watch them skid and slide, and I took the opportunity to share my spiritual learning. "Slow down, chickens," I counseled. "You'll get there better if you don't try so hard."

Our primary outdoor chore involved José Mario's cows.

José Mario lived way up the hill from us, but his dairy cows grazed by our house. A post-and-wire fence ran up the field, about twenty meters from our kitchen window. This feeble fencing was meant to keep the cows on their side, but the cows didn't understand this and sometimes one would stick her head between the wires to get at the grass on our side. (Our grass was quite tall and lush, on account of no cows.) Naturally she'd want to get a little farther in, so she'd work one hoof through, and pretty soon would be munching happily toward the orchard.

Sally and Glen had planted maybe forty trees, avocado, guava, papaya. The trees were still tiny babies, somewhere between Ivy and Harry in height, and certainly not strong enough to withstand becoming cud. Anthony and I had sworn to protect these trees.

So of course, when I glanced out the window over the top of *Harry Potter y la Cámara Secreta ("Soy Dobby, Señor—el elfo doméstico.")* and saw a cow on our side of the fence, I sounded the alarm.

"Cow! Cow!"

Anthony paused to arm himself with one of Glen's hummingbird-identification pamphlets. He rolled it up and we headed out.

Keeping a safe distance from the cow, who for the occasion we named, Anthony was empathetic yet stern.

"Hey Blackie, I can see why you'd want to be over here. It's nice, right? But you really have to...Shoo! Go home! Home, Blackie, home!" Anthony grew up with dogs.

Surprisingly, we had to escalate. Anthony brandished the pamphlet in a manner that made it clear he was not afraid to use it. He told me, "Yell at him!"

"If I yell, will he paw the ground and come at me with smoke coming out his nostrils?"

"I don't think that's a dairy cow thing."

"But do you KNOW it's not? I want to KNOW it's not!"

A few days later, Blackie watched me from her side of the fence. I was following my own instincts and Sally's desires by putting in a vegetable garden.

In Seattle, I'd get so circle-of-life about feeding us from the garden that the kids could hardly stand me. I persevered. I'd always felt that growing things— tulips, tomatoes, baby chicks, children—was the perfect combination of meddling and miracle. I loved setting the stage and creating the conditions. I loved clearing weeds away from fragile shoots, giving the good stuff room to breathe. But mostly I loved that the real work, the something-from-nothing part, was entirely out of my control.

Before we left I had tucked seeds into a tiny secret corner of my trunk, just in case we ended up with a yard. Lettuces, beans, peas, carrots, tomatoes. This year, I would be one of those garden-positive mamas who spent so much time with her hands in the dirt she could never quite get clean.

I had noticed Luis's hands were that kind of dirty. Not unwashed. Earthy. When we first met him, he'd moved forward to shake our hands but then thought better of it. He looked at his palm, laughed, and held it up for Anthony and me to see. *"Muy sucio,"* he said—very dirty. He kept the hand in the air and gave us a friendly wave.

But I'd never seen Luis actually working in dirt. There was no garden near his little house, and at ours he mostly machete'd things.

I planned to clear a big plot this morning, so that when the kids got home from school I could create an idyllic moment in which our whole family planted a garden in the sunshine. I was prepared to bribe my way into this and had already laid in our most extravagant treat: we would toss the chocolate chips into the jar of peanut butter and eat them out with a spoon.

Luis rounded the house, banging his leg with his machete in a swashbuckling manner. When he saw me digging in the soft earth, shaking soil off grass clods and tossing them aside, his eyes lit up and his face broke into his huge gappy grin. *"¡Huerta! ¿Le gusta?"* he croaked—did I like gardens?

"¡Sí! ¡Sí! ¡Mucho! ¡Me gusta mucho las huertas!" I answered.

"¡Venga, Señora! ¡Venga!" Come!

Exclamation points boinged out of us, we were so excited. I would see this phenomenon repeated throughout the year, with varying casts and circumstances: When people basically liked each other but language barriers restricted conversation, enthusiasm filled the spaces that words might otherwise have occupied.

I followed Luis down the side of the hill—not down the driveway, but out past the edge of the laundry line. As we passed the house, Luis caught Anthony's eye through the plate-glass window of the living room and waved him out to join us. Anthony was happy to ditch his Spanish homework. The two of us gamely followed Luis down the hill on a path I had never noticed. We forded the stream and, after climbing the next hill over, came to a clearing.

Luis stood to the side and spread his hand in the universal gesture of, "After you, because what you are about to see is so fantastic that I do not want to block your view."

In a sunny secluded spot that must have been owned by someone who didn't really care, who was just quietly and distantly owning this hill, Luis had created a secret garden.

He walked us among the rows, master of all. Even Capitán and Tonto seemed to know not to step on the plants. Luis told us that he planted new things every week, in the spaces just harvested, and that his family ate something from the garden every day. We walked past fifty feet of cilantro, fifty of radishes. Stout, sturdy spinach and cabbages. Rows bursting with lettuce, greener than green, responding with exuberance to the daily mistings of the weather. Luis had planted more garden than I knew how to recognize, and the entire patch was ringed by an enormous vine that spread like morning glory and held dozens of light green, eggplant-sized fruits. I'd read that a single *chayote* plant could produce two hundred pounds of fruit in a year. I felt like I could see at least that much right then.

Luis picked several radishes and shook them off, smiling. *"Yo los siembro. Dios los trae."* I sow them. God brings them.

"Sí," I said. *"Sí. Exactamente."*

To the bundle of radishes, Luis added cilantro, carrots, and a cabbage. He had Anthony take off his sweatshirt and filled it with chayote. Luis would not let us pay him. The three of us went back the way we'd come, laden and chatting, idiot dogs running circles around us.

"We're getting the hang of this, right?" I said to Anthony a couple of hours later. He had made soup from Luis's chayote and Gungo's chicken, and it bubbled on the woodstove.

"Totalmente," he said, stirring.

I was regularly getting our sunshine-clean laundry before the raindrops did. It was no surprise that our cow relations had improved; Anthony had established us as the Alpha species, which is very important in the wild. We thought we might want to be cattle rustlers or at least ranch hands when we got back to the States.

If we go back, I had started to say. Very secretly and only to myself.

22

¡No Hablo Español Conmigo!

Ivy's refusal to speak Spanish continued unabated. The situation was, without question, entirely *mi culpa*.

As excited as Ivy had been about Costa Rica back in Seattle, when we talked about monkeys, butterflies, and going to school with the big kids, rebellion had set in the moment she realized the Spanish thing was going to be way bigger than *Dora the Explorer*. I'd spared no expense with the language learning aids and had surrounded us with opportunities. In the car, before bedtime. I was always happy to read Ivy an extra bedtime story—*Oso Pequeño* or *Jorge el Curioso*. At T-minus-three weeks, I even amended our family's strict, three-hours-a-week of screen time policy. *Unlimited DVD watching!* I decreed. *So long as you have the Spanish soundtrack on. Wheee!*

Rabid, really, would not be an inaccurate way to describe my behavior during this period.

But despite poor Ivy's best intentions to thwart her mother's best intentions, language started seeping in. The first time I heard her speak Spanish was at school, three weeks in. Fabio picked up the marker Ivy had just set down, and zoomed it along an imaginary runway while he made airplane noises. Just after takeoff, poor Fabio lost his grip. Ivy ran to snatch the marker from the floor.

"Es mío!" (Survival Spanish: Kindergarten Edition.) I was debating whether to bust Ivy for the snottiness or praise her for the language, when out of the corner of my eye I saw Isabella turn her head to hide a smile. Isa had been doing this a long time; I followed suit and ignored the whole thing.

Ivy watched *Newsies* as often as she could. She loved the dancing and the rosy-cheeked, pre-gaunt Christian Bale. But mostly she loved *Newsies* because, even with the Spanish soundtrack on, the singing stayed in English. In the non-singing parts, she was starting to get it despite herself. *"Huelga!"* she'd yell with the newsboys, indignant at the injustice of old man Pulitzer.

In October, at our first parent-teacher conference (called *charlas,* or chats), Isabella told us Ivy's Spanish was really coming along and that she frequently translated for the Tico kids on English days. Anthony and I tried not to look too surprised. We assumed the truth had gotten lost in translation, or that Isabella was just too sweet to tell us the truth.

"Yo quiero a Iby," Isabella told us that day. I never got the hang of when Spanish used the "b" sound for the "v" letter, but Ivy was "Iby" all year long to most native speakers. Ivy loved Isabella, too. Once when Isabella corrected her own pronunciation of Ivy's name, I heard my daughter say, "No, Isa. I am *Iby* when it's you." If anyone was going to make Spanish okay, it was going to be Isabella.

Then, soon after Isabella's mysterious comment at *charlas*, Ivy made a new friend.

Sofia was possibly the most adorable child on earth, like an even-more-miniature version of Lola, from the *Casa de Arte*. Sofi had the same dancing dark eyes and pixie-mischief look, the same rushed way of talking, as if everything that came out of her mouth was the biggest and best news ever. (So far, no cigarette.) Sofia's family, we knew, spoke only Spanish.

When Sofia turned six, she invited aunts, uncles, cousins, and Ivy to her party. Anthony and I weren't sure what the protocol was for Tico kid parties but we both wanted to see what one looked like. We accompanied Ivy to the door.

As we were all three ushered in, Sofi broke from an admiring throng of relatives to run toward us.

"Iby! Iby! Quiere jugar a Snow White, Iby?"

The Snow White dress my mom had made for Ivy had taken *prepa* by storm, and now Sofia had one, too. She'd also received a karaoke machine. We crammed in the tiny living room, watching the kids dance to Spanish pop while some cousins sang. (*Mi Primer Millón!* I knew this one! Should I grab the mike?) An aunt laughed when she saw Anthony's jaw drop at Sofia—this tiny kid inhabited the music, with expert moves and perfect rhythm that would be sexy if she weren't a little girl in a princess dress.

"La musica . . ." the aunt smiled over the music. *"Para las Ticas, corre en la sangre."* Together, Anthony and I looked at Ivy, who was also dancing. Gringas did not have music in their blood. Anthony grimace-smiled back at the aunt and gave a "Sorry, we can't help it" shrug. The girls, oblivious, boogied in their Disney frocks.

After that, Ivy played frequently at Sofi's house. We heard no stories about language confusion or misunderstandings, but within our earshot Ivy was still all English, all the time.

Duh is I believe what Ivy was thinking. *Have you not noticed that we all have a perfectly good language in which we can communicate quite well?* (I never found a Spanish equivalent for *duh*. Sad.)

Then one day, she couldn't help herself.

Across the street from the church, a lady gave away ice cream cones every Sunday after Mass. It was universally understood that this was only for little kids, and only if they'd attended church. One day in November the lady handed Ivy her cone and asked if she spoke Spanish.

"¿Habla español, mi amor?"

"No, no puedo," Ivy answered. *"Gracias por el helado."* No, I can't. Thanks for the ice cream.

But the Ivy-est moment of all came on the driveway, one perfect afternoon in late October.

After the bus dropped her off, we'd stopped at the *pulperia* for an ice cream bar and were on our way up the hill to the house. When we rounded the bend, crossed the stream, and burst into the sunlight that marked the first steep ascent, two *morphos* greeted us as we exited the shade. They kept pace with us for a while, playing tag up the hill. I basked in the perfection that was my life.

Up to that point, we'd been playing our standard driveway-walking game, "What do you like better?" I'd had no problem picking Swiss Almond Vanilla over Peanut Butter & Chocolate, and Ivy had dispensed with "School Uniform or Wear What You Want?" a gimme I'd thrown in to fulfill my own agenda. With Ivy, it was never a bad idea to release the pressure of the school day in a controlled manner. My question gave her an opening to gripe about uniforms for a while, and we moved on.

We got to the hard part of the walk chattering and in good spirits, then fell silent with the effort of the hill. This was the sweaty, miserable part, the part that no game could make fun. And then she fell.

She went down hard. A large stone had dislodged beneath her dusty little ladybug boot, which had long since lost its antennae. The smaller gravel slid beneath her, and Ivy slammed to her knees, tipped over, and rolled for a few feet. She stopped splayed face up like a beetle, sprawled atop her backpack and dusty from head to toe. She howled with pain and injustice. I could see the blood starting to seep through the dust on her knee. I ran-slid down to gather her up.

For once, I wasn't trying for the Spanish. It just came. It's such a good little word, sweet, and without the condescending subtext of its English equivalent, "poor little thing." I'd heard mothers use it dozens of times, for the minor injuries and indignities of childhood. Truly, I wasn't making a point.

"*Pobrecita,*" I soothed, rubbing her head, holding her tight.

In an instant Ivy was out of my arms, fists clenched, stamping the dusty boot below her bloodied knee.

"*NO HABLO ESPANOL CONMIGO! NUNCA!*" Ivy shouted.

DON'T SPEAK SPANISH WITH ME! EVER!

23

Visitors and Vacations

Togetherness-toshmetherness, as the family counselors say. It wasn't just the language that was getting us down: Ivy and I needed some new people. Fortunately, we were about to get some.

First Erin, in late October. Then Lizzie, Nick, Lucy, and Galen, our closest family of friends, would come for what was, in the States, Thanksgiving week.

After Nicaragua, we were all excited for a vacation whose only challenge would be getting to it. Puerto Viejo, on Costa Rica's Caribbean side, promised all the standard ingredients—sand, sun, and someone else making our beds. A twenty-something volunteer at the school had recommended a set of cabins in the ocean-side jungle, all built by Jason, a hippie expat. The price was right. But far more important than destination was the fact that this trip would include Erin. Auntie En would be laden, I promised the children, with all manner of auntie-presents. We'd pick her up on the way to the coast.

Backpacks on, the five of us started down the driveway. It was 5:45 a.m. I'd stayed up late filling an extra fanny pack with nuts, cheese, Pringles, and avocados that were hard enough to travel, soft enough to eat. As we got everyone out the door, Anthony and I were mutually and mildly annoyed with each other—I because Anthony never thinks to feed anyone; he because I make packing harder than it has to be, and then I complain about it.

Long walk down the driveway—bump bump bump went our backpacks against our backs. And into Santa Elena to board the 6:30 bus –bump bump bump went the bus down the mountain. The twisty trip made us too woozy for snacks. By the time we reached the relative smoothness of the sun-softened highway, we'd been awake for five sustenance-free hours. I offered cheese and cashews, but it was too late. Hunger-mind had set in.

Hannah fired first. "Now it's too hot to eat," she said. "I hate Puntarenas." This little town sat at the bottom of the mountain where our road joined the highway. Its low altitude was Puntarenas' biggest crime; after crisp, clean Monteverde, Puntarenas always felt oppressive.

Harry got off the next shot.

"That's dumb. You can't be too hot to eat. That's not even possible. If you're not hungry, just say you're not hungry. Don't make it Puntarenas' fault."

Ivy: "I hate cheese. How come you *never* bring anything I like?"

And so on. Everyone reloaded and let off a few more rounds.

On the ancient public buses that grumble down the Pan-American Highway, vendors get on at one stop, move up the aisle selling treats, and step off when they're sold out. Then they walk back along the blistering asphalt to the starting point, refill their beaten-up coolers, and start again on the next bus. Fruit, chips, empanadas, soft drinks and this time, miracle of miracles, things that were frozen. An ancient *Señor* was selling homemade otter pops— long, narrow tubes of plastic, filled with icy concoctions.

For Anthony, street food is in the same food group as raw cookie dough; he declined politely.

But the kids were melting, Witch-of-the-West-like, into puddles of their own sweat, and everyone needed some calories whether they thought so or not. I bought mango and guava and something that maybe would translate to root beer, two apiece for the kidlets. For me, a flavor that was strange, yes, but in the moment oddly appealing: *rompope.*

"Omigosh this feels incredible." Hannah had the idea first, and the rest of us quickly followed suit. We rubbed the unopened tubes behind our ears, then slid them down the backs of our shirts, along our spines. Cold condensation replaced trickles of sweat. Ivy giggled as she touched hers to her tummy, and more when the big kids did the same.

Finally, much cheered, we ate them.

My pop turned out to be even more delicious than advertised. When I took my first big bite of crunchy-slushy ice-cold eggnog, I understood the twinkle in senor's eye as he'd recommended this creamy pop with a hint of a coffee-colored swirl.

"Muy rico, MUY, MUY rico, Señora."

Rico indeed: My frozen eggnog was definitely *con ron.*

Harry waxed scientific on the miracle pops as he munched through the can of Pringles.

"You know what's weird? My root beer one was actually colder than the mango one. Isn't that weird? Do you think root beer has a lower freezing point than mango?"

"Your mom has a lower freezing point than mango."

"Ar ar ar."

"Aire frío! Aire frío!" the van drivers promised, and I was tempted. We were off the first bus and at the airport. I shot a hopeful glance at Anthony. He said nothing, but I could feel him oozing judgment. The two-hour wait for Erin's flight felt manageable, but the NINE MORE HOURS on the public bus to Puerto Viejo felt longer now than it had when I planned the trip. I was hot. I wanted to hire a driver. The bus was a steal at four bucks a head, but the *aire* on the bus was so, so not *frío.*

Anthony and his smugly fastened bandana wanted to tough it out. Anthony thought we should snag Erin, get into San José, and take the 4 p.m. bus to Puerto Viejo. I thought, of course, that someone who routinely forgets that traveling children need to be fed should shut up. Stop oozing. Whatever.

The hovering drivers circled like sharks, underbidding each other on the only two variables in play: timing and cost. I ducked out of the scrum to find Anthony, making him talk an offer over with me as if we were scheming. It turned out we were; Anthony had had a scrum of his own.

What? I thought you were against the whole plan!

But Anthony was trying to follow instructions, to stop oozing and be helpful, and now we had arrangements with two different guys. Someone was going to be mad at us, no matter what. To offset this, and because I had been in management so I knew how to deal productively in uncomfortable situations, I got mad at Anthony for a little while.

In the end, Elmer (Anthony's guy) won the grand prize of seven hours (he swore he could make it in six) in his van with our family, for US $120. It was a great price—Elmer must have had a sense about what joy it would be to hang out with us, post-otter-pop.

"Puerto Viejo," Anthony told Elmer, who raised an eyebrow and said in English "If that's what you wants."

At last Erin arrived with one small duffel packed with her clothes and one large suitcase filled with presents. She dug Luna bars out before anyone could even ask. The kids fought over who'd carry her bags and clung to her as we walked. We climbed into Elmer's van, happily munching on Erin's treats. She asked about our vacation spot.

Up and down Central America, the Caribbean coast has a different flavor from the Pacific side. The language is just as likely to be Creole or English as it is Spanish. The soundtrack is the Jimmy Buffet/Bob Marley mix tape and the *gallo pinto* is made with coconut milk. Most families who visit the Caribbean side tend to head to Tortuguero, a wildlife refuge famous for the tens of thousands of sea turtles that hatch on its beaches every year. Turtles are fine, but I wanted to steer us clear of teeming tourists.

"Apparently, it's the alternative-lifestyle Gringo hangout," I told Erin. "I think we can expect to see the standard Unconventional Uniform—African colors on blond surfers, beaded braids, toe rings."

"It's not so bad a look," she smiled. She gave her attention back to her nieces and nephew, still talking over each other and wrapping themselves up in her. The four of them looked like a litter of puppies.

I sat in front and chatted with Elmer. My Spanish had come a long way since Marco had shown me what a cow was. I told him we were looking forward to relaxing in Puerto Viejo.

"Los de Puerto Viejo realmente se saben relajar." So the people of Puerto Viejo really knew how to relax?

I'd seen that smile before, on Seattle moms learning about my crazy take-the-bus philosophy. "Who am I to say how you should raise your children?" that smile says. "Even though you are clearly blowing it." At least Magda said these things out loud. Feeling judged and uncomfortable, I stopped trying with Elmer and turned my attention back to the puppies.

Sometime after ten, Elmer navigated us down an unlit road and pulled to a stop by a hand lettered sign that I never would have found. The windows of a cabin that must be Jason's glowed a short distance away.

We piled out of the van into a multi-sensory extravaganza of relaxed. Waves lapped gently and stars shone calm in the black, black sky. The warm night air caressed but did not cling. I inhaled the night breeze deeply. And understood

Elmer's smile. The breeze smelled exactly as if it had wafted in from the sea, then stopped on the beach to take several mellow hits off a really big bong.

Our driver also breathed in and touched his nose. "You and your children will be able to relax, I think." Elmer thought I was going to get stoned with my five-year-old! No wonder he'd given me that prissy smile! I was starting to explain myself when a voice came through the darkness,

"You found us! Right ON. Come in, come in."

Elmer helped with the bags, bringing them to the door. Jason tried to usher him in, too, but Elmer declined. I picked Ivy up and walked past him, my upright carriage conveying the truth that I would not be rolling my daughter a joint later. Once our family was in the kitchen, Jason blinked a few times in confused wonder before saying,

"Awesome to have you guys. And now it's time for your *cuba libres*—that's rum and Coke. Except for the midgets. For them, I think just . . ." he looked to the ceiling for inspiration. The pause lengthened.

"Coke?" offered Harry.

"Yes! Stellar insight, midget-man. Exemplary. That is indeed the answer to our problem."

If Jason had been high when he'd built the cabins, more power to him. Our wraparound porch was so deep that Erin and the kids took measurements to determine whether our two-bedroom cabin had more indoor space or outdoor space (tie). The kids squealed when they discovered they had CANOPY BEDS, which is what any regular bed turns into when there's a ring of mosquito netting hanging from the ceiling. Mornings, we walked down the road for gallo pinto with coconut milk. Every afternoon, Jason delivered a new bottle of fresh water. He saluted the kids, who were still in orbit around Erin, as he turned it upside down and it went glug glug.

"Hey, midgets. So glad you're here. Everything cool?"

Even the ocean was family-friendly—the gentle waves were perfect for toddlers and completely unsurfable. And far from being a misfit nuclear family in a haze of stoned dropouts, it turned out that we took over the place. Courtney's family was there. Hannah's English teacher, whom she adored, had come with her two kids, and another teacher we did not know well was there with his family.

"Let the good times roll!" said Jason, when he realized an entire community had unknowingly booked his whole place.

When we walked into town, it was indeed all toe rings and Bob Marley t-shirts. Puerto Viejo was a Gringo-ridden paradise, and that was okay. We were, after all, Gringos.

Shortly after we returned from Puerto Viejo, the United States would celebrate Thanksgiving. We'd now had visits from my dad and sister, but Lizzie & Co. were our first friends to make the trip. Hannah and Harry were ecstatic. Ivy was sad none of her friends were coming, but Courtney was a consolation prize for all manner of heartaches. She came over several times that week, solemn in her own Snow White dress, to play with Ivy. I realized with a start how long it had been since Ivy had required external distraction.

Our friends arrived the Friday before Thanksgiving. Hannah and Lucy immediately vanished into the loft, emerging for long meanders over and around our hillsides. Harry and Galen spent the weekend carving bows and arrows. The boys had always shared a certain money-loving sensibility, and now they made big plans that involved free materials (the rainforest), cheap labor (their own), and outrageous markups back in Seattle.

The kids couldn't wait to show *jupo* to their friends. Ivy and Harry showed off their tandem routine. Ivy leaned back and waved to the astonished newbies back on the stump, while Harry spun their twosome off the far tree with a practiced leg. Lucy said, "You guys have the best life I have ever seen," but her mom hugged my shoulders and said "God, how do you stand watching Ivy on that thing?"

But then Liz went, too, and couldn't stop laughing.

On Monday, Lucy and Galen went to school and agreed that it was perfect. Fewer kids, more freedom. As Hannah had told me more than once, "There's less stress, but also I learn more." Can't argue with that.

Lizzie came with me to the gallery that morning. Walking through town, she asked how the Anthony-Margot togetherness experiment was working out. I told her, "It's nice. We cook and shop and go for walks and, I dunno, just do things together that we used to do separately for efficiency's sake. But he seems so much quieter than before we got here. It's like he never talks."

"Huh," she said, because she is brilliant. "I haven't noticed a difference. Do you think maybe...what if he's not actually talking less, but you're together so much more that the ratio's off?"

Huh indeed. Maybe Anthony just had a certain number of words he could generate in a week. Whereas I tended to fill in any silence. Worth considering.

Back in Seattle, Lizzie's Spanish had been much better than mine. (She had some, I had none.) She had generously drilled me in key phrases before we left. Now, I was pleasantly stunned to find that Lola, Beatriz, and I needed to slow down our coffee-break chatter for Liz to keep up. I even had to translate a couple of times. Over coffee, Lizzie told me that Lucy told her Hannah was different, somehow, at first. That it was hard for the two of them to get into a rhythm, and Hannah had seemed distant.

"I think she's out of the habit of friends," I told her. "It scares me."

"They got past it. Lucy says it's all good now," Lizzie was quick to reassure.

I showed Lizzie the painting I'd been working on—wildly colored animals, including parrots and cows floating in a starry sky.

"Honey," she said to me in English, "How are you ever going to leave?"

We pulled the kids from school for three days. We had sworn to minimize this kind of behavior, as we really did want to live a real life here. But it was LUCY and GALEN, and we can't go to school on Thanksgiving! We hit the beach at Playa Hermosa, on the Pacific side. Costa Rica definitely contained multitudes; on a map, the Spanish-speaking Pacific coast is just a pinky-finger away from where we'd been a month before. But no dreadlocks, no toe rings.

My new backpack philosophy suited Lizzie, as did traveling by bus and generally on a shoestring, while recognizing the importance of spontaneous, parent-sponsored ice cream stops.

It had stopped mattering to Ivy that she didn't get her own friend. On the bus, she sat on Lizzie's knees and hugged her, then leaned back to look and make sure she was really, truly, there, then hugged her some more.

We'd rented a large, rickety beach house of weathered dark wood, with porches big enough for two queen-sized beds (more mosquito-net canopies). It was the kind of house you find things in, and Harry cheered capitalistically as Galen pulled a dusty Monopoly game from the back of a closet. One evening on the beach, I made the ten-second trek from shore to house to see if the boys wanted to take a break from the game they'd been playing for a day and a half and join the rest of us at the water.

"We're good," said Harry, scooping up the money on Free Parking. "Your turn, G."

Then he glanced at the water and touched my arm. "Mom, look at Ivy."

Ivy stood at the edge of the twilit waves, naked, her little white butt cheeks contrasting with the bronze of her legs. The sun was setting in front of her. In that instant she turned her head back toward us and smiled. She was a twenty-first-century Coppertone girl, all deep tan lines and curly pigtails, bare in the sunset with the shining eyes and unselfconscious glee of a girl who has been adored in every moment since the day she arrived. (I was in no mood to see the strong-minded spitfire who couldn't care less about being adored, who would turn from hugging to kicking in an instant, for reasons of her own.)

"She's so . . ." Harry said. And then, "Awesome. I own three railroads—dude, you owe me seventy-five bucks."

Back in the States, loved ones were sharing turkey and cranberries. That evening we, also with loved ones, ate perfect grilled tilapia at a tiny café. Afterward, Anthony and I swam out past the wave line and soon all nine of us were out there. We bobbed in the gentle Pacific and chatted the sun down, talking about everything and nothing. Hannah and Lucy let Ivy, in her life vest, hang out in their little circle and join in their big-girl gossip. Galen and Harry spat water at each other and talked profits. We adults admired our children, haloed in the sun.

The saline ocean lifted us up, lowered us, lifted us again. Our bellies were full, and we were floating in the sea, catching up on four months of conversation with beloved friends. The warm ocean took on a pink glow all around us.

Stars winked on in a green-blue sky, and we fell quiet. Spread out on our backs, we let the waves roll beneath us. Harry said,

"This seems like the time we should talk about what we're thankful for."

So we did, and what we all came up with was this exact moment. It was all we could remember, as if time began with this sunset, and these people.

By late November we had been down the mountain four times—three vacations and a thirty-minute/two-day appointment with Dr. de la Rosa. Returning from the beach, we knew to expect the temperature drop as the bus climbed the twisty, rocky road toward Monteverde. It was starting to feel a little like a homecoming, and we breathed in deeply.

24

Season of Waiting

"*M*eddy Chreesmos!*" Luis and Paula hollered and waved from their front porch on the first day of Advent. The four thousand miles between us and Seattle felt farther at Christmas. Our neighbors tried to make us feel more at home, gamely wrapping their mouths around the English.

We waved and called back, *"Feliz Navidad!"*

Our whole family was striding down the driveway. Erin had called to say that she mailed a Christmas box shortly after her October visit. All our Seattle people had gotten their presents to Erin and she'd handled the logistics, and we should start checking the post office today. Once we had the box, she said, we'd want to take a taxi back.

"It is not a *small* box," Auntie En had told Harry in a smiling voice.

Two hours later found us still on foot, trudging back up the hill. No biggie, I told the kids. There was still lots of time.

But it was a biggie. That box was going to bridge those miles, connect us back. We were four months in. The new and shiny had worn off, we still weren't fluent, and visits from Erin and the Lizzie crew had reminded us what deep, easy relationships felt like. When they left, we felt their absence harder than we had before. We were all a little lonelier, now.

We scaled the driveway, and I felt the homesickness settling over us like the omnipresent fucking mist. I looked away from the riot of cosmos and oversized impatiens all around us.

"Those are summer flowers," I muttered to Anthony.

"And they're too big," he agreed. "It's obscene."

Harry was looking at the rainforest, too. "Hey, there are no pine trees here," he said. "What are we going to do for a Christmas tree?"

Anthony and I broke the news: No pines, Norfolk or otherwise, grew in Monteverde.

Back at the house, the kids drifted into poor uses of time. They watched *Princess Bride* in English and grumbled at each other, while I took my own mind off Costa Rica not being Seattle by planning a post-Christmas trip to Panama. Between the school's regular breaks and our own Thanksgiving cheat, even vacations were getting tiresome. But Panama would be a brand-new place, totally exotic, sure to be distracting, etc. We'd go to Bocas del Toro, an archipelago on the Caribbean side.

I called a rustic guesthouse that looked good on the Internet. Bob Marley or maybe it was Jimmy Cliff answered the phone. He took my credit card number before he warned me:

"Missus, I got to tell you, aldo de electrics come standahd, sahmtimes it stop wahking. But it always come back."

Okay. We could handle no electrics, so long as it was just for sahmtimes.

For the next week I dove into making it exciting to celebrate Christmas away from home. I mostly did this by saying, "This is so exciting!" several times each day. I found soccer socks in red and green in town and glued felt letters on. Harry scaled the cold wood stove to tape these stockings to its flue. Ivy looked on, worried and directive.

"Don't put mine low! What if he misses it?"

So Hannah climbed up and raised Ivy's stocking as high as she could reach, protective of the one who still believed.

Everyone was trying.

If the kids were missing the spacious, hand-knit-by-Grandma stockings that had hung from the mantle every other year of their lives, I didn't notice.

I imagine that our family has pretty much a standard amount of dysfunction. We have money problems and divorces and secret addictions, seething jealousies and the very occasional act of pure cruelty: my wealthy dentist grandfather ran off with his secretary, leaving my grandmother to raise four daughters in near poverty, in the dreary green-gray of southeastern Alaska. When he died forty years later, he left each of them one dollar in his will.

Mostly we're not like that, but you do get the outlier. That's family.

But there's one thing about us that's full-on Norman Rockwell, and it's our Christmas stockings. Gramma knits one ahead of each baby's arrival, right up to the cuff, which she leaves unfinished until the newest adorable gets here and gets named. Then she knits the letters in. My sister and I grew up with these, and all our cousins had them, and now the next generation. All created by my mother from the same pattern she'd found in the early '60s, when her big sister Heather got pregnant with the first of us cousins: Gordon, clear-eyed artistic genius who would later become my favorite cokehead.

But wacky cousins and Gramma's stockings were on another continent, and our soccer socks hung on the wood stove with care. Phone calls to and from the States increased.

The kids worried that Auntie En's box wouldn't arrive in time. The giant parcel from home, of home. I thought of Laura and Mary Ingalls, waiting for the Christmas barrel from the folks back East. I didn't mention to the kids how it all went down in *The Long Winter*. How the blizzards stacked themselves so thickly that it was April before the trains came through and Laura finally got to read her copies of *Youth's Companion*.

The kids and I needed a project. Something thrilling to get worked up about and that would hold our attention. And I needed a gift for Anthony. Clearly, what the situation called for was a motorcycle.

People in the *Zona* seemed to learn to drive a *moto* right about the time they gave up the binky. It was the preferred vehicle, far ahead of the automobile. Serviceable bikes, nothing fancy or tricked out.

Thanks to my mother and her years as an ER nurse, I had grown up believing motorcycles lived high on the certain-ruin scale, not too far from crystal meth. Yet regularly in Monteverde, I'd see a man on his motorcycle, woman on the back, holding their baby over one arm, no helmets in sight. I'm not *recommending* this. Just pointing out that, you know, perhaps I'd been wound unnecessarily tightly *vis à vis* these particular vehicles.

Our friend Mike had bought a motorcycle when he and Kelly first arrived— he practically had to, I guessed, with all those tattoos.

The family and girly vehicle was a *cuadra*, a four-wheeled open-air vehicle. (I believed in the States this was known as an ATV.) Perfectly crisp ladies in white hotel uniforms rumbled down the streets astride *cuadras*. As did impossibly tidy mamas with a gaggle of grinning children, who themselves began driving *cuadras* at about age twelve. (Fourteen was the age for legal licenses, but we were pretty far above the law up here.)

Early on, I had done a little cost research and lobbied weakly for a *cuadra*, but Anthony was against it.

"That doesn't look very safe," he said, channeling Courtney, my mother, and every eldest child on the planet.

"With everyone else zipping around on *motos*," I had argued, "an ATV is practically a Volvo."

But Anthony had never explicitly vetoed a *moto*. He knew how to ride, having owned some kind of a dirt bike as a teenager. (Didn't his mother even *like* him?)

I began making inquiries.

Increasingly minimalist Anthony, when asked what he wanted for Christmas, repeatedly said "Nothing." But I knew better.

I was itching to do something fantastic. And beneath that, on a level so deep I didn't quite give it words, I was tired of all the calm radiating from my husband. In every day, in every hour. Nothing made Anthony miserable, nothing made him furious, and most of all, nothing, ever, made him ecstatic. Maybe with a motorcycle, I could finally get some exclamation points out of this man.

And the kids really did need something to get excited about.

Suck it, minimalism. Sometimes you just have to take one for the team.

Three weeks before Christmas, Ezmeralda invited us all to share the holiday with her family. Ezmeralda's parents and younger brother lived in El Dos, a community of about twenty families, mostly coffee farmers, an hour's bus ride away. The house was small, Ezmeralda said, but would we come? They would splurge and buy a pig this year, and we would spend four days enjoying soups, tamales, and other delicacies from all its parts.

Now we really had a focus (although I kept pursuing the motorcycle. The school secretary told me she had a brother whose wife had a *primo* who might want to sell). As we started making gifts for a family we'd never met, the non-arrival of our Christmas box became less of a daily issue. I plunged us into the idea of Christmas in El Dos, with new customs, new foods, and a surrogate family.

Also, I had to have a little meltdown.

Two weeks before Christmas, on a day that couldn't decide how it was going to be—cloudy, then bright-bright, the strong breeze changing the outlook by the minute—I found a wrinkled note under Ivy's pillow. One side held a meticulously detailed drawing of a Christmas tree.

Christmas is a series of totems. We had *Charlie Brown Christmas* on TV and Hannah's special music box with the skater that went 'round and 'round. Gramma's stockings. Cousins.

But the tree was the center. The tree ushered the rest of it in. Since Harry's tree question on the driveway, Ivy had kept asking, and I'd kept explaining, until apparently Ivy had given up and drawn her own. I looked at the ornaments for a while, crayoned balls and candy canes. Then I turned the paper over and saw the blocked, uneven letters of a five-year-old:

DEAR SANTA

I AM SAD SANTA.

FORMM IVY

I had not noticed, what with being so festive and all, what was really going on in my family. What I had done to them?

Suddenly, the whole adventure came unmasked. I had had an idea and whisked us all off on a whim, to a land where we didn't even know what season it was going to be. The naked truth was that I'd simply tired of waiting. I had hauled my family along on an updated version of the adventure I'd put aside the day I learned I was pregnant.

Me and my poster board and lists and "Let's decide this as a family." Ho. *Fucking. Ho.* You can talk kids into anything if you frame it right. Sure, I'd had lots of good reasons. But the advantages I'd hyped looked threadbare in comparison to Ivy's solid black letters.

This year was selfish wish-fulfillment, all dressed up as parenting.

Poor Hannah. Friendship was hard enough at thirteen in a world you knew. How had I expected her to navigate being the new kid in middle school, *in Spanish?* When I'd asked Lola, she had explained to me why the distance between Hannah and the girls at school seemed to be expanding, rather than contracting, as time went by.

"*Hannah es preciosa, pero todavía es niña,*" Lola explained. "*Es niña, m'entiendes, MarGOTE?*" Lola always repeated her important words, to make sure I understood. "*M'entiendes?*" she asked me several times a day at the *Casa.* Do you understand me?

Yes, Hannah was darling—and yes, in body and attitude, she was still a little girl.

"Y las otras...ya son chicas." The other girls had new bodies and gossip and makeup and boyfriends. Hannah didn't have the hang of any of that. In Seattle, Hannah had peers who felt like she did. In bringing her here, I had isolated her—and now she was digging in further. But, you know...Merry Christmas! The day before, I'd actually pulled Hannah away from an email to Lucy so we could hang paper snowflakes from the hummingbird feeders.

Visions of therapy flashed before my eyes. Hannah in her twenties, telling a clucking professional about how she grew up putting a brave face on, acting like she loved whatever insane adventure her mother had concocted. Ivy unloading about the shame that surrounded anyone in our house who just wanted to be normal, to watch stupid shit on television, eat Cheetos, and then maybe go to the mall. Harry would have questions about spending the first half of his childhood in the comfortable glow of uninterrupted success, only to have his mother yank it all out from under him. "What was so terrible about a little invincibility?" I could hear him saying. "I was *nine years old!*" I saw Harry looking lost at the blackboard on the first day of school, looking small in his alone spot, getting yelled at on the soccer pitch. Harry's power had always lain in his ability to communicate, and I had stripped him of his words.

Even Anthony had told me very clearly what he wanted, perhaps what he needed: nothing at all. But I hadn't listened. I kept wanting him to talk more, but didn't heed the things he said. And now a used motorcycle was bought, paid for, and on its way.

I pulled the concocted stockings off the wood stove. *Look everyone! You can make Christmas out of* **anything***!*

My breakdown took most of the morning. Anthony was at a hotel by the Reserve, helping them figure out why their Internet was so slow. (Answer: Dial-up is really slow.) The kids were at school and Magda was, thank heavens, not coming today. The last thing I needed was Magda pursing her perfect lips and harassing me about hot breakfast while I tried not to cry.

If you're going to stage a full-on fiesta of self-loathing, no point holding back. The lack of witnesses freed me to pick up the nearest emblem of my selfish focus, a bundle of Harry Potter flashcards grown so fat it was beginning to challenge its ponytail holder. I threw it out the open door at the guava tree. While I'd been preening about getting to the second book in the series, my five-year-old had figured her best bet for a little sympathy was Santa Claus.

In Seattle I had agonized about whether my working full-time was wrecking the children. Here, I'd been striving so hard to be the perfect NON-working mother, with my stockings and my gardens and my sleight-of-hand Christmas. Chess game my ass. There wasn't a conference room for a hundred miles, but my kids were lonely and tired, and I hadn't noticed.

After a while, I ran out of sad. Whatever my motives had been, however secretly selfish, here we were.

What next?

I'd always loved Emily Dickinson's lines about the post-grief body: *After great pain/A formal feeling comes/The nerves sit ceremonious/Like tombs.* As the clouds and sunshine jockeyed for position outside our giant windows, I moved through the house with my ceremonious nerves. I watched my hands with mild curiosity as they smoothed the cotton/poly threads of the soccer/Christmas stockings (red for the girls, green for Harry) and hung them back up. I drank a glass of water. I took some aspirin.

I would be gentler. I would make space for something other than my own unrelenting *Navidad* cheer.

I made some calls to see about canceling the motorcycle, but when the secretary at the school answered, she launched immediately into how excited her brother's *primo* was to have found a buyer, that he really needed the money right now, and that he would even give us his two helmets. Fine.

I met Ivy at the bus stop and asked her what she wanted to do.

"Let's check for Auntie En's box."

The post office, which was also the bus station, was a tiny room with a high counter and a single chair. A couple of scruffy Euro tourists were trying to sort out their tickets back to San José, so I sat in the chair and pulled Ivy onto my lap. We listened to the omnipresent Spanish pop. A song came on we kind of knew, and we kind of sang along.

The young man at the counter knew from visits past what we were after. When he saw Ivy, he made a big show of looking high and low to be sure he hadn't missed anything. He invited her behind the counter to take a look.

"*Lo siento, chiquita. La caja no está aquí, pero la Navidad—vendra todavía.*"

I'm sorry, sweetie. Your package isn't here, but Christmas will still come.

And Ivy seemed okay. We walked home, stopping for an ice cream bar.

When we got back to the house, Luis was just finishing up keeping the grasses at bay. He whacked them back weekly, keeping space open for Harry to play *fútbol*, for Anthony and the girls to read in the hammock while stacking mango skins on their tummies, for me to hang laundry. I paid Luis and thanked him. We chitchatted idly as he lit his cigarette and took a deep drag, gazing beyond me.

Luis took his leave and he, his immaculate white t-shirt, and Bruce-Springsteen jeans began their slow saunter down the driveway. Capitán and Tonto ran ahead, bumping into each other sidekick-style. After a few steps, I noticed Luis had stopped. He looked up and down the driveway's side jungle, then swiped his machete at a batch of errant foliage that had dared creep into the lane. Then he stood, cigarette dangling, searching for more.

It suddenly occurred to me that Luis walked the way he did not because he was so relaxed, so *pura vida* that he never needed to hurry. Luis moved slowly through the world because he was always, every minute, on the lookout for something to fix.

I knew what that felt like.

25

Christmas in El Dos

"I t'll be fun to open it when we get back," Anthony told the kids as we waited for the bus to El Dos. "Like a Christmas extension." Erin's box still hadn't arrived by December 22. I noticed that Anthony could be upbeat without sounding maniacal.

Ninety minutes later, we stepped off the bus at a tiny dirt-road intersection. We'd lost altitude again, and the temperature had risen accordingly. Heat didn't feel Christmasy, but we were troopers.

Ezmeralda had said her parents' house was right by the bus stop, and now she stepped out a front door and waved. The kids shouldered their backpacks and headed over. And then they started shouting, and rushed the house.

Christmas in Victorian England played out on every window. Icicles hung from snow-covered gables. In the glow of iron street lamps, bundled carolers held songbooks with mittened hands. Evergreen trees by the dozen, some decorated with balls and candy canes, and some just being evergreen trees.

Somehow, some way, Ezme's family had gotten their hands on Dickensian window decals. The kids pointed and talked over each other, an energy in their voices that we hadn't heard in weeks.

A tiny woman with a black bun, black eyes, and a dress of riotous color stood on the front step. I looked from her to my resuscitated children and swallowed, and couldn't make words. I smiled and she patted my arm. Odalie. Ezmeralda's mother.

Ten minutes later, over *empanadas,* Ezmeralda's nineteen-year-old brother, Pedrito, pointed at the window scenes and asked us to describe things. Mostly he wanted to know what snow felt like. Our Spanish was up to "cold" and "soft," but not "fluffy" or "crunchy," and certainly nothing like "exhilarating." I knew "magical"—thank you, J. K. Rowling—which helped. The kids tried to tell Pedrito about catching flakes on your tongue. I think Harry got it done.

Pedrito was...frail. Papery and delicate, with high cheekbones and a gentle voice. Our kids adored him instantly. My generally reliable gaydar registered a hit, and I wondered what that must be like for Pedrito in tiny El Dos, Catholic church at the center.

Ezmeralda had mentioned that Pedrito was sensitive, but I don't think it ever occurred to her that her sweet little brother might have something else going on. Over the course of our sessions and in our search for topics, Ezme and I had begun to broach politics and religion. She'd told me she was starting to think that perhaps being gay wasn't something you could help, but obviously you can't let those people around children.

Ezmeralda's father, Pedro, looked like a Latino Clint Eastwood. Handsome and lanky, with square shoulders and a don't-try-any-funny-stuff gaze. Pedro took very little notice of his own son, but made a big deal over the athleticism of mine. Soon Pedro and Harry were arm wrestling. Harry held his own, and my heart broke a little when I saw Pedrito turn away.

Ezmeralda saw it too, and piped up to suggest that Pedrito show us where we'd all be sleeping. It wasn't until then that I truly *got* the size of their house.

Hannah would just fit on the couch that just fit in the living room. Anthony, Ivy, and I would share Ezmeralda's bedroom, whose door was right at the end of Hannah's couch. Our hosts had put a two-foot-by-six-foot strip of foam next to Ezme's twin mattress, and together these two beds took up the entire floor. At the other end of the couch, another bedroom door, where Ezmeralda would share her parents' double bed. Harry would take Pedrito's narrow cot on the enclosed back porch while Pedrito himself slept on the half-meter-wide floor space next to it.

In the face of this staggering display of hospitality, this opening of their cozy home, without apology or embarrassment, I knew I had to warn our hosts about our family's nighttimes.

When she was tiny, Ivy was a terrible sleeper. But so are a lot of babies. How could we know she had demons?

Ivy never remembered her dreams the next morning, but as she became verbal we'd gotten some clues. "The monkeys! The monkeys!" she would scream. Or just, "No, no, please, NO!"

Ivy's eczema, always worse with stress, created a vicious cycle: A nightmare increased her heart rate, which lit her skin on fire, which in turn must have exacerbated whatever the hell was going on in her head.

Time and again we found Ivy scratching wildly in her sleep, hands everywhere at once, body drenched in sweat. It was impossible to keep her nails short enough; for years now she'd had tiny scratch marks all over her little tummy, legs, back.

It was wrenching, yes. But you can take almost anything in stride when it happens a couple hundred nights a year. Once, I took a little longer than usual to get my bearings at the two a.m. shrieking. When I finally entered their bedroom, I saw seven-year-old Harry crouched by toddler Ivy in their shared room, patting her back and saying, "It's okay, Ivy. I promise. You're safe."

But as good as we'd all gotten at coping, I knew this wasn't normal. Lizzie once took all three of our kids overnight. The next day she said, "You'd warned me, but God. I honestly thought she was being murdered in her bed."

I had hoped we could contain things at Ezmeralda's--sleep close to Ivy, keep the sounds to a minimum. Now, realizing that the whole house would hear everything, I outlined the routine and told Ezme's family not to worry: Ivy would be okay, this always happened.

"*Déjame pedir una bendición para la niña.*" said Odalie. She wanted to ask a blessing for Ivy. She went on, and I looked to Ezmeralda. Our tutor spoke no English, but was great at slowing down the Spanish. She told me that her mother was very close to God. She had cast out many demons and cloaked people in holy protection.

Over the years, straight-up western medicine had prescribed an antihistamine that would ostensibly treat Ivy's eczema, and had the charming side benefit of sedating her. A naturopath had prescribed borage, which turned Ivy's pee bright green but had no other effect. We'd greased her itchy skin nightly, with everything from Crisco to hardcore prescription steroid cream.

"What do you think?" I asked Anthony. "It kind of seems like there's nothing to lose."

"I don't really know what an exorcism looks like," he said. "But it can't be as bad as the movie."

When asked, Ivy was eager and unafraid.

Odalie turned out the light in Ezmeralda's bedroom. She lit a candle. The three of us climbed over the extra mattress to the bed. Ivy's face registered excitement; she was enchanted by this black-haired, beetle-eyed grandmother who ran her hands gently over Ivy's own fine curls, saying, *"Empezemos"*—let's begin.

I sat behind Ivy, my arms loose around her torso. Ivy was not a child you wanted to hold too tightly. Odalie placed her hands once again on Ivy's head, then shoulders, and finally held both of Ivy's hands. Then she began to pray, so softly I couldn't understand. This troubled me a moment, as I had understood that part of my role there was translator. But this first prayer was not for public consumption. Odalie was centering herself. When she was done, she smiled at Ivy and pulled a tiny bottle from the front of her shirt. *Is this how it works?* I wondered. *Catholic women keep holy oil in their BRA?* Focus.

Odalie took the stopper off the little bottle and turned it over on her finger. Her ring finger, I noticed. Was that significant? She dabbed oil onto each of Ivy's wrists, then put the bottle back where it came from. Clasping Ivy's hands again, she began:

"Jesús," she prayed. Pronounced, of course, "Haysoos."

Odalie kept her eyes closed but I could not; maybe through a combination of lip reading and hearing I could get more of the Spanish. Or maybe I was just fascinated. Odalie held Ivy's hands. I held the rest of Ivy and watched Odalie.

Jesús . . .

In my church and my Christianity, we tend to be pretty vague about what God might do; when we speak of miracles at all, we're long on metaphor and short on literal interpretation. We take care to avoid the presumption that we have all the facts. Odalie, though, didn't pussyfoot around. Boldly laying claim to specific promises and power, Odalie prayed:

"We bring you this little child, Jesus, because you love the little children. We know there are demons everywhere who want your world, and these demons are entering this child through her sleep. She needs your protection, Jesus. This little girl, this beautiful *niña*, she is yours. She belongs to you, and she requires your attention. We are asking you to come into her sleep. Leave no room for the devil. Come into her sleep, and give her beautiful thoughts. Do not let her be afraid, Jesus. We trust that you want no child to fear. You love Ivy, Jesus. Drive the devils from her. Protect her in her sleep. She is yours."

Odalie murmured her prayer first with urgency, then slowly, waiting for me to catch up. I translated as best I could.

I could hardly wait for bedtime and kept checking my watch. At 8:30 on the dot, "Okay, Small! Time for hugs and kisses—I'll read two books. Off we go."

Ivy slept through.

Had the excitement of the day wiped her out? Was it because she got to sleep with Anthony and me? Power of suggestion? Straight-up coincidence?

I had no reasoned response to what happened. Just wonder and gratitude, gratitude, gratitude.

The next day, Pedrito approached me nervously.

"*Lo siento mucho,*" he started to say. Pedrito apologized if he had seemed distant and perhaps like he did not want us there. Quite the opposite—he was happy we'd come and he wanted us to have a wonderful time. It was just that he felt very shy, Pedrito explained. He wasn't good with people and had never met Americans and didn't want to say anything that might offend us.

Hannah happened to be across the room. She had a book on her lap, but I saw she had stopped turning pages. She sat still as Pedrito and I talked, as he confessed his awkwardness and fear.

Later I suggested to Anthony that he try to spend some time with Pedrito. It seemed like this gentle young fellow could stand to be around a grown man whose personality didn't stomp all over his. As frustrated as I often was by Anthony's stillness, even I could see that it was also a gift.

Odalie might have been great at exorcism, but Hannah's vegetarianism had her flummoxed. For the first few meals, Odalie offered to make Hannah special dishes of chicken or fish.

"*Pollo? No? Pescado? No?*"

I felt terrible. Odalie felt she couldn't nourish our child, and nourishing children was the thing that Odalie loved most of all.

Finally, Odalie settled for feeding Hannah an egg at every meal while the rest of us ate some new segment of pig. Eggs were a poor substitute, in Odalie's opinion, but she sighed and kept on scrambling. I wanted to hug her every minute.

With the pig, Odalie and Ezmeralda taught us to make tamales.

In most Tico farmhouses, we learned, cooking is done over a kind of stone or brick indoor fireplace called a *fogón*. While we were at Ezmeralda's, the *fogón* burned most of the day. There was always a cast iron pot of water on to boil; if it wasn't needed now, it would be soon enough.

For tamales, we kept the *fogón* well stoked, cooking the pork on a grill and the cornmeal in boiling water in the big pot. Odalie had made tomatillo sauce ahead of time, and Ezme stepped out the back door to pick fragrant handfuls of cilantro. Pedro brought piles of banana leaves from his *finca*. In the States, I'd always seen tamales wrapped in corn husks; banana leaves, I learned, are the wrapper in much of Latin America.

Ezmeralda showed Hannah how to cut the leaves and put the rest of us on an assembly line. Ezme spooned corn mush, Anthony and Harry added pork, and Ivy and I pinched and placed cilantro. Odalie tried to teach us to tie the tamales just tightly enough. My packets never reached supreme Tico tidiness, but Hannah turned out to be something of a natural.

Ezme's dad was amused that Harry and Anthony wanted to help. Pedrito looked as if he hadn't realized such a thing was possible. When he made tentative moves to join in, Ezmeralda and Odalie cocked identical perfect eyebrows, but nodded.

Hannah, on seeing Pedrito work so hard to come out of his shell, seemed to be poking her head out, too. She moved over to make room at the table, then fake-scolded Pedrito as she retied his first tamales. Anthony switched jobs to join them, and the three chatted amiably at their end of the table. Across the kitchen, the rest of us guffawed and threw corn mush at each other.

Odalie asked us about our post-*Navidad* plans. When I told her about Panama, she, Ezmeralda, and Pedrito issued simultaneous clicks of their tongues.

"Los de Panama...no son muy educados," Odalie broke the news gently. The worst! Panamanians, she was sorry to tell us, were not very polite. We were in for it.

While the Ticos we knew reserved their highest contempt for Nicaraguans, they tended to adopt a somewhat doleful attitude toward the rest of Central America as well. It was hard for Costa Rica to be surrounded by such trashy countries. Like a parent whose son brings home prodigious SAT scores and terrible grades, our Costa Rican friends weren't *angry* with Honduras, El Salvador, and the rest—just so disappointed. All that potential.

Odalie insisted we make fifty tamales without any pork for Hannah. The poor child might not find anyone to feed her, once we hit the road.

On Christmas afternoon, I was talking with Ezmeralda when Harry begged to climb a guava tree he'd found by the church across the street. Filled with the bonhomie born of my best sleep in half a decade —it had been three nights now—I said sure and went back to my conversation.

Over the past few months, it had become clear to me that the beautiful Ez was also quite brilliant. Sleeping in her room, I had noticed her bookshelves filled with Isabelle Allende, Gabriel Garcia-Marquez, Jorge-Luis Borges. I'd read these guys in college, and asked Ezmeralda if she'd ever considered going to the university in San Jose.

"I did go, a little," she told me. She'd enjoyed herself, but it didn't make a lot of sense to her. "I asked myself, why should I *spend* money learning to do something I love, when I can *make* money actually doing it?" She loved teaching and she was able to earn a living tutoring. She loved reading, and there were her books. She was living independently but was close enough to her family to see them on weekends.

"I don't see how college would make my life any better," she said.

I was starting to recognize the assumptions I'd never been aware of making. I added "Formal education is basically mandatory unless you want to be broke and miserable" to my mental list. Then Harry came in, crying and cradling his arm.

"I fell at least two meters," he wailed, and I am sorry to say that my internal response was *Harry has gone metric! We are totally local!*

I pulled him on my lap and sent Ivy running to Odalie to see about ice. Harry continued to gulp and snuffle. Ez was scandalized. She shook a polished nail.

"Harry! You are too old to be such a crybaby!" That was not a Seattle word. I wasn't sure Harry had even heard it before. But he knew what it meant all right. Harry dried his tears immediately.

Odalie had a doctorish friend, and after Christmas Eve Mass he put oil on Harry's arm. I was beginning to have a lot of faith in oil. *Plus, he carries his doctorish stuff with him,* I thought. *That is so legit.* Señor Mora pressed his fingers very slowly all along Harry's forearm, looking for a break. *"No hay,"* he told us—there's none. He recommended ibuprofen for pain and swelling, and to keep the arm still.

I fell in love with Odalie when she invited us into her home and cooked pig and pig and pig, and eggs for Hannah. And along with loving Odalie herself, I admired her for keeping holy oil down the front of her shirt, and for her belief, without qualification or equivocation.

Pedro took Harry fishing and taught Hannah and me to milk a cow. Pedrito worked hard to be social, and my elder daughter met him halfway across an abyss of awkwardness. By Christmas morning, the two were comparing good reads and Pedrito asked Hannah to teach him to knit. Ezmeralda's family gave us their beds, and window stickers that looked like home, and the first solid week of sleep Ivy had ever had.

These strangers made the choice to love my homesick children fiercely. They were different from us. But by the time we kissed goodbye and climbed back on the bus, there was no question that we had had Christmas with family.

When we got back to Canitas, the box still hadn't come, but the motorcycle had. Anthony's reaction was mild. I tried not to let this hurt my feelings. He took me to the end of the driveway on a test drive, and I was more afraid than I'd thought I would be.

"*Meddy Chreesmos!*" shouted Luis, waving.

"*Feliz Navidad,*" yelled Anthony. He removed his hand from the handlebar to wave back, and nobody died.

Later, we all walked to Santa Elena to run Harry's arm diagnosis past someone with a little more medical degree. The gleaming office/pharmacy felt comfortingly institutional, and Doctor Doogie felt Harry's arm very carefully—just as *Señor* Mora had, though Doogie took less time and used no oil. The slightly perfunctory quality of the care added to Doogie's credibility with Harry, as did the presence of a padded table with a roll of tissue paper on it. Harry felt that in El Dos, I'd taken him to a witch doctor or perhaps a faith healer.

"The ulna might have a little crack in it," said the Doog. "You can take him to San José for x-rays, which would show you for certain. If there is a crack, they will immobilize the arm for a couple of weeks. We can do that now, just in case."

All this in Spanish. I was getting good.

I think Harry was pleased with Dr. Doogie's diagnosis. A boy who cried in Latin America had to take a lot of shit; it was nice to get a doctor's validation that something bad had maybe happened.

Anthony and I felt comfortable getting the sling and bagging the two-day trip. Harry accepted this solution in the moment. In later months, though, he would bring it up as proof that he was being raised by reckless boobs, the Moe and Curly of parenting.

"I had a broken arm, and you didn't get me x-rayed!"

"Harry. If we'd gone to San José, you might or might not have ended up in a splint for two weeks. Instead, you ended up in a splint for three weeks, just to make sure. Would you not argue that we, in fact, provided more medical care than was necessary?"

"I HAD A BROKEN ARM, AND YOU DIDN'T GET ME X-RAYED!"

True.

Three days after Christmas, everyone but Anthony got the flu. The *moto* proved helpful as he ferried crackers and ginger ale up to our house/infirmary. I relished his attentiveness, and considered the upsides of breaking a bone of my own. But now I was skeptical—could I be trusted to get myself the appropriate medical attention?

One afternoon, Anthony's errand took too long—an hour, then two. I curled up in a chair next to the woodstove and semi-hallucinated to the sound of the rain on our corrugated roof. I imagined someone stretching a drum the size of Kansas, and letting everybody in the world toss pebbles onto it.

Along with the rain, the mists were as dense as I'd ever seen them—no guava tree, no hillside. Every one of our picture windows told the same story: The universe contained just me, the Kansas-drum, and three feverish children, alone inside a cloud.

I resolved not to look at the clock, not to think about the terrible things that happen when foolish children *will* buy their husband a motorcycle, though warned by their mothers not to. Instead, I let my mind traverse the last five months.

Yes, our year was having moments that were...other...than the wondrous adventure I had advertised. But was it really the festival of narcissism I'd identified in my pre-Christmas meltdown? Had I done my children wrong while I chased my misspent youth?

True, the kids weren't happy every second. But endless joy is a vacation fantasy. We were living real life, where adolescence happens and Mommy gets it wrong and sometimes the Christmas box doesn't come. September had been awful and the kids missed home at Christmas—for real life, was that really so out of whack?

Not that adjustments shouldn't be made. It was selfish of me to foist an expensive gift on Anthony just when he was exploring his inner Spartan. Maybe I should look into selling the *moto*.

The *moto*. My mind dealt out images of legs, mangled like the ones in my mother's stories. I saw Anthony pulling himself up our rocky driveway on his elbows, hands cradling a box of saltines.

I had tugged on my boots and was heading out to look for him when I heard the chug-chug that was just becoming familiar. Anthony burst forth from the cloud, cresting the last, steep stretch of driveway. He rolled under the shelter and tugged off his helmet. His grin—in that ever-open, ever-sincere face of his—was electric.

"Sorry I'm late," he said. "I thought I'd go the long way around, see what's down by San Luis. And then I ran into Mike, and he was on his bike, too, and we went for a ride."

"It's pouring . . ."

Now he was wringing out his socks. I jumped back from a muddy waterfall. "Yeah, I don't think I've ever seen it rain this hard. It was *awesome!*"

January – April

26

Things I Knew and Didn't Know

All systems go for a mountaintop experience.

Back from our week in Panama, I stood alone by the picture window. Mists rose up from the distant sea, and my skin glowed outdoorsily. Six days at the beach, on top of my five-months-walking-everywhere life, had me looking more enlightened in general. I felt I had the air of a yogini or a for-real Buddhist (as opposed to the once-you've-made-your-first-million kind). Even my hair was having a spiritually receptive kind of day. Frizzy hair was anxious hair, but the strand I inspected as the mists began their approach was a serene wavy-curly.

In the Christian liturgical year, the sixth of January marks the Feast of Epiphany. Two thousand years ago, three travelers suddenly knew that the little manger-baby, with his tattered blanket and confused parents, was something special. This new data changed the wise men's return route, perhaps even their destination.

I had long neverminded Epiphany, tending to observe instead a post-holiday Festival of Exhaustion. My special day to heave a martyred sigh and start tidying up what Christmas had wrought in the living room.

This year was different. For the first January in my adult life, I had time. Time to be watchful. Time to listen. Time to Epiph.

And so I sat at the top of our mountain. Nagging questions, hidden for years in the black tangle of my too-busy brain, had very recently revealed themselves. This unlikely clarity had come to me as I stared, spellbound, at the mangrove forests near Bocas del Toros, Panama. In the mangroves, I'd understood the questions. Today, I was ready for some answers.

It was a miracle we'd gotten to Panama at all.

One week earlier, we had boarded the Ticabus. This was the trip I'd planned in early December as a distraction from all the homesick.

Bocas, as its friends called it, was supposed to be absolutely beautiful. We'd have snorkeling and language classes, as well as a return to the Caribbean-side, rasta kind of vibe that allowed for lazing and reading and nothing at all. To get to the main island, we'd take a tiny motorboat through mangrove forests. I wasn't sure what mangroves were, but I was excited; whatever they were, I felt certain that island forests of them would have a very Dr. Seussian feel.

Lining everything up back in December, I'd felt smug about finding a win for everyone. But Ivy's hidden Santa note had humbled the smug right out of me. Now, I just hoped all of us would have a nice time.

It would take us from before dawn until after dark to get to our boat ride. The border would close at seven p.m., half an hour after our bus's scheduled arrival.

Everyone should hurry, the driver of the Ticabus said as he dropped us off, *because the Panamanian immigration guys would not stay one minute past seven.* I thought I heard a little attitude in his tone. A sly implication that if Panamanians would just put in some overtime, they'd be famous for more than a pockmarked dictator and a canal built by somebody else.

Anthony said that what he'd heard was that we should hurry, because the guys on the Panama side would leave at seven.

It must be nice, being Anthony.

At the northernmost point of their meeting, Costa Rica becomes Panama right down the middle of the *Rio Sixoala*. Travelers pass through Costa Rican immigration on one side of the river, and Panamanian immigration on the other. There are no services on either side—motels, stores, or even restrooms. Immigration officials sit in two cement-block buildings, separated by a railroad trestle over the warm, brown *rio*.

We had heard that this crossing, between the tiny settlements of Sixaola on the Costa Rica side and Guabito in Panama, was pretty hassle-free. Someone had mentioned that the railroad-trestle bridge was charmingly rickety but not dangerous. After the bridge and our quick stamps at Panamanian immigration, a taxi would take us to the closest real town, where we would catch our much-anticipated water taxi.

My family's collective instinct to move as slowly as possible in the sticky heat trumped our desire to hustle for a good place in line. We were mountain people now, and Pacific Northwesterners before that, and we'd never gotten good at heat. And so we waited, dead last in the long line. The kids sat on their backpacks, disinterested and exhausted. Hannah buried her head in her crossed arms, trying for a nap. I wondered again whose needs I was serving, hauling my family away from a life that had been perfectly lovely.

Hannah gave up on the nap idea when she realized her body was too hot to bear any form of curling in on itself.

While the children wilted, Anthony and I read a plywood sign nailed to the outside of the building. The trestle was almost a hundred years old, we learned. No trains used it anymore, but cars could cross one at a time. The letters were furry-edged where the magic marker bled into the wood, but were still clear enough to ensure us of our safety: The one-vehicle rule was very strict. *("Muy, MUY estricto,"* promised the sign.)

Another sign, newer-looking and posted below the first, informed us that the bridge was also missing some railroad ties. Not many, but crossers should take care. *Pura vida.*

After a twenty-minute wait, as a cheerful immigration official stamped our passports, I asked him about a backup plan if we couldn't get into Panama. Was there a way to call a taxi on the Costa Rica side? He shrugged, smiling. There was never a need, he told me—everyone got in. Again, I heard the attitude. "It's *Panama,*" he said, as if the entire country was like community college or something.

"Pura vida," he said, and promised us cheerfully that with tonight's bright moon, we should be able to spot crocodiles!

"Mira bien," he told the kids. *"Pueden verlos cuando los colas hacen splash!"*

Look carefully. You can see them by the splash of their tails.

Anthony and I exchanged startled looks. Hannah would be fine and Ivy was in my arms, but we both instinctively grabbed for Harry.

Together we approached the bridge, and then we inched out onto it.

Someone had thoughtfully placed planks along the outer edge of the rails. Running lengthwise, the planks allowed a person to cross the creaky bridge without stepping tie-to-tie. I appreciated this gesture, as the railroad ties themselves appeared to be positioned just about Hannah-width apart. We inched.

But crossing a rail trestle in the dark, several feet above across a croc-infested river, turned out not to be the hard part of getting to Panama.

We made it to Panamanian immigration a few minutes before closing. Everyone else from our bus had already been loaded into taxis and whisked away. A single *taxista* remained. His expression said, "I will wait three minutes, no longer, for these idiot Gringos."

My family trooped in and sat on the single bench. Anthony was entertaining Harry by listening to him, and Ivy was losing it. She whimpered and fussed in Hannah's arms, hair plastered to her sweaty head.

A round, no-longer-white clock with black hands read 6:56 as I approached, opened our passports and laid them in a tidy, helpful line on the Formica countertop.

And hassle-free Panamanian Immigration Guy, all politeness (remember to tell Odalie!), nodded once, twice, and then shook his head three times—once for each of the kids' passports. Hannah, Harry, and Ivy couldn't enter, not tonight. There was a problem. He smiled. Panama would be happy to host all five of us after we had straightened everything out at the Embassy in San José. Or *Señor* and *Señora* could enter right now, no problem.

Were they really going to make us cross back over the crocodile river and spend the sweltering night on the benches outside the Costa Rican immigration office? Odalie was right! That is not a polite thing to do! I swelled with a new fellow-feeling for my Tico brothers and sisters.

"*Los pasaportes* are *buenos*!" I insisted. "*Son*...current! Really!"

My Spanish always fled when the going got tough. I had mentioned this issue to Anthony months before, shortly after I propositioned the hardware boy.

"It seems like my Spanish is kind of cowardly."

His voice was mild. "Maybe it just doesn't like to be pushed."

I thought the language and I had worked something out since then. Yet here I was at the Panamanian border, minutes before closing, family spent and miserable—and my Spanish had fled the scene.

Immigration Guy seemed to feel that maintaining eye contact would only increase my shame. He shifted his gaze down to the little blue booklets, splayed on the gold-flecked counter.

The faces of my family smiled up at us, cheery and uncounterfeitable behind the patriotic overlays of stars and stripes. I pointed at the expiration dates, five months away. "They're *buenos!*"

Immigration Guy shook his head again.

I repeated my Spanglish at increasing volumes, and soon I had a small band of Immigration Guys not helping me. My family waited on the single bench at the back of the room. Ivy had long since passed explosive and was now just a moist, whimpering mess. Hannah rocked her, singing softly. Anthony continued to feign interest in Harry's account of a baseball game. I stood at the counter, alone.

Our main Immigration Guy patiently pointed at dates. His backups nodded vigorously. I caught, *"Embajada. Me entiendes? San José."* His chorus looked at me solemnly and nodded with vigor.

Yes, but San José was an inaccessible eight hours behind us.

"Los pasaportes are *buenos!"* I said, louder, so he would know how much I meant it.

Immigration Guy slid our passports gently back to my side of the counter and gave me a sad smile. His regret seemed remarkably sincere given the temper fit I continued to have in his building.

"The kids' passports are fine!"

I looked up at the stained squares of the ceiling and bit the insides of my cheeks. I had promised this trip would be fun. A sunny consolation prize for being far from home at Christmas. I kept the tears balanced on my lower lids; I did not let them fall.

Suddenly, Hannah stood up. She adjusted sweaty, wretched Ivy on her hip. She touched my arm to get me to move over, parked Ivy right on top of the gaggle of passports, and said...something in Spanish. She delivered a little speech that was so fast and so fluent I couldn't catch a word. The official shifted all of his attention to this ponytailed, freckled child whose left hand never stopped rubbing her little sister's back.

Hannah spoke. Immigration Guy spoke. Hannah shook her head, pointed at Ivy, and became more emphatic. Immigration Guy huddled with the chorus, then came back with a long speech. When it ended, Hannah tipped her head to one side, then gave a single, firm nod. Very formally, she extended her hand.

He stamped all five passports. Then, although I was still standing right there, he handed the pile to Hannah.

He whistled for the remaining taxis and helped us stuff ourselves in, reaching out one more time to shake Hannah's hand.

"We have to go to the American Embassy next week," words tumbled out of Hannah as she bounced on the seat. Harry looked at her funny—bouncing was kind of *his* move.

"He kept trying to tell you, Mom. He wouldn't let us in unless we promised. The passports aren't expired but it's within six months and they don't like that. At first he didn't want to make an agreement with me. He was all 'She's just a little girl,' but the other guys told him it was dumb to shake on anything with some lady who doesn't know what you're saying—that's you, sorry. I promised we'd go to the embassy on our way back, after Boca. Then he told me to enjoy our stay in Guabito."

"But..."

"Mom, it was a *joke!* Guabito's a hole—nobody stays there any longer than it takes to get their passport stamped! He joked with me in Spanish! No one's ever done that before!"

I didn't know anymore whether to worry about Hannah or to ask Hannah to worry about me. So I hugged her and tucked her hair behind her ear. I knew how to do that, still.

By nine that night, we'd been traveling for fifteen hours and it wasn't awful. We'd dealt with the heat, we'd dealt with immigration (fine—Hannah had dealt with immigration), and now we were ready for the fun leg of our journey.

Our water taxi was bigger than a rowboat, smaller than a big boat, and had a vinyl canopy. During our ride, the moon got brighter, which did not at first seem possible. There were a ridiculous number of stars—the night sky, as drawn by a preschooler who didn't know when to stop.

The air was a mixture of earth and sea, plant life and salt water.

We slipped through still, protected water, navigating between islets that seemed to be comprised entirely of twisted trunks. At first we were enthralled by the lack of motion around us.

"I can't believe we're on the ocean." Anthony was amazed. Oceans were muscle and strength and movement, but this water was still as a pond. The kids trailed their fingers, creating tiny wakes. No one barked rules about keeping arms inside the boat.

Before long, its glassiness made the water a nonevent, and I turned my attention to the mesmerizing mangroves.

In my world, roots provide offstage support for the amazing show that is a tree. I'd noticed them mostly when they cracked the sidewalk. Roots in my experience were very occasional and mostly kept to themselves.

But mangroves don't behave like that. Mangroves put their whole selves right there for us to see, branches and leaves and roots, in and out of the water. The staging area *is* the show. So at first you might think mangroves have no secrets, everything being so aboveboard and all. But soon I got the feeling that mangroves are nothing but secrets. That their outward show of self-revealing was a trick. At first I was all "Look, I can see the whole tree at once," but then I realized that was just the outermost shell of each island. The islets were dense, and I couldn't see very far in—just a twisting black tangle, back and back, until darkness.

The giant moon beamed silver in a cloudless sky, and the mangroves cast their shadows on a silent ocean. Everything looked imaginary.

I felt like I was witnessing mystery that we above-ground folks weren't supposed to be privy to. I turned to do a status check of my family. Hannah looked like she, too, was imagining the fairy stories that went on inside this gnarled, underworldly overworld. Anthony was enjoying the wind in his face, the soft putt-putt of the small motor, the calm, emerging nighttime. I nearly reached for Ivy and Harry, to hold them close. But they were trailing fingers, making moonlit wakes. I reminded myself that my children are not my security blankets, and I let them be.

In this mysterious setting, my own mysteries crowded to the fore. It was suddenly clear to me that I'd had reasons for this year that weren't the ones I'd talked about. Yes, we'd come to learn Spanish and get away from Bush II. Of course, we wanted to spend more time together as a family and to live a simpler life. All of that was true.

"I want my kids to be less materialistic," I had said, and meant it. But sweet Jesus, who doesn't?

I saw that, like the mangroves, my own outward show of self-revealing had been incomplete. I'd sat on those baseball bleachers and leaned forward earnestly to tell Beth, "There are so many ways to live a life."

The reasons I gave for our trip always showed what a good person I was, how honestly I grappled. ("*What do we do with our privilege?*") I'd given the good-looking issues all the air time. But what else was back there in the tangle, what had I never said, not even to Erin, to Vic, to Lizzie, myself?

- In good-mother math, which counted more: the love or the mistakes?
- What was the secret of being less tightly wound?
- How could I pull words or even feelings out of my silent husband, and what would I do if I never could?
- If we went back to Seattle and I worked full time again, exactly how badly would I damage the kids?
- Or would I just go bitter and crazy, lost in my envy of the mommies who, war or not, got to *choose*?

And then we were in Bocas del Toro, where everything was lovely and everything was fine. White sand is no place for raggedy, black-tangle questions. They tucked themselves back again, in the wrinkles of my brain. Smoother, tidier thoughts rose to the surface while all of us played in the surf.

Three men arrive at a barn, bearing gifts.

Artists through the ages, great and tacky, have taken that on and set sky-high expectations for the rest of us—lots of light and singing. Haloes. Bugles. In Costco Nativity scenes, the shepherds all but smack their foreheads in wonder.

All of this makes it harder to recognize an epiphany that arrives without melodrama. I returned to Monteverde alert for subtler insights. About my marriage, my mothering, and how I might address some of the more irksome aspects of my personality.

We'd come back yesterday—January fifth—by way of the U.S. embassy and three new passports. This morning I'd awakened with an Epiphany feeling, then worked at the *Casa de Arte*. Anthony and I met Ivy at the bus stop. The two of them jumped on the *moto* and took off for the library. I hung laundry in the sunshine, then settled into the hammock with Harry Potter. I'd been working for an hour or so *("El basilisco tiene Ginny!")* when I looked up and saw, past the socks and t-shirts waving in the breeze, that the Gulf of Nicoya had gone.

Today I'm going to get some answers. I thought. My new (old), black-tangle questions moved forward, and my anticipation climbed along with the gray. *Wisdom is coming, borne on a million tiny droplets of cloud-forest mist.*

As the foothills disappeared, I left the hammock and bustled around, setting the stage for my impending enlightenment. I set one of our barstools next to the window and sat with a plate of homemade tortillas and avocado, feeling culturally authentic. I noted with a pang that the mists were going to get to the laundry before I would.

Now the pasture was gone, and the scheming cows. Any moment, it would just be me and my snack, inside a white cloud. I set down my plate and closed my eyes, awaiting revelation.

None came.

I finished my avo, paused a moment, and went for a mango as well.

I wandered outside. The mango was perfectly ripe. I stuck out my chin so the juice would drip in the grass and not on my boobs.

Sometimes, I told myself, *maybe I don't get to know.*

27

Halfway Between Everything

"Hey. We've been here six months."
Anthony noted this with some alarm as we picked our way down from the fence. Blackie still wasn't getting it about property lines. The sun blazed.

When I'd heard "dry season" back in July, my mind had gone straight to arid, an equal and opposite reaction to the downpours that had greeted our arrival. Without thinking about it much, I'd assumed withered, dusty plants. Cow skulls, probably.

But January in Monteverde was glorious, not grim. The temperature was always excellent, though I never had the faintest idea what it was. (Celsius temperatures are an academic exercise, indicating nothing. Say 75 and I know what you mean. But there's higher math between 23°C and me knowing whether to put on a jacket or a tank top.) No worries; *pura vida*. Pure, clear skies and fresh mountain air. We were basically living in a Mountain Dew commercial.

Which was why Anthony's comment caught me off guard. Were we really entering the downward slope of the year, just when everything was getting perfect?

The problems our new life had introduced were resolving with increasing quickness. Friendships were evolving, loneliness abating. Beatriz had helped me settle down about Anthony; I was trying not to require noise of him, and to better attend to the words he did produce. For feelings and whatnot, I had my friends at the *Casa*.

Since reaching out to Pedrito in December, Hannah was spending a little less time in the mists. A new girl joined her class at the beginning of the term in January. Sharon, from Vermont, had come for one semester with her mother and had the eager sociability of a short-termer. She and Hannah were forging a friendship that included Liliana, who seemed to be smiling more and shrugging less. Lola and I were grateful for the changes in our daughters. I figured I'd know soon enough whether Hannah would retreat again, or whether I'd just witnessed the shortest moody adolescence in human history.

And I had at last stopped trying to speak Spanish with Ivy. In chasing the dream of brilliantly bilingual children, I'd been pushing so hard I had completely missed the obvious. (Yet again! Go, me!) This child had been surrounded from birth by grandparents, aunties, friends, and neighbors, talking to her and listening to her. Now she lived with the four of us, on a mountaintop.

Ivy was five years old and she'd only recently mastered her first language. With the people she had left, Ivy needed all the words she could get her hands on.

When Ivy needed Spanish—to get a toy back, play with Sofia, be polite—she used it. But language for Ivy was a real, working tool; I'd been trying to make her play with it in the sandbox.

Harry was Harry again. We knew it for sure the Saturday we walked up to the Friends School for a pick-up soccer game. Harry ran ahead and as the rest of us approached, we heard kids from both teams shouting his arrival:

"Pa-gi-NA! Pa-gi-NA!" –the Spanish word for "Page."

Hannah said, "In Seattle, I kind of hated Harry for stuff like that. Now, I'm just glad he's ours."

Our new life was addressing a handful of our old-life issues, too.

Ivy's nights were vastly improved. She'd slept through the night for the duration of our stay in El Dos, and for about three weeks following. Never in her life had she had so many restful nights. Some nights, out of five years of habituation, I'd wake up and go look at her unfurrowed brow. She'd look angelic or drooly, but utterly relaxed in either case. Her fingers lay on the covers, not twitching.

What is a person to do with this information? I didn't do much. When the dreams started coming back, I wondered aloud to Anthony the glib, vaguely insulting questions of a person who does not want to probe too deeply: *Does Jesus' protection expire, so that you have to keep re-upping your request?* I could see it. If I were God, I'd be annoyed if people started to take my protection for granted.

In answer to an older, thornier problem, Anthony and I now lived in a better economic balance than we ever had. Instead of his income being helpful, with my salary doing the heavy lifting, his hours on the hotel computers trumped my occasional teaching money and had a tangible effect. Anthony's earnings were the difference between eating at a restaurant or not, between gas for the *moto* or walking everywhere that week. We felt Anthony's fiscal contribution in a way we never had before.

Anthony never spoke of this. To me, though, it mattered.

We did talk about how, the first year of anything new, you're really just finding your feet. This first twelve months we would get through so much: homesickness, finding friends, learning the language, and a host of firsts: first Christmas away from Seattle, first time taking two days to go to the orthodontist.

Finally, I said it out loud as we crunched down the driveway to get Ivy at the bus stop.

"If we stayed another year..."

Silence. But I knew he was listening.

"We'd be the experts, not the newbies," I went on. "In year two, friendships deepen. Teachers know you."

I bit my tongue and waited for a reaction. We were past the coffee bushes now, just about to the road.

When we got there, Anthony stopped and looked both ways—old habits die hard. He spoke as we crossed the dusty pathway, "It does seem like a waste to just up and leave, now that paradise finally has Internet."

Paradise? Kinda.

At three-thirty most days, I split an avocado and handed half to Hannah. She grabbed the saltshaker, and we lolled in the hammock eating avo on the half shell while we recounted our days to each other. With Ivy it was ice cream bars from the *pulperia* and the walk from the bus. Harry and I chatted free-range, on no particular schedule, and sang Spanish pop at the top of our lungs whenever we walked down the driveway. Mostly Juanes and Bacilos.

My starry animal painting was coming along, and now included a surreal gecko. Lola was forcing the rapid expansion of my *oeuvre*. She'd concocted a seven-layer exercise in which she had me make a piece of art—drawing, painting, or collage—inspired by each of the body's seven systems. I was currently on respiratory, and planned to combine words and images. I had drawn a giant pair of lungs that looked (not on purpose) like ears without a head. I was pondering whether to mitigate the issue by working hearing into my prose-poem about holding one's breath. I had done digestive already—batik on rice paper. For reasons I couldn't quite pinpoint, I found myself looking forward to circulatory and very much dreading skeletal.

Anthony still loved walking, but the *moto* joy rides continued, too. He was always happy to throw one of us on the back (or between his arms, if it was Ivy) for a ride to school, a milkshake, a library book. Still safety marshal, Anthony always insisted on helmets. (Even I would do *that*.)

Hannah said, "This whole year is worth it, if only for the chance to see a five-year-old in a cow slicker, ladybug boots, and a motorcycle helmet."

Anthony took Harry on an overnight motorcycle trip to Tilarán, two hours away, a major metropolis of at least fifteen thousand people. The boys went to the public pool and out to dinner, while the girls and I stayed on our hill and had Kelly and her daughters over. As if to underline that we all were living lives both foreign and familiar, we turned baskets of mangos and chili peppers into old-fashioned cooked jam.

Just as we were halfway through the year, I still felt suspended between visitor and local. In so many ways I was at home, but I hadn't gotten past what I felt was a very Seattle-mom flavor of sissy: I was still terrified of the *moto*.

A motorcycle, like a bicycle and I think also wolves, can smell fear. The motorcycle's response to fear is to wobble, but with Anthony at the controls we never did, not even on that rocky terrain. I would sit behind Anthony, clutching and stiff, waiting for the end. I squeezed my eyes shut. I worried that a pack of Rainforest Wolves might sniff out my wispy terror and come snarling out from behind the giant impatiens blossoms.

Anthony on his *moto* had the grace and balance borne of deep confidence. He and his enormous cloud of boldness sailed down the dappled concrete, deep into the shade of the creek, and up the other lovely side. With my eyes closed I missed most of this, but what a nice time he must have had.

I feared the motorcycle, and, because I'm me, I wanted to conquer that fear. Why come to paradise, if not to improve myself, and to really *be* here? I wanted to be just as good as Anthony, to feel that exhilaration, like the kids on the *jupo* vine.

If on some level I was entertaining this notion because I knew it would make my mother batshit, that was deeply, deeply subconscious.

But I wasn't going to conquer anything on our roads-o-rock. Tilarán was the closest town with real pavement, and when Anthony's mom visited in February, we created a win-win-win: LoraLee would get the kids to herself. Anthony and I would take a jaunt to Tilarán on the *moto* and, once there, I would learn to drive it.

That Thursday afternoon (not having an office job never stopped being fantastic, not for one second) we found a stretch of road where no one seemed to be. It was mostly straight, which eliminated turning as a point of failure. All I'd have to manage was the throttle and the speed and the shifting and the balance.

Tilarán was halfway down the mountain—hot. The pavement shimmered in front of me. Anthony was very patient. First he had me sit behind him and feel what his hands were doing. It turns out that, on a motorcycle, you manage the gas with your hands. Making my hands responsible for the gas at the same time they had to steer the whole enterprise seemed very dicey. Plus, the gas was on the right. I'm left-handed practically to the point of disability, and have always thought of my right hand as my Bob Dole hand. I nearly packed it in right there, but Anthony was gently encouraging.

"You'll get used to it. It's really not hard. I'm left handed, and I do fine."

"You're not left handed like I'm left handed! You throw right! You catch right! You use scissors right! The best thing I can do with that hand is to stuff a pen in it and tell it to look busy."

He waited. I considered. I asked,

"Do you think Bob Dole can ride a motorcycle?"

To further mess with me, the *moto*-makers moved shifting down to the feet. There was kicking involved, and you had to do it with authority or the motorcycle wouldn't believe you. I practiced kicking with authority, as if I felt at home.

Hannah had recently pointed out something interesting: Like most families in the *Zona,* Lola and Liliana had no car. They generally walked everywhere, or rode on the back of a friend's *moto.* Yet when Hannah hung out at the *Casa,* even if it was still light when the time came to leave, Lola put her in a cab. And each time, Hannah said, Lola thrust her oxymoronic (fierce, yet shaped like a perfect heart) face in the driver's side window, looked the *taxista* in the eye, and said, *"Ya lo conozco"*—I know you. Lola always made sure *he* knew that *she* knew exactly who he was, before letting him drive off with the white family's daughter.

"I think I'm as close with Liliana as anyone at school is," Hannah said. "Maybe even closer. But I'll always be treated a little differently, as long as I'm white."

This difference felt neither good nor bad; just true.

Of course, Magda never made any pretense that we fit in. Her honesty was not always refreshing. One day as she was gathering laundry, Magda passed through the living room where I was helping Ivy sound out words. When she got to the washing machine, Magda called back to me, apropos of nothing at all, that she'd heard from her taxi-driving friend that the *taxistas* in the area thought I was strange. I ditched Ivy and walked back to where Magda was stuffing our sheets in the machine.

"Wait, what? Strange how?" I asked her. Suddenly I was frumpy again, the oldest mom in *prepa*. I tried to think of strange things I might have done in a taxi.

"No sé," she answered and continued shoving sheets in the washer, not looking up. *I don't know.*

Well, that was going to fester. Had I been doing the Margot equivalent of telling people to wash their monkeys? What would that even be?

"Who are those people who say they'd keep their jobs if they won the lottery?" Anthony asked one night.

"And are they impressively devoted, or depressingly unimaginative?" I added.

Once I'd broached the subject, Anthony and I had an ongoing conversation about the possibility of staying. Quietly, after the kids were sleeping. We told no one.

Back in the States, Abu Ghraib had broken in all its awfulness and George W. Bush was gearing up to launch a full-on assault on those who would try to demean my marriage by...committing to someone they loved? Living in Monteverde, I could hear about all that without fury. It wasn't really of us anymore. We didn't have to be embarrassed, and we didn't have to be furious, because—*look, toucan!*

At the same time, America was my country—a sentence I probably would not have uttered last May. But I felt it now, strongly. I found myself increasingly proud of its schools and its safety nets, its Constitution that had stood the test of time.

"That stuff doesn't just happen out of nowhere," Anthony said the next afternoon. Exactly. America had gotten a lot of stuff right, and it was our land, too. If we didn't go back, were we letting the bigots just *have* it? Part of me wanted to return to Seattle just to fly a flag on my porch.

The Jensens had recently decided to stay a second year. Kelly and Mike started making practical moves that showed their deeper commitment. They bought a car, and Mike built bunk beds for their twins. I wondered about Molly and Ivy's funny friendship of opposites, and whether Molly would start to gravitate toward kids who would stick around, now that she had longer-term options.

What would we do? How would we decide?

"I'm going to sleep on it," Anthony told me, heading for a hammock. "And don't you have yoga with that new chick? You can look for your sloth."

28

The *Pura Vida* Continuum

Anthony settled into the hammock, which both annoyed and did not annoy me. How much sleep does one person need? I headed off to yoga, hoping to see the sloth that had been hanging out above the bus stop lately. I found him very inspirational.

Slothy quiet is neither clenched nor manly, repressed nor judgmental. Sloths aren't quiet for the purpose of attaining stillness. My sloth had located no chakras and did not say *Namaste* when he was done. He was just...Yup. Nice branch.

I didn't know whether the animal sloth was named after the deadly sin, or vice versa, but no one seemed to take issue with a sloth's slothfulness. Tourists sought the sloth out. Marveled. They weren't agitated by his lack of agitation. They didn't find him sinful.

"They should make a new inspirational stone," I had said to Anthony, when I took him to the bus stop to marvel at my sloth. "And put it in one of those baskets by the register."

"Patience, Friendship, Sloth," he said. "I'd buy that."

Now, Anthony was snoring the soft, whistling snores of a man who refuses to take Claritin for his allergies. I tried to marvel.

"Tranquility" is a nice enough word, but it tries too hard. I was trying to remember not to be so effortful about everything. In the meantime, because not all of us have the gift of sloth, I was going to aggressively pursue some stillness at Shridevi's yoga class.

Yoga was one of my standard attempts at becoming a better person. I'd take up running, or eating right, or being patient with people who bugged the shit out of me, and stick with it for a while. When the new yogini started tacking up flyers, I figured I might as well dabble in a little Shridevi.

Shridevi was a massage therapist, and she taught yoga to boot. Although she was blond, toned, tanned, twenty-eight, and a former gymnast, the rest of us Gringas were willing to forgive this combination once she got her hands on us. She'd come to town after Christmas. One by one, we all found our way to a Shridevi class and fell in love.

Her yoga wasn't like other yoga. Shridevi did yoga to you. She moved constantly around the room, making our clumsy bodies right. When Shridevi adjusted my hips in downward dog, she held them hard and lifted strong, and her fingers dug in in a mini deep-tissue massage. And my downward dog became perfect, and I realized I should probably be in a yoga DVD or maybe open my own studio.

And it wasn't just her yoga that was great. Shridevi's post-gymnast body had an unintimidating kind of muscularity. She was a regular thickness, like a soccer player or a swimmer, so the rest of us didn't have that whole size-twoness to contend with. Her skin was smooth and bronze, but her nose was large for her face. Plus, she had a hyperactive eight-year-old named Sunshine or something, who was kind of a pain in the ass.

Shridevi was a manageable mixture of the human and the sublime, such that when her brilliant strong hands manipulated me into a pose, I thought about leaving my regular life behind and just doing yoga eight hours a day, but then having ice cream and maybe a beer.

Shridevi had taught yoga to rich fancy people back in the States, but in Monteverde she just wanted to make a living. She adjusted her prices to what most of the expat community could afford. More than once I saw Shridevi go straight from a class to the grocery store, turning the cash she'd just earned with her triangle pose into beans and avocados and milk. At five dollars a class, I could afford to go regularly.

"Bye, sweetie," I whispered to hammocked Anthony, just in case he was a little bit awake.

In response, he actually, seriously, snored louder.

When I returned, Anthony was awake and heading out to a computer-fixing gig. Perfect timing, because class had been so good that I wanted to check in on an even bigger Shridevi expense. A Shridevi massage cost thirty bucks an hour, and she made house calls.

"Go for it," Anthony said.

The next day, Shridevi taxi'd her table up our hill and set it up in the living room. Massage with a view. We got started, and Shridevi clucked her tongue.

"Your back's pretty out of whack. And what's going on up here? Jesus." She poked and prodded at the top of my spine, the place where you can feel a bony bump when you're slouching. Which, it seemed, I frequently was.

"Yeah, I'm pretty sore there." Was I supposed to apologize? I tried not to feel a little bit proud that I could quit my job, move to a tropical paradise, and still win at stress.

"We can fix it if you want," she said.

"Absolutely. Do me." I lay patiently, face down, and waited for her magic fingers to get to work.

To my surprise, Shridevi hopped up on the table. Slowly, she assumed the Crow pose, right there on my back. If you've never seen Crow, imagine squatting, planting your palms on the floor so that your bent knees kind of graze your armpits, and then leaning forward to balance on just your hands. Not many people are stable in Crow; I usually ended up on my nose. Crow was certainly not among the yoga poses I would have considered doing on top of a naked person, on top of a narrow table, on top of a hardwood floor, on top of a mountain.

Bit by bit and with utter smoothness, Shridevi shifted her weight onto just her two hands, which she had placed so perfectly across my shoulders and along my spine that a series of little pops filled the room. They reverberated off the walls and then off the hillsides and down, I was sure, to the sea.

Crow plus back-cracking took place at about minute seven, and things went on from there. I felt as if not just my muscles got a treatment, but each of my organs as well. Pancreas and gall bladder ceased to be squishy viscera and became objects of cheerful reverence. Liver and kidneys were taken out and held to the light. Shridevi's nimble fingers worked off the congealed gunk and scrubbed each bit of me. Then she took each transformed organ and molded it back to the way it was meant to be from before I was a baby, before original sin. She put me back together in a better, more breathable body than the one I had settled into over the years.

202 January - April

Then she said *"Namaste,"* left the music on, and got me a glass of water. She said she'd come back later for the table and whistled down the hill.

Sloths had a good thing going, no question, and so did my husband. I admired their gift of temperament, and knew I would never, ever have it. But those of us who weren't born *pura vida* could still get there. And if I could make my own relaxation, I might never have had Shridevi bring her table to my living room.

I lay there in my body, grateful for every bone, sinew, synapse, and freckle. I vowed to walk everywhere, straight and beautiful and poised, with my shoulders thrown back, and to be a wholly good person for the rest of my life.

It was helpful to have Shridevi doling out energy and wellness, because Ivy's nights were brutal again. This made my head fuzzy, my limbs heavy, and my temper short. The nocturnal shrieking had even begun to bug Harry, so we put a mattress on the loft-landing right outside Hannah's bedroom.

One morning, it wasn't Ivy but Harry who curdled the night.

"I'm freezing!" he yelled from his loft. I felt my way out of our bedroom. Man, it got dark here.

Harry's covers had gone missing. After a thorough search of the loft and the space below it yielded nothing, I went into Hannah's room. I found her beneath two enormous down comforters, faking sleep with diabolical vigor.

"Hannah! What the hell?"

She yawned extravagantly, blinked, feigned confusion. "Mm? What's going on?"

Hannah's defense was a highly logical offense.

"Well, Harry's so active, and you know how he always sleeps so hot, with one leg on top of the covers? I figured I would be doing us both a favor. And I didn't want to wake him up to ask—I know he really needs his rest."

Then Ivy yelled in her sleep. I was speechless, anyway. I redistributed covers and headed downstairs, unsure whether the quiet daughter or the noisy one was the more demonic.

A few hours later, Lola was laughing hard.

"It's good for Hannah to be bad once in a while," she told me "That's what *hermanos* are for, to get all that out." Lola said the thing she felt worst about as a parent was not giving Liliana siblings, who gave a child opportunity to behave badly without dire consequence. Lola worried that, as an only child, Liliana would feel compelled to step out in other, more dangerous ways.

"Perhaps as a rebellion, Liliana will learn to cook," Beatriz murmured, not looking up from a meticulous painting of a hummingbird. Lola threw a rag at her, and threatened that the next missile, if Beatriz couldn't be nice, would be a can of *espaghettis*. (Spaghetti-Os!)

Over coffee, I lamented the return of Ivy's nightmares.

"You tried God," said Beatriz, a sort-of Catholic. "Now you should try tree."

Lola nodded emphatically. Definitely, tree.

They were both surprised I hadn't thought of this.

"*Árbol?*" I asked.

"Tree. *Definitamente.*" I realized they were not using the Spanish word. Tree was not a botanical remedy. Tree was a person.

Ivy's second exorcism was, in the end, not unlike the first. Instead of sitting on a bed, Ivy lay on a converted massage table.

Our exorcist's name used to be something like Linda or Marsha but she had changed it. She was in her mid-forties, and looked and sounded like she was, back in her Marsha days, a nice Jewish girl from Long Island. She'd probably gone to Barnard, or maybe Mount Holyoke, but like the rest of Layer Two, she was over it. She wrapped her short, salt-and-pepper hair with a light-blue scarf that trailed down her back. Tree's jewelry involved a lot more feathers than I was used to.

I learned that Tree had earned a living in Monteverde for years as a massage therapist and jack-of-all-New Agey stuff. However, when serious competition came to town, in the form of Shridevi (*née*, one assumed, Traci or perhaps Susan), Tree wisely acknowledged that rebuilding people from the guts outward is a rare talent. As the Shridevi revolution swept through Monteverde, Tree branched out. She'd shifted focus to her other, non-massage gifts.

When I told her of Ivy's nights, Tree offered me a trade—she'd get Ivy's aura all straightened up, kick out whatever bad juju was sneaking through to demonize our little girl's sleep. And I would build Tree a web site, so she could better snag tourists in their planning phases. It was all very Monteverde, everyone doing what they did best, filling each other's gaps.

Tuesday, four o'clock. The small room was tapestried in cloth the same light blue as Tree's long-tailed scarf. Tree had placed a tiny stool in the corner so that I could be present for the extraction.

She explained to Ivy that this wouldn't hurt, that she would work only with Ivy's aura, which was not part of her body but just outside it. Tree would remove the bad forces that were clinging to Ivy's outermost layer and wrap Ivy in metaphysical protection. It was quite a lot like Exorcism I, if you replaced "aura" with "spirit" and "metaphysical" with "Jesus."

Ivy lay on her back. Tree told her to close her eyes and concentrate on the color light blue—a *very protective* color, emphasis Tree's. Light blue is the color of goodness, of the forces of light. Ivy cut Tree off mid-lecture, snapped her eyes shut, and said, "Okay, I'm thinking about sky. Now you go."

Tree went. As a kickoff, she ran her hands all around Ivy, an inch away, never touching. Head to feet, arm to arm, back and forth. Sometimes there were circles.

Because I am very accepting of that which I do not understand, I didn't snicker even a little bit when Tree started to grab the air around Ivy between her thumb and forefinger and cast it aside. Pinch, toss, pinch, toss. I noted that there seemed to be a lot of pinching around Ivy's knees. I had never really considered knees a spiritual trouble spot, but I was not the professional here. More than anything, it looked like Tree was hunting gnats, which had decided to convene around this small child. Occasionally, Tree shook her hand vigorously, as if to shake supernatural yuck off her fingers. Sometimes she grabbed with her whole hand and flung away a fistful of air. Tree worked quickly; fingers flew. Pinch, toss, grab, toss. Begone! In a few minutes, she was done.

"Okay Ivy. Good girl."

Ivy hopped off the table, looking no cleaner. But again—I was not the professional.

Tree turned to me. "Tie something blue around her head when she sleeps. Also, have her envision light blue for a few minutes before bed. You should do it too, both of you in her bedroom, thinking light blue."

Start to finish, Exorcism #2 clocked in at less than six minutes. And now I owed Tree a web site. I kind of felt like she should do Hannah for free, just in case.

We did the blue thing. Again, for about three weeks, everyone at our house slept through the night. Again, the trip back to normal was slow.

In February, Anthony and I were still privately batting ideas around for what it could look like to become permanent expats. As part of our surreptitious research, we asked each of the kids separately what they liked best about living in Monteverde. Harry and Hannah said the same thing, right off:

1) having Anthony and me around so much, and

2) the freedom to go where they wanted, when they wanted.

An interesting pairing, I thought. Our kids loved having us more available in general, but less directly tethered.

In Seattle we'd had Hannah take the bus, but we always knew where she was. Here, our knowledge of our big kids' whereabouts was far less specific. For example, the other day Hannah had told us she wasn't coming home after school, but would definitely be home before dark. Wandering downtown, she'd come across one of those enormous SAT books at the book exchange. She grabbed it and crossed the street to the Blue Morpho café, where she ate a toasted avocado sandwich and took a practice test for yuks. All of this was predicated on her having oceans of time to herself, and no particular plan. On having time and space to wander, and see what might happen next.

When we asked Ivy what she liked best, she said milkshakes.

During this period, Hannah had Vermont Sharon, the girl who'd arrived in January, over after school. That night, over breakfast for dinner—*gallo pinto* with eggs—I ran Sharon through the standard grilling about life back home, what had brought them here, etc.

It turned out she'd come to Monteverde with just her mom. Her dad didn't feel he could leave his job, but they both wanted Sharon to be able to go straight into Spanish II when she got to high school.

"I've been taking French since third grade, so that's already covered," she told us.

Sharon told us about her private school back home. "It's not that the public schools are bad," she explained. "But a lot of the kids there aren't parented very carefully. Also, my mom wanted to get me away from our culture of violence."

Anthony cocked his head at me across the table. "Vermont has a culture of violence?" said his eyebrows.

I was concerned. Harry was his own culture of violence, and his arsenal had taken over our kindling bucket. Using Ivy's picture books, he had fashioned a divider to keep the slingshots separate from the arrows.

"We came to learn Spanish, too," Harry was saying to Sharon. "And blah blah blah, family time." He reached out and patted his sisters on their shoulders, ever happy in the middle of his pack.

I got up to get dessert. "You can't do anything else when you're making flan," Beatriz had cautioned me. "It takes only a second for your caramel to go from *perfecto* to useless." I had never seen Beatriz multitask.

I was announcing that everyone's caramel should be *perfecto* when we heard a taxi puffing up our hill. On arrival, it disgorged a medium-large woman with very red cheeks. She, too, was puffing.

"Oh my God, that's my mom," said Sharon, dropping her spoon and running to yank on her shoes.

I opened the door prepared to be pleasant and perhaps apologetic. Had Sharon's mom found out about the arsenal?!

"Hi! I'm Margot. I'm so glad the girls . . ."

Sharon's mom's mouth opened and shut once, but no words came. I saw that the poor woman was too furious for pleasantries, but too well bred to be unpleasant.

Eventually she was able to take herself off mute, and we pieced together the situation. Apparently, Sharon had promised to call her mom when she got here and to be home by six. I hadn't known of either requirement, and assumed Sharon would stay for dinner. Our phone was having one of its off days—a kilometer of telephone lines for just one house made us a low priority for maintenance—so Mama Sharon hadn't been able to get through.

I tried to explain the mistake. I apologized for her stress and for the misunderstanding. I joked about how the mountain air just blows things from your mind. The girls were having so much fun. Sharon must have lost track of time. I tried to sound like someone who parented carefully.

"I'm so sorry for your worry..." I was saying once more, as Sharon's mother stuffed her daughter in the cab. She turned to me.

"I'm sure you are," she said. And then to Sharon, "You need to practice your French, or you'll get behind." And off they went.

The rest of my family had pretty much frozen during the entire scene. Now Harry jabbed his spoon into his flan. "Why did they even bother to come here?"

I was trying not to be too judgmental—at least not where the kids could see. But in silent agreement with Harry, I fumed in Sharon's mom's general direction. *Costa Rica is not just a fast-track to AP Spanish. It's a different, amazing world. If you don't want to be different in it, what the hell are you doing?*

Out loud I said, "It's really hard being a mom, and stressful when you don't know where your kid is, or if she's okay." Which is also true.

I had been used to envisioning *pura vida* as a spectrum that extended from sloths—and Anthony, Shridevi, Tree—to me, all the way out with the high-strung parrots. Sharon's mom provided an instructive data point. Perhaps I was not, actually, the polar opposite of a sloth.

Anthony and I kept comparing notes. Casual non sequiturs whose subjects we dropped as quickly as we'd picked them up.

"Today Harry and Ivy spent three hours in the back yard, making slingshots then doing target practice at the guava tree..."

"People keep saying we'd better get back and start college-prepping Hannah. But you know what I bet colleges would like? A well-read kid who spoke fluent Spanish and could actually find the Latin American countries on a map..."

"John from Hotel Santa Elena called today wondering if I could troubleshoot their network. I could make a living here, if I wanted..."

What do you like better? Time to talk with friends and play with your family, to paint purple-spotted geckos and get a massage, in a life you can afford? Or an hour a day in traffic to work in front of a screen, then come home to hound people about chores?

It felt hard to think ahead, and we set these questions aside. Here, in the life right in front of us, Harry and I had to put ourselves in mortal danger.

29

Falling Off Things

Harry didn't die and I didn't either, but both of us gave it a legitimate shot. Harry went first. He later found a way to blame it on Hannah, because she loved to gallop.

Hannah on a fast horse was like Hannah nowhere else. She stood up in the stirrups, she whooped and hollered, she couldn't get enough. Hannah loved speed on a live thing. She just didn't want to, you know, ever manufacture it herself.

The first time we'd gone fast on horses was early in our time in Monteverde. That night, Hannah chattered on, trying to explain the feeling.

"It was so energizing, and the whole time I was doing it I was thinking *I'm not old enough to be doing this! I can't believe they're letting me do this!*"

I had attended horse camp with the Girl Scouts when I was ten. So as practically a professional equestrienne, I could tell that Costa Rica horses seemed a lot less ploddy than the kind back home. Brighter. Like fresh green beans compared to the canned ones, Tico horses hadn't had all the flavor cooked out of them.

Horses were to Anthony what the motorcycle was to me: He understood that that they were both safe *and* dangerous, and that a lot of people enjoyed them. But on a fundamental level horses made him nervous. Unlike me, Anthony felt no need to conquer his fear.

So Anthony, who had no interest, and Ivy, who even I had the sense to know was too little, stayed home. But Hannah, Harry, and I all loved to gallop. Ezmeralda came with us, as well as Ramón, the guide.

First, Ramón walked us through areas so scenic we didn't want to zoom through them. Up and down hills, around the outer edges of mountains from which we could admire the mountains beyond. Ramón took us places we didn't recognize, even though we were locals now. We arrived at a broad meadow, wide open save for a single tree, and miles from any road navigable by car—or ambulance. Ramón grinned and asked us, *"¿Rápido?"*

"¡Sí!"

Hannah's horse sped around the giant field and when she stopped near me I got a view of every cliché of exhilaration: Hannah was smiling so widely it split her face. Eyes shining. Completely breathless. She spoke a single word, like a toddler:

"More?" She was asking the horse, not me. They were a team now.

Harry's whoops were a much more normal part of life, so it's possible I paid less attention. He was going fast fast fast over here while Hannah became a blur over there, and then I turned to find him again and as I did the world jerked to a stop and picked up in slow motion. Harry was coming off his horse.

The high-mountain air had become an invisible semi-solid. Harry and the horse swam through it at a distance, with great effort. The girth was loose, the saddle had slipped. I couldn't move.

Harry was sideways and bouncing. His torso stuck straight out from the horse's flank, and his head swung up and down, one ear pointing toward the sky, one toward the grass. I flashed on an image from forever ago: that same cheek, that same ear, pressed to the grass in Volunteer Park, in the year all we watched was *The Lion King*; Harry was listening for the wildebeest stampede. But now he *was* the stampede. I could see the hair feather up from his skyward ear and then settle, indicating much faster movement than I seemed to be computing. My boy was slipping down the side of a horse, closer now to belly than back. He was heading right down among the hooves.

"¡Salte!" yelled Ramón—Jump! and the air turned normal again, and child and animal were moving way too quickly. The horse's legs were a galloping blur.

There were two problems with following Ramón's instruction. In his terror, would Harry recognize the Spanish? And, even if he understood, would he be able to get himself out of the stirrups?

And if he managed to jump—what next? Would he be able to push away, or would getting out of the saddle only deliver him more quickly to the frenzy of hooves?

I had no time to worry about this because in the millisecond after Ramón yelled, I saw a threat that our guide had noticed, but I had not. Not a risk, like galloping, like motorcycles, like moving your family to a country where you know no one and none of you can speak the language—but a certain peril. Harry's horse was heading toward that single tree.

Harry atop the horse would have cleared the lowest branch easily, but he wasn't atop the horse and branches weren't the problem. In about three seconds, Harry's head was going to hit the trunk.

And then he was on the ground. I stopped being paralyzed and screamed, once, for long as I had breath.

There must be a limit to how much terror a body can hold. The fear tore out of me now, in the biggest noise I could make.

I couldn't tell if Harry had jumped or fallen. He hadn't ended up in the hooves and I knew he hadn't hit the tree, but all I saw was a blue lump on the ground. A Mariners T-shirt, size ten. After a beat, Harry got to his hands and knees. He stayed there a moment; then he rose to just his knees and waved to show he was okay.

I noticed next that Hannah was staring at me, not at Harry. As was Ezmeralda. My scream hadn't stopped yet. It was still coming out.

A few minutes later, I suggested we all walk our horses back. Harry looked at me with sympathy but said very firmly, "Mom, it is so obvious what I'm supposed to do right now that there's even a saying about it."

The guide wouldn't let Harry back on his own horse, with the troublesome girth and the questionable judgment. But they traded, and Harry got right back up on our guide's horse. We went home.

When I didn't die, at least it was out of necessity.

Anthony's annual Men's Retreat stood as my crowning achievement of meddling. Years ago, because I couldn't imagine life without my own close friends, I decided Anthony must need some, too.

"You need to take care of your friendships, and if you guys won't make it happen in regular life, just go away together!"

Every spring since, Anthony had taken a trip with his best friends from college. I got to feel brilliant for putting the initial plan in motion and noble for being a single parent for a week. This year, the boys were coming to Costa Rica.

We'd come to count on the motorcycle for grocery shopping, and for getting to the library when we didn't have all day. I'd been practicing since our trip to Tilarán, and I knew I could do it. The *moto* was bigger than I was, and I never felt completely comfortable. But I was no sissy, and I aimed to prove it.

A ship in a harbor is safe, goes the saying, *but that is not what ships are built for.* I was going to ride out of the motherfucking harbor, and I was going to do it on a motorcycle.

Mike had told me once, during one of the merry evenings when he was failing to teach us to play bridge, "If you're going to learn to ride, and I think it's cool that you are, you ARE going to lay it down at least once. You just gotta accept it." So while Anthony was away at the beach, I did.

It happened on our driveway, on a perfect afternoon. I navigated the really steep part beautifully, but down near the stream I just forgot to do all the stuff at once. The *moto* landed hard on my left knee. I lay for a few minutes under this huge collection of metal that I had never, ever trusted, wondering whether I was mangled. Eventually, two blue morphos came and fluttered around my head. I was Wile E. Coyote, post-anvil.

I blamed Mike, naturally.

I wasn't mangled, but there was road rash. And pain. And I didn't have time to clean up before hobbling to get Ivy at the bus. I stood with all the tidy Tica moms who were waiting for their immaculate little people to jump smiling into their arms. These ever-polite mamas in their spotless white jeans and bracelets that coordinated with their earrings chatted away with me as if I looked just like them. Probably they didn't think I looked much different than I usually did. When Ivy saw my muddy grossness and I told her what had happened, she responded as follows: "Can we still get ice cream?"

We did. We also took my knee to visit Dr. Doogie, who prescribed ice.

The next day Anthony and his posse came up the mountain to spend some time at our house. I told them about my motorcycle crash, but Colin had fallen off a horse at the beach. He and Harry compared notes, and that was all anyone could talk about.

A few days after the boys left, Anthony offered to help me get my groove back.

"What do you think? Ready to get right back up on that *moto*?"

"Actually, I think the bike won," I told him. I thought a little more. "And I think *jupo* frightens me more than it thrills me. From now on, I'm just going to love that you guys love it."

Since my time beneath all that metal, watching the butterflies circle, I'd given risk some thought. What if I didn't let it rule me in either direction? I didn't want to become risk-averse, but maybe I didn't need to hurl myself at it, either. What if I let anxiety call a shot or two? Perhaps—just perhaps—the entire universe wasn't issuing me a challenge with every fear that crossed my path.

A ship in a harbor is safe, and sometimes that's nice. Sometimes there are neighbors, there in the quiet bay. We could visit and have some snack. Maybe one of my neighbors would say, "Adventure!" and I would go along. But I could also say, "Have a great time. I am going to stay here in the harbor and play some checkers."

I stopped riding the *moto* when I realized I had nothing to prove. But I kept galloping—not out of some juvenile contrarian instinct, but because I loved to gallop.

Not long after I swore off *jupo* and the *moto,* Harry made a statement that seemed to come from nowhere.

"You know what? I think sometimes when I go riding, I'm going to gallop. And sometimes, even if Hannah gallops, I won't feel like it. I think those times are okay, too."

30

Opportunity Knocks

"I heard there's a little farm for sale down in San Luis," said Anthony. "We could afford land there and still be close enough that the kids could stay at the school."

By mid-March, Monteverde had treated us to two months of deep blue skies and a steamy-clean smell when the sunshine zapped the mists. Still no cow skulls. Just the chirping-buzzing background hum of the forest, the infinite variations on green.

"Sure is nice here," I said.

Anthony and I were winding up an epic morning walk, up and over the hill behind our house, through pastures and forest trails, past the house where a former president of Uruguay waved cheerily as we passed. We tramped through the hills, on paths used more often by cows than by people.

Continuing home we passed José Mario's house. Jose Mario lived with his wife, son, and daughter, in a house of maybe seven hundred square feet, with a concrete floor. Sally and Glen had purchased their gorgeous, multi-hectare parcel for $500,000 from José Mario. His current house was on a parcel at least as nice, and bigger. Hotels were always making offers. It turned me upside-down a little, knowing that José Mario had a lot more money than we did. He didn't need to keep cows anymore. His wife had told me once why they didn't move, or build,

"A big house is more to keep clean," she said simply. "Why would I want that?"

We were grateful for their decision, of course. Without José Mario's marauding cows, we would never have learned to be ranch hands.

We'd told everyone, and promised the kids, that this was a one-year adventure. Plus, a decision either way meant taking some kind of action. Staying meant disappointing, even hurting, people we loved. (Also, finding another house.) Going back meant truly considering the financial implications of returning to an expensive life with no means to support it. (And getting Harry signed up for fifth grade. I wouldn't mind sidestepping that.)

We kept poking at the decision, but not making it. When a former boss of Anthony's in Seattle called him out of the blue in March and said *we need help, we think you'd be perfect, can you start right away?* Anthony and I should have been delighted. It took all the stress out of returning.

"But this was our year," I whined. "It still has four months to go."

"It would have killed them to wait two months to contact me?" said Anthony.

But while we were definitely entitled whiners, we weren't completely stupid entitled whiners. To be able to return to the States and land on our feet was almost beyond imagining. And Anthony could be the one with a job, the one whose income we could count on.

A Seattle market-research company was opening an office and wanted Anthony to run it. He negotiated that he would return to the States at the beginning of April and stay five weeks. During that time, he would set up the new office, and all parties would think about whether this gig was a good fit. Then Anthony would return to Monteverde. If everyone agreed he should stay on permanently, Anthony would work just enough by email to keep things progressing, until our family returned together in July. The trial basis offered the perfect escape clause. We were still fantasizing about farmland in San Luis and welcomed the postponement of hard decisions.

School was humming along, everyone spoke Spanish and had friends, and I loved my world with Lola and Beatriz at the *Casa de Arte*. I had finished my painting of colored rainforest animals. I brought it home, and Anthony hung it right next to Vic's. The children, who had always been parented appropriately, knew just how to react to my masterpiece:

"I really like how you used lots of color," Harry told me, nodding and patting my hand.

"Tell me *your* favorite thing about your painting, Mama," added Hannah. She was not smirking so much as failing to hide a very tiny smile.

The prospect of Anthony leaving for over a month didn't scare me in an all-alone-in-a-foreign-country kind of way. But I was terrified in your garden variety *I have three kids and two hands and single parenting is hard and five weeks sounds long* kind of way.

So we set up some defenses. Since Anthony would be making an income for the month, I arranged to have Magda pick Ivy up at the bus stop two days a week. This let me continue "working" a few hours each week at the *Casa*, which would keep me as sane as I was ever likely to get. Plus, they needed me there—my coloring inside the lines was excellent now.

Before Anthony's job offer, Hannah and I had made a plan to try homeschooling for a month. She wanted to learn about the U.S. Constitution, which seemed unlikely to be part of the CEC curriculum. The school was great about the plan and Hannah and I had been looking forward it, so we decided to go ahead. I was slightly nervous about the workload.

I was also, guiltily, looking forward to Anthony's absence. For a couple of reasons.

The first thing I looked forward to was being a dictator. Any honest Quaker will tell you that consensus is an enormous time suck. As Supreme Dictator, I'd make all decisions quickly and efficiently. I hoped I would use my power for good, but made no promises.

Second, I wanted to be Fun Parent. I wasn't good at that when Anthony was around. His orchestrating the nightly kitchen cleaning was helpful, but insufficient. If everyone was going to get teeth brushed, homework finished, and bother to wear underwear to school, it was pretty much up to me. This pissed me off; I was not, congenitally, a drudge.

"I hate being the bad guy all the time." My standard opening gambit.

"So don't do it," Anthony always said.

I maintained that that left me with two crappy options. "I shouldn't have to choose between nagging and stuff not getting done. You and I both want the kids to be responsible, right?"

He knew better than to deny this.

"So why don't YOU badger them?" I always asked.

"Okay," Anthony would say at last. "I will."

But kids know when Daddy is only making them pick up their crap because Mommy is making him make them. They see Mom's eyes darting between Dad and the untouched algebra book. They see Dad trying to figure out what the hell she's getting at, then clicking in with a start. I was the nag even when I wasn't the nag.

I wanted Anthony to notice what needed doing, and make it happen. Then I could be the one to go, "Hey everyone, let's play tag!" or whatever it is you say when you're really fun. Sometimes I forget.

Some fun was about to happen to us anyway, and the Fun Parent turned out to be Erin.

On March 31st, Ivy and I were in town buying airplane snacks for Anthony when the *muchacho* from the post office left his post and ran across the street. He crouched down in front of Ivy, smiling, and put his hand on her shoulder.

"Hay una caja, mi amor," he told her. *"En la oficina. De Puntarenas."*

"EN SERIO?!" she cried. *"Gracias, Señor! Gracias!"*

Erin's Christmas box had spent nearly six months in Puntarenas, the town at the bottom of the mountain. A zealous customs official had gone through every item in the package and then forgotten all about it. Somehow our guy found out. Anthony jumped on the *moto* that afternoon and made the several-hour round trip under a blazing sky.

And so it happened that the day before we said goodbye to Anthony, our family held a great celebration. We put on Christmas carols and our jammies. We took turns opening books, clothing, and toys. The fudge would have to go, but the boxes and boxes of Luna bars were still perfect. Hannah hugged the just-released-on-DVD first season of *The West Wing* to her chest. Dressups for Ivy, a new baseball for Harry. Every single item had been carefully opened in customs, and then re-taped, whole and perfect. Even the tiny boxes with spending money for the kids had near-invisible slits where the wrapping had been sliced; inside, the cash was intact.

Late that night, Anthony's last act before heading down the mountain was to spill a *cuba libre* all over the keyboard of our single laptop. All written communication from our house would henceforth be free from interference by the lower-left corner of the keyboard. The spacebar, as well as letters Z, X, and B, were dead to me.

Anthony had never been chatty, but really. Was it necessary to cripple the rest of us?

The X key was the best—when pressed, it didn't just neglect to make a letter. Depressing the X also kicked off a spell check, and woke up the obnoxious Microsoft Word 2003 "Clippy" from his automated slumber to see if he could be of service.

"It looks like you're writing a letter," Clippy said in his dialog balloon. "Do you want to write a letter?"

"Yes, you little freak." Hannah yelled. "And the letter I want to write is called X. Can you bring me an X?" But Clippy just folded himself up and went back to sleep.

So everything I wrote while Anthony was gone took on the flavor of a ransom note. In the mood, I began composing my emails in Courier. One email after *cuba libre* met Toshiba was even about murder.

A *manigordo*—ocelot—had been eating our chickens, methodically working through the flock at the rate of one per night. Our hens had actually become terrified to go home in the evenings, which was the first sign of intelligence I'd seen in them. For a couple of nights, I let them sleep in our house.

What to do? Make them stay outside and face the huge cat? Spend every morning cleaning chicken poo *inside my house?*

Or...have Magda teach me what a real Tica does with a chicken.

We used a machete, which Harry had been begging to wield since he started watching Luis. The girls hid inside. Magda demonstrated on the first hen, then handed the machete to Harry, who was suddenly reticent. Magda laughed and laughed. She almost died when I expressed wonder at the large and perfect egg we found within a freshly-beheaded chicken.

"Did you think the hens went to *Esperanza* every morning?"

The resulting stew was delicious and *muy típica*—very Costa Rican. Neither Harry nor I could bring ourselves to eat it. This surprised me. I thought I was a much harder hardass than that. I wrote to Vic that night:

```
HarryAndIAreDeciding.ShouldWeGoOutInSecretAndTossThe
UneatenChickenConSopaThatMagdaMadeUsAndPretendWeLoved
ItSoMuchWeAteItAllUp?
OrShouldWeOFFERItToHer.
TheSecondIsClearlyTheRightThingToDo.
-utWeDon'tWantHerToLaughAtUsEvenMore.
```

EcksOEcks,

Margot

(P.S.SorryIHaveNoSpaceKey.AnthonyHasADrinkingPro-
lem.)

The birds took Anthony's disappearance hard and began flying into our windows.

It turns out that when you build a house that is mostly windows, and you live on a mountain in a clearing, and April comes along —migration season— your beautiful house becomes an instrument of death.

Thunk went the birds into the living room windows, several times a day. We cut yellow rain ponchos into strips and set them waving in front of the windows, and we made scary crows out of black construction paper. We created warning signs *"¡CUIDADO, PÁJAROS!"* and some in English just in case some of the birds were U.S. natives, going home. I spent much of the month going back and forth with our landlord, trying to figure out a solution. Poor Glen. He wanted to know what he was, um, getting, so I took his bird-book from the shelf and got to work. Yellow-olive Flycatcher. Spotted Barbtail. Sooty-capped Bush Tanager. Knowing their names made me feel even worse, but I will say it's pretty easy to ID a bird when it's just lying there on the deck.

We all got good at going outside when we heard a thunk, and finding the little fellow, who was usually dazed, not dead. We would upright it, move it far from the house, and point it north. Most seemed to end up okay, but I officiated at what I felt was more than my share of bird funerals.

It would turn out that the first parenting curve balls I got in Anthony's absence were so girly that Anthony wouldn't have known how to react, anyway.

Fashion in Costa Rica put forth a standard look for all females of the species: clothes tight and revealing, eyebrows plucked, mouth lipsticked. Ivy was by nature well suited for Latina adolescence, so I was happy we'd get her out of there well before then. But the first week of Anthony's absence, she emerged from her bedroom modeling a short-short skirt that a classmate had given her and asked me, "Don't I look sexy in this?"

I opened and closed my mouth a few times, then asked Ivy if she was hungry. Good job, Mom.

The next one was harder.

If you're ever feeling nosy about your family, get everyone the same language tutor. Ezmeralda and I talked about my children and husband constantly. The best way to acquire language is to talk, talk, talk, and family provides unlimited content, manageable complexity, and a wide range of verb tenses. While I'm sure Ezme never broke any serious confidences—I never got anything scandalous is how I know—she did provide insights I could never have gotten on my own.

By March, the giggling Tica *chiquitas* who had so mystified Hannah early on had become a decent group of friends, with whom she was spending more time. Vermont Sharon and Hannah loved hanging out with Liliana at the *Casa de Arte*. Either out front, with the *arte*, or in the tiny back living quarters. The girls would lie on the bed and gossip, and Lola would without embarrassment or guilt heat them *espaghettis* from a can.

The *chica* boobs, alas, had yet to arrive. Hannah had seemed to be rolling with this as well.

"I found an upside," she said one day as we sat down to parse the Fourth Amendment. She looked pointedly down at the unbroken plane of her uniform shirt; the CEC insignia lay flat and wrinkle-free above the place where other girls had started keeping their left breast. "I'm pushing fourteen, but the lady at Esperanza still hands me an ice cream cone if I happen to be hanging around after Mass. And of course, I can get into movies for the under-twelve price."

"Of course, that's kind of an abstract upside," she added, pulling out the tattered copy of the Constitution that we'd found at the Friends Library. "Since there's nowhere to go to see a movie on this godforsaken mountain."

Hannah's easy joking told me she was okay. The upswing had started back in December, in El Dos, and continued when we got home and there was still no box from Erin. Hannah had put her arms around me from behind, pressed her cheek against my shoulder, and whispered, "I know you feel bad, Mama. So I will tell you my secret. I love it here, and I love what it's doing to our family. If we'd gone home for Christmas, when we came back we'd just have to start from scratch again."

So I wasn't too worried about Hannah anymore, but I felt a new pang in April when Ezmeralda related a conversation.

Hannah was learning the conditional simple verb tenses. To give her practice, Ezme asked, "What would you change if you could?" Hannah answered according to type: no more wars, everyone having enough to eat, and so on. But then she stopped and was quiet for a moment. She told Ezmeralda, in a near whisper, "You know what? I'm not being honest with you. If I could change anything, I'd want to be pretty."

Oh, my girl.

And Ezme said, "Hannah! You ARE pretty! Not just outside, where you are nice to look at, but on the inside, for which there are no words. But if you want to feel better about it, there are some things you can do, and I will help you. Because I was thirteen once too, and I didn't have anybody to show me this stuff, and moms are of course useless."

Ezmeralda was twenty-five—old enough to be trustworthy, young enough to be credible. And hot enough to make it clear she knew girly secrets Hannah's mother had never unlocked.

The two of them planned a day trip to Tilarán. They would shop for clothes and nail polish and maybe get Hannah's hair cut. Hannah was beside herself, as was Ezmeralda.

"I always wanted a little sister," she confided.

I had misgivings. I loved the Hannah who threw her hair in a ponytail and sucked the end of it, and who loved a school uniform because it saved her the hassle of thinking about clothes. My little girl with the giant vocabulary. Hannah's twiggy body had let her stay *niña* in my mind, but she wasn't, really.

I was a Seattle crunchy mom. I could barely handle my five-year old in this culture. I was happy to let Ezmeralda help Hannah do thirteen. Happy and sad.

I wanted to tell Anthony, but he was off in Seattle—being even sadder, I would learn.

The day arrived. Hannah had gathered every dollar and *colón* in her possession and put them in a purse she thought might pass as cute. Ezmeralda was right on time, but Hannah was pacing by the time Ez tootled up our hill on a borrowed scooter. She tossed Hannah a helmet like they were two gorgeous chicks in a movie. Down the hill they went. I stood outside and waved them off, feeling like Billy Crystal and Carol Kane in our overwatched copy of *The Princess Bride*. "Goodbye you two! Goodbye! Have fun storming Hannah's innocence . . ."

31

Holes

Once again, culture shock didn't come the way we expected it would. Why would we expect it at all? Four-fifths of us were staying put. It took Magda to alert me to what was going on.

I think Magda knew her gorgeousness flipped the white ladies out, and she held herself in a bit of reserve when a husband was near. But with Anthony away, Magda started to stick around after cleaning. The two of us would chat, and she loosened up with the kids as well. The most fun thing we all did in April was dig a hole.

The day after our chicken massacre, when Anthony had been gone about a week, Magda suggested we bury the entrails and carcasses deep, where the ocelot would not dig them up. Harry, Ivy, and Magda went up the hill away from the house and took turns with the shovel. Soon, the kids dragged me up to witness their accomplishment.

"It goes all the way up to Ivy's neck!"

I admired. Harry jumped in to show me the hole came to his waist. He climbed out, and Magda had just begun dumping the bucket of guts in when Ivy began to howl.

She had planned to jump into the hole and show me the neck thing. We tried to convince her that since there was really not much in there yet, and since she was wearing her ladybug boots, she could jump in anyway. No dice.

Ivy stomped and stormed at Harry for always ruining everything, then at me for always taking his side, and ran off crying. I heaved a sigh. *Ivy.*

The three of us filled in the hole and trooped back to the house in silence. When we got there, Magda, whom I had never heard apologize for anything, found Ivy curled in a chair. Magda crouched beside her and spoke in Spanish:

"I'm sorry, Ivy. I think we should dig another hole. I think we should start right now, and the new hole should be just to play in. We will make it so big you cannot even see out of it."

!!!

Ivy's eyes got bigger with every word. *"Sí! Sí! Sí!"*

Magda caught me watching. She seemed embarrassed by her warmth, so made up for it by snapping at me. "It's hard for the children when the family has a change." Now I was embarrassed. Of course. I hadn't thought.

Harry got excited, too, and even though it was raining by then, the three of them donned slickers and went out to get started. I watched them from the kitchen. They were digging in the rain, laughing and throwing dirt. And I realized: Hey! I'm Supreme Dictator, and I have no job. Yet here I am working on dinner, while Magda is playing in the rain with my kids.

"So don't be," Anthony had always said when I grumped about being the drudge. But kids have to eat, and now, there really *was* no one but me to feed them. I kept grating yucca.

I went out later to look. They had made the hole so deep that they had to tie knots in a rope, then tie the rope to the *sapote* tree, so that Ivy could climb out on her own.

Anthony and I had set things up carefully to avoid a Single Parent Freakout. Imagine our surprise when instead, Anthony flipped. Honestly, I don't think either of us thought he had it in him.

His emails were fine at first—got here, safe, sound, job seems good, very busy. I didn't know he was having a hard time, which was his way. But then I did know, which wasn't.

Shortly after we started the hole, I got a mail from Anthony that sounded like a textbook case of first-world reentry. He wrote:

> There's just so much stuff here. It's everywhere. And I can't believe how much people eat. The portion sizes are disgusting.

A couple of days later, he was even grumpier. My accepting, it's-all-good husband was highly un-*pura vida* about the state of the States:

It's weird here, very weird. People are rushing places in their cars, but I don't see the urgency. They leave their boxes each morning and get into their boxes with wheels. Then they ride their boxes with wheels to a bigger box where they can go sit in smaller subdivided boxes, until the end of the day when they get into their boxes with wheels so that they can return to their sleeping boxes.

Unflappable Anthony...had finally flapped.

I guessed that the unplanned nature of his re-entry must be exacerbating the culture shock. Anthony had gone back to the States four months ahead of schedule, and with a single week's warning. He was home but not, living in a tiny, furnished apartment the company had found him, several miles from anyone he knew.

Also, while the rest of us had adapted to the downsizing of our lives, Anthony had actively relished it. How much worse, then, would the supersizing be for him?

I shared some bits of Anthony's freakout with Vic, who told me,

Yeah, when I got back from India when I was 20, culture shock hit hard and my parents hauled me off to therapy. They thought I was suicidal. And I told them, "I don't want to be DEAD. I just don't want to look at all this PLASTIC."

I urged Anthony to look up some friends, and told him not to hesitate to call me if he needed to talk. Yes, long distance was expensive. We'd figure it out. And we could always IM, for free.

For a few days, I didn't hear back. Which was okay, as I was pretty busy getting schooled by Magda.

My Spanish was decent by now, but Magda could still stump me. One sparkling morning as I returned from speaking firmly to Blackie about the avocado seedlings, Magda shook a bathmat off the end of the deck with a snap so sharp it got my attention. When I looked over, Magda shoved her hand on her hip and called out a question that would have been fraught even coming from a person who didn't have quite so much contempt for my people as a whole:

"Mar*GOTE,* how come your girls don't play with Barbies? I see that the Gringo families, none of them have Barbies for their *chiquitas.*"

"I'll be right in," I answered, buying time.

I was hotly aware of the rich-person values I carried around, of the luxury implicit in choosing an anatomically feasible, racially indeterminate, child-labor-negative doll wearing an organic hemp tunic, all the while turning up my nose at Malibu Barbie.

Vocabularily speaking, "self esteem" was still beyond me, as were "misogyny" and "disproportionate boobies." It was time to get my earnest on, in very simple words. Magda was getting out the wood polish.

"I want my girls to be happy with their bodies," I said, hoping *cuerpo* didn't only mean corpse. "And a body like Barbie isn't real. Besides, um, there are lots of other toys to play with," I trailed off.

Hilda pulled on rubber gloves and arched a perfect eyebrow.

"Mar*GOTE*. Ivy plays with an elephant. Do you think Ivy will grow up and want to be an elephant?"

"Yes, I see, but . . ."

Magda wasn't done. Magda had a speech. Clearly, she'd been stewing for a while about the contradictory ways of the people whose houses she cleaned. Magda was about to tell me what was what. I missed reserved Magda.

She was on the stairs now, rubbing oil into the rich mahogany.

"All girls want to play with Barbies," she began. "*Es normale.* Is hating Barbie because of the anorexia?"

"Um . . ."

"*Los Gringos,* they are all so worried about the anorexia. They eat all the time, then they worry about not eating. Only the United States could make it a disease not to eat. If you ask me, a little bit of anorexia is good for North American girls! What man wants to be with a *gordita?* You cannot climb hills, you cannot do anything. No boy will want you if you are too *gorda.* You see on television all the time how fat *los Gringos* are getting. If more girls in your country played with Barbies, maybe they would not be so ugly. In Costa Rica, all the *chiquitas* play with their Barbies. Costa Rican girls are small and beautiful, because if they are too fat we tease them. But *los Gringos* won't let their girls play with Barbies, and soon their houses will need bigger doors."

"Except you and your girls," Magda finished charitably. "You are not very fat." She went to her bag and produced a Barbie. "My niece is done with this Barbie. Does Ivy want it?"

Was this whole thing Magda's way of giving a gift?

"She'll love it. Thank you, Magda—that's very thoughtful."

Then Magda seemed to remember another strange habit of the Gringos. "Not Harry, though. Don't let him play with the Barbie. You do not want to make him a homosexual!" She laughed, brushed a gorgeous wisp of hair out of her flawless face, and went back to polishing my stairs.

I couldn't wait to tell Anthony about this, but he kept not being here.

That night, the phone rang just after I'd finished putting the kids to bed. Anthony was on the other end, crying. Initially, this did not compute to such an extent that I thought he had a cold.

"I can barely hear you," I told him. "I hope you're taking something for that."

What Anthony was going through sounded like not quite, but alarmingly close to, a nervous breakdown. Within spitting distance, as I understood the condition. Definitely some kind of crisis.

Anthony wasn't just crying on the phone, he told me. He was crying all the time. Nothing he thought was sure seemed sure. He hated Seattle. He didn't want to see anyone. Work seemed pointless. Why were we married?

It did not escape me that many spouses in my position—sane women, smart women—would get a little panicky at this point. I didn't, because:

1. Anthony was finally having some emotions, and
2. He wanted to talk about them, and
3. He wanted to talk about them with ME.

Was it selfish of me to be a little bit grateful for Anthony's pain, since it gave me a chance to feel closer to him, and useful to him? Probably. I tried to help Anthony, and encouraged him to get help. But while I wanted him to *get through* this hard time, I couldn't bring myself to want him not to have it at all.

There was a rawness to my husband that I had never seen before. I felt possibility in it, the potential for a shifted emotional balance. My ears had become accustomed to a cheerful but monotonic hum from my husband. This—the crying, the absolute bewilderment in his voice—was a sad and scary music. But still: music.

I tried to give him some tips from my lifelong experience of having feelings. I tried to imagine what it would be like to live my whole life without inexplicable tears, then have them sneak up on me when I was pushing forty. I'd be terrified. For Anthony, that initial terror was joined by embarrassment at being terrified, and then of course there were the actual tears, and the accompanying mortification. The two of us began to IM, email, or talk on the phone at least once a day.

One Saturday about three weeks into Anthony's awayness, a Seattle neighbor stopped through for a single day and night. The kids and I gave her a crash course in Monteverde and returned home, exhausted, in the evening. I turned on the laptop to a multi-page email of what it was like for Anthony to be in the world that particular day. (Condensed version: hard.)

I left Maude yakking with the kids and hid in the bedroom to IM with Anthony. I wrote him a *Things to Note When You're Losing It* list. The difficulty of typing on our crippled laptop should serve as a barometer of how much I wanted to help:

Margot says:
1… CultureShockIsARealThing--- MaybeGiveYourselfA-reak,LetYourselfHaveFeelingsWithoutRecrimination?

2…YouAreHavingTheCultureShockWallopALONE.IKnow You'veNeverQuite-lievedThis,-utAloneCan-e WAYHARDERthanNotAlone.

3…YouMissYrFamily.ThisIsAppropriateAsWeAre QuiteDelightful….KnowThatWeMissYouToo.SoMuch.

4…YouHaveNOTHINGTo-eAshamedOf. YouCanTellMeWhatIsUpWithoutWorryingIWillFlip. IAmFeelingSolidAndNotFlippy.

Anthony says:
It is very good to IM with you. You are smart and so empathetic and I don't think I give you the opportunity to demonstrate that very much.
Margot says:
ThankYou.WhatANiceThingToSay.
Anthony says:
Also, here are some more spaces: I think you're out again.

Yes, my communications looked like a painfully wrought manifesto. Anthony getting the keyboard wasted had sabotaged my ability to form comprehensible sentences. But if we combined my new disability with the words suddenly pouring forth from Anthony, maybe we were finally even.

Maude and I stayed up late talking. We covered her marriage, my marriage, finances, work-life balance—a Seattle-style, multi-topic conversation blast.

I needed some sleep, so when Maude and I finally turned in at two a.m., I said goodbye. We had arranged for an early taxi to take her down the mountain in just a couple of hours. But Harry wanted to get up to see her off (of course Harry wanted to get up to see her off), and after she was gone he found himself without much to do.

It was 5:00 AM when he sat on the edge of my bed.

"Good morning, Mommy," Harry whispered, touching my shoulder. "She left at 4:30. I talked to the *taxista* to make sure he knew what she needed. Maude told me you wanted to sleep in, so I waited to ask you. Can I take a bath?"

Yesyesyes, of course. I asked Harry if he could get himself to school today. Ivy had the day off for *charlas*, so if he could handle himself I could get some sleep.

"Sure! I'll even make my own lunch!"

"Thanks, sweetie. I love you. Have a great morning. See you after school." I was asleep again before he reached the bedroom door.

5:25: "Can I put the last of the granola in my lunch?"

5:32: "Okay, my bath is ready, so I'll just be getting in now. I'll be really quiet."

5:55: "Guess what, Mom? You were right! I am really enjoying *Ender's Game*. I guess I should have just believed you. Also, I picked my clothes up off your bathroom floor so you won't have to."

At 6:15, Harry stood by my bedside with a cup of water and some bread and butter, as well as my toothbrush, all prepared. "Can I bring my breakfast in, too? We can have breakfast in bed together!"

For the next half our, our conversation ranged from what he should be when he grows up ("Do you think I would make an okay actor? Not the singing kind."), to Diego/Miles problems ("Sometimes I feel like Diego doesn't want me to be friends with Miles, and Miles told me he doesn't like Diego. I want to be both their friend but this really seems like it's going to end up bad."), to the birds outside the window ("How come we never see toucans or parrots in the morning? Are there morning birds and afternoon birds? It seems like the afternoon birds hit the window a lot more—maybe morning birds are smarter.")

6:45: "Now that you've gotten to sleep in, do you think you could help me just a little bit, to get my things together for school?

7:00: Bye Mommy! Love you! See you after school and we can talk some more!

It was too late for sleeping. Before facing another day without Anthony, I wrote him a quick mail:

Jaysus,Everyone'sAllTalkTalkTalk---
WhatDoesAGirlHaveToDoAroundHereToGetALittlePeaceW
ithHerThoughts?

Anthony replied:

No zealot like a convert.

Back in Canitas, our magnificent hole had consumed much of a week. It was a hole among holes, a champion, so deep now that all of us needed the rope to get out. We'd sculpted shelves in the side and the kids were storing things on them—tools, snacks. Pedro and Diego heard the legend and came up the hill to play in it. Ivy ringed the top with rocks for fancy effect. Four people at a time could be down there—two, if they wanted to sit down.

Hannah amused herself: she descended, via rope, with an avocado, a pillow, and the book *Holes*, Spanish translation. She stayed down there all afternoon.

I thought of Anthony's latest email. He had written:

I predict that the kids will be hardest hit by coming back because I don't think they'll be able to articulate what they're feeling. They'll feel life being different, but will they be able to give voice to it?

What will they do when we return to the States and the busy lives from before we left?

What indeed.

By three weeks in to the extended stint of Anthonylessness, I wasn't just longing for a parenting break. I missed the Anthony of Anthony. I was discovering in Anthony's absence that I had felt his presence keenly.

I missed him. I missed our walks. I missed lying in bed after everyone was finally asleep, listening to the chirps and whirrs and absence of traffic that filled our hilltop nighttimes. And being able to say, as I had after one particularly drama-filled day before he left, "Don't you just hate the children?"

And him saying, "We should look into Vic's idea, sell them on eBay. Hannah's got the blue eyes and the work ethic, Ivy's entertaining, and Harry can make slingshots."

He paused, then had a flash of insight. "Bilingual! We could charge extra!"

I was in that place now, the place in which my adorables were wearing on my last nerve. But I had no Anthony to banter with, no dark hilarity to temper my frustration.

By the time he'd been gone a month, Anthony was still having emotions, but he was far less whacked out about it and sounding more like himself. I told him over IM about the night I had stayed up too late talking to Maude, and a surprising discovery I'd made:

Margot says:
TurnsOutSheAndGrantAreEvenMoreFuckedUpThanWeAre!

Anthony says:
Oh no! I really wanted to win. Well, I am getting more fucked up every day, so we might still pull it out.

I wanted to say, *Please, please can I sleep in tomorrow?* but there was no one to say it to. Plus, I wanted someone to know, *my motorcycle knee still really hurts even though I am being very stoic.*

Three meals times three picky children. At least two walks to the bus stop, totaling five kilometers. Groceries on foot. Homework. Get them all in bed, then wake them all up and start again. Come up with creative, exciting curriculum for Hannah, and review her work. I'd nursed some crankiness this year about Anthony not helping out enough, he'd clearly been doing something; I was exponentially more exhausted with him gone.

At least the bird plague had subsided. Was migration season waning? Or had Darwin prevailed, and the dumbest birds were no longer on the wing? No time to sit and wonder; we had a new plague. Ivy had lice.

The two of us walked to town for that nasty shampoo. A couple of hours and six kilometers later, I paused while bent over Ivy's head to gaze out the window and get the nit off my fingernail. I laundered all of our sheets. The mists came in. We'd sleep on bare mattresses tonight because oops, no dryer and no backups.

Harry was furious I wasn't digging with him more. That afternoon, he'd hit me with, "Dad would dig! You never want to do anything fun!"

I did want to, I really did. But there was always another dinner to think of, and Ivy needed help with everything. She was little.

Best Life Lesson from a Movie: *Broadcast News,* when Holly Hunter unplugs the phone, sobs for about ninety seconds, then wipes her face and gets back to the day. Early that evening I snuck away to let it out for a minute, making a mental note to share with Anthony the benefits of doing a Holly.

Harry appeared a minute later.

"What's wrong? Did someone make you mad, or did someone make you sad?"

I wiped my eyes. "Oh, honey. It's not you. It's not anything that anyone is or isn't doing. I think I had an idea of a year when everything was special and different, but it turns out I still spend an awful lot of time washing dishes." I tried to laugh.

"I'm sorry." Harry waited, awash in sympathy, for what I'm sure he thought was a polite amount of time. Probably three seconds. Then he asked, did I remember I had promised to dig with him?

The tears sprang back.

Harry backed out of the room. "Yeah, okay," he said. "I know you're busy." Oh. Oh no.

Harry was that boy in the Harry Chapin song, who wants to play ball with his dad! The dad is always busy, but the boy is super understanding. But then he grows up and is just as self-involved and jerky as his father had been. "Cat's in the Cradle" does not end well for the father.

I was doing it again. I'd spent so many years thinking that the distance between me and motherhood nirvana was exactly as wide as my full-time job. That *if only I didn't have to work,* I would be astonishing, magical, perfect. "I just can't do it and work in high-tech," I had said to Anthony that night.

Here I was, with world enough and time—sitting on my bed doing Holly Hunter. Or cooking dinner. Or studying Spanish. Jobless in Costa Rica, I had found plenty of ways to not play ball.

How many times was I going to have to learn this lesson?

"Harry! Wait!"

I worked my body hard. I lifted and dumped and pulled and got dirt in my hair. For dinner, we ate the Cheerios I had found at Esperanza, next to the hair dye. Afterward, I said we'd all clean for the duration of two songs. I put Frank Sinatra on loud. I explained to the children the importance of music with really good horns in it when you're having a hard day, and they pretended that was interesting.

Later, I was sitting at our lovely table, composing a lice update for Anthony, when Ivy came out of her bedroom. She'd been quiet for a while, and instead of being suspicious, like a good parent would, I had just been enjoying it. Turns out she had cut Barbie's hair. I told Anthony about it, not even trying to make the word "Barbie" intelligible with no letter b:

```
TheSkinnyDollWithHuge-reastsAndPointyFeet—

YouKnowTheOne,FromMagda—

IsNearlyHairlessAndIvyIsFREAKINGMEOUT.

ShePutTheShornDollHairInHerUnderwear.NowSheIsMarching

Around,DELIGHTED,WithHerPu-icHair.

Jaysus.ThatKid.

Plus:That'sAllINeedRightNow:MoreFuckingHAIR.
```

As was my custom, I had lied to the children about when their dad would get home. Today was Tuesday, and I'd told them Friday. Anthony's Thursday arrival—with the replacement part for our drunken laptop—would thus come quickly.

He called that night, completely himself. By which I mean that he wanted me to do most of the talking.

I told him about Hannah's trip to Tilarán with Ezmeralda, which I had forgotten about in all the crises on his side and exhaustion on mine. She'd come back with cute new shirts and Tica-tight jeans, several colors of nail polish, and a haircut. For a second, as she was pirouetting one of her new outfits, a trick of the light me made think I'd seen...

"Omigosh Hannah—did you buy a *thong?*"

Anthony started to gross out, but I ssh'd him for the punch line.

"Eeew!" Hannah had answered. "I'd never buy a thong. I mean, I want to look good and normal and maybe a little bit hot, but it's not like I want to be a *wonton!*"

She was still our girl.

The night before he got on the plane to come...home? back? I didn't know the wording...I told Anthony about the Easter preparations in town, and how it threw into stark relief the spotty religious training we had provided. Harry was particularly curious about the Jesus statue he'd seen; Our Lord had been planted face down in a coffin, on the back of a flatbed truck.

"What about rolling the stone away?" Harry had wondered. "Do Catholics have a coffin instead?"

Anthony and I went back and forth a little about whether the resurrection story would be more impressive or less so if Jesus had escaped a grave rather than a tomb.

"I don't think just breaking out of a wooden box is all that," said Anthony. "The stone-rolling thing is definitely more badass."

"If he'd been actually buried, though? I mean, digging up out of a hole— that's pretty hard."

It struck me that we both had some recent experience with this.

May – July

32

What's Next

When Anthony returned in the first week of May, all trace of emotional crisis was gone. Poof. He was exactly his old self. I looked carefully for signs of fragility, or perhaps a need to process.

"You okay?"

"Sure! Why? Oh that. Yeah, that was weird."

I realized then that I'd always assumed every human existed along the basic emotional spectrum that went from "heart on sleeve" to "all bottled up." I'd long assumed Anthony was just an incredibly good bottler, and I tried not to get hurt that he hid his feelings. But did I have the metaphor wrong? Perhaps my husband wasn't *holding in* his doubt, fears, and tears. Maybe those things were just really far away most of the time—more of a comet-type situation. I considered marking the calendar for a dozen years out, reminding myself to keep watch in case Anthony's Emotions and Need To Discuss Them came back around.

It was weird to me. But Anthony insisted he was fine, so there didn't seem to be much else to do except to figure out what to do next.

The kids were asleep. Anthony and I were sitting up in bed with *cuba libres* and talking about the job. His employers hadn't seemed to notice that Anthony was mostly unhinged; they'd loved his work and made him a permanent offer.

Anthony sipped his drink and clicked open the laptop. (Really, Anthony? Three days after we got the spacebar back?)

I wormed my cold feet under his warm knees.

"So this would seal the deal," I said.

"Hey!" Anthony extricated me from his legs but held my frigid toes. "Do your feet not get that they're living in the tropics?"

"The torrids," I corrected.

"The thing is," he said, "if the grandparents were all spread out, they might as well fly here as anywhere else. But we might be the last family in the States with its roots in one place. It feels important."

But it wasn't just family. It was everyone who'd made a stepping-stone quilt patch. It was Lizzie, Vic, Lucy. It was Harry's teammates, and their parents on the bleachers, with whom we shivered and then sweated through baseball springs, reversing the order each soccer fall, until it turned out we were friends. It was the college buddies who had stuck with us when we had kids a decade early, and the parent friends who'd joined them. We had a whole world up there.

"But we have a world here now, too." Lola and Beatriz. Pedro and his parents. Sofia. Everyone at the school.

The situation made me fussy.

"Why can't our roots come here? Stupid roots."

"That's not really how roots work," said Anthony. We sat in silence a minute.

"I think . . ." I said, "I think we're going back. And I also think we can be confident that it's right, but still be a little sad about thing we didn't choose."

Any hard choice means closing the door on something you really wanted. I thought a minute more and amended:

"Actually, I will probably be a lot sad."

We would stop fantasizing about staying, about working low-key jobs and raising *pura vida* kids among avocado trees and toucans. We shifted from tantalizing dreams of permanent exile, and began dreaming of the people who had loved us for as long as we could remember. Of the snap and crackle of city living. Of bringing Costa Rica habits to our old yellow house. We'd have *gallo pinto* for breakfast and walk to the library.

Baseball camp, two cars, and a house in the center of town were hardly requirements for a life near our roots. We could downsize, live in the suburbs— even an apartment. But going back wasn't just a geographical choice. It was a cultural one, too, and the culture we were choosing hadn't gotten any less expensive in our absence. As grateful as we both were for Anthony's newfound employment, he'd be earning a little less than he had when we left. I would go back to work.

We wanted the life. This was best for the kids. The grandparents would be so happy.

"I'm glad to know this about us," I said. "That it's the people. That I'd rather live in Lynnwood with the people we love most than in paradise without them. I didn't know that, 'til now." Lynnwood was my least-favorite suburb of Seattle, all box stores and strip malls.

"And we don't actually have to live in Lynnwood," said Anthony.

He was right. Our situation in the States was great. And I'd had this year, this insanely wonderful year. Not many people get that. I could go back to playing chess.

Anthony typed a quick acceptance, "I would be honored . . ." etc., and clicked Send.

"Well, that's done," he said. He drained his drink and laced his fingers in my toes. "Feels good to have it decided."

Anthony snapped the laptop shut. Two minutes later, he was asleep, face as slack and as peaceful as Ivy after an exorcism. The door we hadn't chosen would never trouble Anthony again.

And I? I did what women do. And do and do, until our doing is cliché: I stole to the bathroom. I blasted the faucets and sat down on the cool, slate floor. I hugged my knees. I sobbed and I sobbed and I sobbed.

33

Fireflies

W hen a diver returns from the down-deep world where everything is different, he's cautioned to come up slowly. He's just going back to the place where he started, but he's been changed by where he's been and needs time to adjust. It's dangerous to come back too fast.

"I don't want us to get the bends," I said to Anthony the next morning.

"Agreed," he buried his groggy face in my neck. "Bends bad. No bends good."

Funny, I thought, how at the beginning of the adventure, you can just dive right in. Drop backwards off the boat. Use those big fins to immerse yourself, get to the good stuff as fast as you can.

But coming back...*that's* the big adjustment. Take it slow.

The obvious way home was pretty fast. Head down the mountain at dawn, to the airport in San José. With a decent connection in Dallas, we'd be high-fiving all of Seattle by sunset.

But we'd lived down deep a long time. We moved to the rhythms of this other place, now. With Anthony's jarring experience as warning, I decided to seek alternate, slower routes home.

At this point, the moderately self-aware Gringa might have made a mental note: *Something of a milestone, no? Actively seeking a less efficient way to complete a necessary task?*

I rejected driving (hot, hard to cross borders). Trains rejected me (none went where I wanted to go). I began to concoct a sailing adventure, but my loved ones rolled their eyes so far back in their heads I feared someone was going to seize. I'd pocket that.

I vaguely remembered a Seattle friend mentioning that, in the 1950s and '60s, her missionary father would book passage on freighters as an affordable way to haul their family from place to place. Preliminary research indicated that *some* freighters would still take *some* passengers. But I'd have to really want it; this was not an Expedia thing.

I emailed polite requests, then slightly desperate ones.

By the end of May I had a plan: On or about July 5 (freighters come when they come, so be ready), we'd board the good ship *Rosario* in Colón, Panama and head North through the Caribbean and into the Gulf of Mexico. A quick left into the Port of Galveston. From there, flying from Houston to Seattle wasn't hard.

Perfect. No bends. All set.

In early June, Harry gave a demonstration on soil erosion for the school's end-of-year open house. All morning he switched between Spanish and English, depending on the audience. A few teachers from other grades had gathered around, asking, "HOW long has that boy been here? We thought just this year, but that can't be . . ."

"He even uses reflexive verbs correctly!" Miss Marti crowed a little.

It was such a clear marker of progress from that first day at the blackboard that I knew I should take stock of the other ways we all had changed. Write things down, make sure we had a record. But when I got home and went to start, the laptop blinked on to display an email Harry had been writing to Galen:

> The other night there was a lightning storm, with no rain or thunder. It was a mix of forked and sheet lightning, but Hannah thinks the sheets might have been just forks behind a cloud. Everything lit up, like in a movie. The wind was so strong our whole house shook like crazy, and we didn't go five seconds without lightning for a whole hour. In between the lightning the night was pure dark and in the pure dark we could see like a million fireflies. And when the lightning ended the night stayed dark but the fireflies were still everywhere. My sisters and I turned out all

the lights. Our parents came up and we watched it, like a show, from the loft.

The tears welled up. "Get a grip," I said aloud.

Screw taking stock. I didn't want to think about the ending, tie everything up with a bow.

My final weeks in Costa Rica marked a conversion—wholly incomplete and probably temporary, equivocal as all hell but I take what I can get. I became someone who could, on occasion, enjoy each moment as it came.

Fireflies blink on for a heartbeat, and then they're gone. Sometimes you try to track one, but by the time you've got it fixed in your sights, it's off again. So you stop and just watch the aggregate, a universe of shooting stars right there at eye level. Together, they make you take in your breath and hold it, not quite believing you get to see.

If I hadn't been in such an anti-stocktaking kind of mood, Ivy's next move would have made a Milestones list for sure. One June evening at Kelly and Mike's, the grownups were putting away a second bottle of wine and playing bridge to humor Mike. We sat at a table that had finally come to rest in a Magda-approved location, and I had a hand that even I could recognize was excellent: lots of high hearts and spades. Harry and the middle Jensen kids were hard at Monopoly, and the Hannahs were discussing whether a boy in eighth grade was cool or just mean. Ivy and Molly were engaged in an elaborate role-play in the middle of the room.

In full Snow White regalia, Ivy was preparing for the ball. Molly, in camouflage pants and Spiderman t-shirt, was the peasant man whose job was to hammer the biggest diamond into the royal tiara. But the princess dropped the central prop.

"Please help me find my diamond," the princess asked the peasant. "It fell into the cawpet."

"The what?"

"Peasant man, my DIAMOND has fallen into the CAWPET."

My attention was divided as Kelly finished the bidding. Molly wasn't getting it. Ivy switched to Spanish, her voice rising:

"Esta en la alfombra!"

Ivy's Spanish R's were as beautiful as always. But Molly didn't know the word.

I was debating whether to head off disaster or lay down an ace when Ivy took a deep breath and gave it a last, heroic effort. Slowly,

"Molly. My diamond. It fell into the CARpet."

Four heads jerked up. Ivy, Harry, Anthony and I exchanged looks from various corners of the room. Finally, Hannah blew a silent kiss at Ivy's back. Harry pumped his fist. I smiled at Anthony and took the trick.

And that was that. The w's were gone. Ivy spoke English, now.

Anthony, with renewed respect for the power of human connection, was out for a ride with Mike. Hannah was sleeping at Sharon's house. (We hadn't worked up the nerve to invite Sharon back to ours.) Harry, Ivy, and I were at home, and they were clamoring for a movie.

Harry had been busy maximizing every moment. That afternoon, he and Pedro had played two hours of basketball up at the Friends School, and then some soccer, after which Harry had walked all the way home. He was exhausted, but I'd never get him to bed—it was only seven o'clock.

A movie would be perfect. I had just the thing.

A couple of months before, my dad had sent us a very grandparent present. *Winged Migration,* a documentary about birds, was surely a lost and boring cause as entertainment. But it would be relevant, given our recent experience as a migration-path booby trap. I'd make the children watch enough of it to write a believable thank-you note.

Riveted, I think is the word. The kids lay on their tummies for two hours of a CGI-free, nearly wordless movie. The birds were not funny and did not speak. There were no sidekicks.

A few minutes in, Harry started saying, "Maybe I'll just shut my eyes and listen. I love this music."

But his eyes wouldn't stay shut. He had to watch the birds flying, landing, diving. Birds, over and over.

There is a terrible moment in this astonishing film: geese in flight, perfectly lit by a setting sun. The movie lets you hear popping sounds, and shows some of the geese, dropping. No voiceover, no visible humans. Just the sound of guns, then birds tumbling out of the sky.

Ivy burst into tears. Harry sat up and pulled her into his lap, and cried a little himself. No one spoke. Ivy spent the next twenty minutes with her head on Harry's shoulder, looking out. He patted her hair.

As Ivy got absorbed again, I started writing down some of her comments; Anthony would want to hear them:

"Omigosh. That is so pretty I think I might just die right now."

"Omigosh. If this were true, I'd pay. I really would." (Harry: "It's true, Ivy! This all really happens, and those are real birds!" Ivy: "Omigosh. I'm paying. I really am.")

"They are so beautiful when they fly all in a group that I just can't stand it."

"This movie reminds me of *A Little Princess*. I can't explain it. I mean, it just makes me FEEL like that movie."

"I wish I had two kinds of newborn birds and I could take care of them and hold them in my arms with two kittens. Only wait—do kittens eat birds?"

A list of things that entertained and delighted us in April and May:

- Digging a hole, then climbing into it and out of it
- Birds—protection, burial, movie about
- Lightning
- Fireflies

One night in mid-June I stayed late at the *Casa de Arte*, gluing scraps of newspaper on balloons destined to become cow udders, and arguing with Lola and Beatriz about my tummy.

"No tiene panza!" said Lola, shocked, and called Beatriz over to look at my belly.

Spanish has a special word for the softy mom-abdomen that is either the badge, curse, or cross, depending on attitude and politics, of most regular-sized women: *panza*. And I was no skinny little thing, but I didn't have one. My ass was impossible and my thighs were close friends, but my tummy, except when filled with baby, had never done the pouchy thing. It's probably my best physical feature. As I pulled my sweatshirt off, my lack of *panza* had flashed itself at Lola. She stopped me right there and called to Beatriz.

Beatriz tucked a paintbrush behind her ear, wiped her hands on a washcloth which she then folded carefully, and came over. The two of them inspected my midsection from all angles, then announced their conclusion: My three children could not possibly have grown in my body.

"Tres hijos! Tres!" I had never seen Beatriz so animated. She brought out her own *panza*, the proud product of four pregnancies, for comparison. She took her brush from behind her ear and waved it at the belly of Lola, mother of one, who obediently lifted her shirt. They made it clear that my belly belonged somewhere on this spectrum. I was very understanding. I patted them both on the *panza* and lifted my shoulders in a fake-apologetic shrug.

We argued for some time about whether I even deserved to be called a mother. Lola and Beatriz made me laugh so hard I peed my pants a little, which, really, should have satisfied everyone

Running late in the last week of school, Hannah bounced down to breakfast in that bouncy-floppy way of the giraffe-legged young adolescent who is not yet too cool to bounce and flop. It was a pristine morning, nothing but blue sky from us to the *Golfo,* and she stopped to hold Ivy up to the kitchen window. They shushed to listen for bellbirds.

Grabbing a banana and stuffing her lunch (avocado sandwich, mango, peanuts) in her backpack, she held up a dog-eared copy of a book, *Surrendering to Marriage.*

Travelers through Monteverde left a wake of life-coaching, how-to-make-everyone-more-pleasing-to-you material at the Santa Elena book exchange, and Hannah took it all in. She liked child-rearing books best; she liked to identify what was being tried on her. But due to extensive inventory, she'd recently begun to explore the vast and contradictory genre of marriage self-help.

"I read in this book that it takes five positive statements to counteract the effects of one nasty insult."

Without looking up from his gallo pinto, Anthony lobbed:

"Gee Hannah, what a dumb thing to say first thing in the morning."

While Hannah fake-kicked her daddy in the shins, I played my part:

"Hannah, you are smart and you are funny; you have a dazzling smile, fantastic freckles, and...what is that, four?...a very lovely mother."

Hannah rolled her eyes. She knew ahead of time exactly how that was going to go, and had magnanimously decided to play the straight man for her parents' morning show. She dropped kisses on our heads and bounce-flopped out the door and down the hill, her brother chattering in Spanish at her side.

Our corny domestic scene made me think about an email I'd recently received Lizzie. I'd written her a bewildered email about Anthony's Seattle emotions and then how they went poof. She wrote:

I know you feel like he's so...absent...sometimes. I don't know if you notice it, but you guys hum like a top. I can't imagine how it would have shocked his system, to be yanked away from the humming.

I read Lizzie's review of us and considered emotion, connectedness, word count. What to think about it all? Anthony would never be the one to throw the emotional life preserver into the depths and pull me up from my innermost fears—lost opportunities, wrecking the kids. When I cried in the bathroom, I'd do it alone.

But as much as I wanted more words, I considered the ones Anthony did produce:

"Hmmm. Yeah. Let's." he had said, when, with no context at all, I had poked him awake and made the wackiest suggestion of our lives. Not a bit of skepticism, not a whiff of fear.

There's power in what isn't there.

I'd never stop wanting deep, married-people conversation. But whether we were moving to another world or just finding ourselves oh-so-hilarious, Anthony's and my briefest exchanges were nonetheless packed with implicit trust and connection.

The rope on a life preserver is stout and strong. But so are the million tiny threads that bind us, every time we are simply kind to one another. Loving the kids, watching the parrots, washing the dishes—little bits of everyday connectedness matter. The everyday is, after all, where we live.

And when that wasn't enough, when I got frustrated that Anthony lacked words and was too unemotional, I needed to remember the month the emotions comet passed. *Remember that time, when Anthony talked?* I was thousands of miles away and he had friends and family nearby. Yet he'd chosen to talk to me.

The following afternoon, the rainy season got serious. No one in the Zone felt like venturing out, but no matter. Mooching around the house with just each other felt, at long last, plenty of thrill for the five of us. As the mousy gray of the day turned to the sooty gray of dusk, our heads popped up from a Christmas-box puzzle when we heard a noise outside.

"What was that?" said Harry, and ran to check.

The dog at our door was a brown and white everydog. If you didn't know dogs well and someone said, "Draw a dog," you'd draw her. Her eyes were so soulful and her fur so dripping wet that we broke Seattle-steadfast rules. We fed her. We let her in the house. We petted her and scratched her behind the ears and named her Manchitas, which means, roughly, Spot.

For the next week, Manchitas's trick was to trot along next to us but just behind, which made her seem ours, and well-trained. If we crossed the street, she'd cross, too. If we entered a store, she'd wait patiently until we came out.

In Seattle we had chickens, which the kids tried to believe were like real pets. But chickens never knew their names. Chickens never made us feel loved, or worth waiting for.

Manchitas lay at the foot of our bed the morning Ivy jumped onto it, thrilled:

"I found more teeth!"

So she had. Ivy hadn't lost any of her baby teeth yet, and with four new ones coming in on the bottom, the only thing the new arrivals could think to do was start a second row behind the first. Rather than letting Ivy grow up to be a shark, I called Dr. de la Rosa for a recommendation, and discovered—glory!— that he had a very high opinion of the traveling pediatric dentist who visited Monteverde for two days every month.

Recently, Dr. de la Rosa had taken a look in Harry's mouth and recommended we start opening things up—our bloodline tends toward fangs. I made an appointment for multiple extractions.

On the day of the dentist, Manchitas followed us in. She wanted to sit in the chair with the kids, but the dentist didn't subscribe to our dog anarchy and suggested she wait outside. From the hallway, Manchitas poked her nose under the door, offering courage.

We left the office about 25,000 colónes ($60) lighter, carrying two little baggies holding eight little teeth, and headed to Monteverde for milkshakes.

"Harry! Harry! *A donde va?* Where are you going, Harry?" Huge smile. Dimples. Both languages, to be thorough. I pictured Diego at the blackboard that first day of school, charming his way out of speaking any English.

"*Fabrica* for a milkshake!" said Harry. "Want to come?"

"*Jes! Jes!*"

As he and Harry ran ahead, I noticed Harry subtly checking his pockets.

When we reached the *fabrica*, I felt Manchitas' patience at the dentist warranted a reward; she seemed like a chocolate-chip-mint kind of girl.

We were falling hard. There was talk of flea shampoo, even a collar, and whether we could take her on the freighter.

The next day, Manchitas was gone. We walked around our hill calling, to no avail. A few weeks later we saw her in town. She was with another family, following next to them but just a little behind.

We learned Manchitas had been playing this game for some time. She'd pick a family and hang out for a while, but she couldn't be tied down. You could name her whatever, and she'd come when she was called. So it turned out Manchitas was a bit of a slut. But she was the first dog we ever had, and we loved her.

Firefly moments, blinking and ungraspable.

When I learned I was pregnant with the zygote who would become Hannah, I felt laid open, like I might fly apart. I felt like that now, but not out of panic. Out of sheer complicated emotion. Joy and sadness and gratitude. I didn't know what I was feeling most; just that I was feeling, a lot.

I was walking back from the *Casa de Arte,* feeling. I'd spent the day chatting, fluidly at last, with Lola and Beatriz. Drinking their coffee. Painting things badly while my friends painted things well. Now, I felt shiny in the reflected light of their competence and camaraderie. Expansive, like skipping.

God I love it here, I thought with every footfall. *I love my time at home. I love my time alone. I love it in my house, I would love it with a mouse.*

It was one of those days when the world is more wonderful than usual, imbued with extra awesome. The road to our house from the *Casa* was purer and humbler than I'd noticed before. The loose stones that tumbled out from under our feet in the dry season now stayed rooted in the damp dirt; how honest they were, how rocky in their rockness.

I crested the hill, where the CEC was even in that moment ladling goodness into my children, handing them back to Anthony and me as stewards of earth and community. I passed the school in gratitude and headed down the back side of the hill, the nobody-uses-it side. The road here was deeply rutted and pitted. The shade deepened as the forest canopy got chummier, trees draping themselves across each other's shoulders. Down where I was, the ruts weren't fooling around. These foot-wide crevasses were the reason this road never had vehicles on it. Also why I had to halt my internal gush-a-thon and concentrate on getting down the hill without falling on my ass.

After about two hundred meters of hilly forest tunnel, the road leveled out and left the canopy behind. My walk now hugged the high side of the valley, almost at the ridge.

On days when there was absolutely no mist, no clouds to create a gray backdrop, if the sky were the most lucid blue and your eyes were having a particularly eagley day, you could sometimes pick out the thread of ziplines in the distance. The tiny tourists whizzing across the gorge always reminded me of parachutists from a Lego set. I looked now but didn't see any.

My mind wandered to my morning at the gallery, and the women who had taken me in.

Lola with her oceanic personality, all forty-foot swells and troughs. She made everyone want to rush with her, headlong, wherever she was going. Compared to the placid pool of Beatriz, with whom I felt so safe and so easy I could happily have curled up with a blankie and taken a nap at her feet. This yinnish/yangish partnership had transformed that little house into a gallery and studio, one room at a time. Now they were makers of and midwives to an incredible body of work. And they let me hang around.

Thinking about all the art they'd given birth to and supported, the birth metaphor went literal and a realization hit me so hard that I sat right down to mull it over.

Lola and Beatriz were mothers. Who worked. Working mothers.

Well now.

A sound broke the silence, and I looked up—a zipliner zzzz'd through the sky, hooting and hollering his adrenaline rush.

Holy shmoley. Lola and Beatriz ran a complex business, supporting their families as well as giving voice and funding to dozens of local artists. Yet they weren't making people crazy, engaging in mental chess just to get through the day. I couldn't imagine either of them indulging in a maudlin festival of guilt if they missed a move. I had never even seen Lola at the school.

Lola and Beatriz didn't play that game. They did what they could do, and moved forward. Liliana was a fantastic kid, and Lola recognized that. She wasn't sitting up nights, wringing her hands about whether she was wrecking her daughter.

A month ago I had resigned myself to going back to work. The chess game, with its daily potential for a win or a loss, was part of that package. I'd assumed that a loss—a crappy dinner, a lost temper—was, *de facto*, a terrible thing.

What if I went back to the job, but not the game? The life, but not the scorekeeping? Suddenly it seemed possible that I wasn't actually failing my kids, in that life. That I was in fact an actively decent mother, a loving, creative one. Perhaps I'd been biting off more angst than I needed to chew. And perhaps I could choose otherwise. Perhaps, just perhaps, going back to work didn't have to mean going back to crazy.

A year ago, I'd wanted to show Harry that there was a vast distance between *being poor* and *not having every high-end consumable on the planet.* Surely there was an equally vast space between *rotten mother* and someone like me: *mother who works—or not—and who might, on occasion, be a bit tightly wound.*

For years I had been frustrated by my husband's innate calm, but I had also envied it. Yet I was not the polar opposite of Anthony. On the spectrum that ran from *pura vida* to parrots, there was still plenty of room to my right.

Since we got to Monteverde, I had been reminding myself to loosen up, be present. Over and over I had kicked myself as I kept not learning that most basic of lessons. But what if I never mastered it? Could I keep reminding, but stop with the kicking?

Did I have to become an entirely different person in order to love my kids well?

Love them. Screw up. Apologize. Move forward. *Tomamos* some freaking *café.*

I stood up and brushed the road off my butt. In that half second of non-thought, Seattle saw its opening and whooshed back in. Vic and Lizzie and grandparents. Year-old, brand-new stepping stones waiting for us in the garden. Crescent-shaped scrapes on fir floors, made by a three-year-old boy with a broken leg who had barely had one language and who now had fully two. Brave girls with bus passes in hand.

Roots. Soon, Hannah would enter the same Garfield High hallways that Courtney's dad and I had left decades before. I would drive down the Alaskan Way viaduct with my sister, Pike Place Market on our left and Puget Sound to the right. We'd sing loud to the radio while state ferries whose names we knew made their green-and-white way across the sparkling blue.

I loved Seattle.

Yes, I'd have moments in conference rooms missing the kids. And I'd zoom around town, delivering them places. But no matter how parroty I got—and I would surely get parroty, squawking and running—we would always have done this. Costa Rica happened. Our togetherness now was marrow deep. We would always have the fireflies, and the memory of how one year, we stopped and took them in. Those golden ungraspable moments of brightness, of light.

Tiny Lego paratroopers zipped across the sky, backlit and glowing. The late-afternoon sun blazed hot and bright.

34

Winding Down

When I got home from the *Casa* that day, Anthony's quiet had a different feel than usual.

"You okay?"

"Oh. Yeah. Just a little sad I guess."

I'd been kind of bursting, but it wasn't the time for my big revelations: that after almost a year, it had dawned on me that my best friends here were working mothers who seemed really happy. That we could take our family out of Costa Rica, but that wouldn't necessarily take Costa Rica out of us.

"I'm sorry," I said to Anthony. "Is it a specific sad, or malaise sad?"

"Um...I don't know," Anthony shook his head. "It's just...I don't know. I guess it's been a pretty good year."

Ah. Super Pollo syndrome. I gave him a hug, sliced him an avo, and went out by the hole to pick lettuce for dinner.

I'd gotten excited about our return to Seattle, but my feelings were still— and would probably always be—mixed.

I didn't want to guilt trip the kids with all the big stuff it meant for me: a return to work and traffic, and needing more than one pair of pants. But I did try to articulate how much I'd miss the scenery.

"Look...just from here, we can look out the window to the Gulf and see the light green of the grass, the dark green of the foothills in the distance, and a dozen different kinds of green in the canopy."

"Mom? Mom? Mom?" said Harry. He'd begun poking my shoulder repeatedly in the middle of my lecture, a self-aware parody of the child who won't leave his mother alone and that exact child.

"Yeeesss?"

"The way I remember it, Seattle is pretty green, too."

Well now. So it is.

But the next day, Harry was humming a different tune. I heard it coming from deep in the hole. Diego and Stefan had just headed home from an afternoon of digging, whittling, and belting out Spanish rap.

I was positioned in the hammock, where I could discuss logical consequences with any bird who might head for the picture window. I called out an innocent question about the rapid-fire *español* lyrics Harry was laying down, which sounded angry. "Hey, what's that song about?"

Harry's head appeared and his voice was ferocious. "What does it matter, when I'll never hear it again?"

At school and through Ezmeralda's teasing, macho Latino culture had made its mark on Harry, and he did not cry. But his face was bright red and his eyes shiny above Ivy's decorative stonework.

"It would have been better not to even come! What was the *point*, Mom? You bring us to this place, we make all these friends, and now we just have to leave!"

He disappeared again.

That night, Anthony and I posed the age-old question at dinner: "Is it better to have loved and lost, or never to have loved at all?"

"That question isn't fair," pointed out Harry, who would always love justice. "They didn't include 'loved and *not* lost.'"

I'd mention it to Shakespeare. In the meantime, it was a classic, "What do you like better?" We all ended up at "loved and lost" that night. Except for Harry, who used his free pass.

Three weeks before we were due to board the freighter, Hannah came downstairs all ready for bed. I sighed, and mentioned that her pj's used to have feet.

"Yes, Mama. Those were certainly the days."

And then she launched into her proposal.

"This has been such an amazing year. I think I've changed a lot."

"You have, honey. You know a whole new language. You have friends who aren't just like you, people you'd never have met in the States. You've grown up so much..."

"Exactly!"

That was quick. I had clearly taken some kind of bait. I looked at Anthony, who looked—surprise— unfazed. This would end.

"The thing is, *you* know I've changed, and *I* know I've changed. But so much has happened to me here...how can I keep it from fading?" Hannah paused, letting the chirping rainforest nighttime do its thing.

"We'll go back to Seattle and at first, all of this," her arm swept our world, from the wood stove to the Gulf of Nicoya, "will be crystal clear. But it'll slip away."

How wise you are, Grasshopper. How articulate, and how true your sentiments. What is it you want, my little daughter? Tell me, and you shall have it...

"So I want a tangible reminder of this year. Something just for me," she added quickly. "It wouldn't be for showing off, or public display. That's just gross."

She had our number all right.

"Doesn't it seem to you like there should be some physical sign? Some tangible change, to always be a reminder of how much this year changed me, intangibly?"

Logic. The subtle invocation of the sacraments, those outward and visible signs of our inward and invisible state. Calm reason and strategic supplication, where a normal teenager would have gone with entitlement, indignation, perhaps a stomped foot. Oh, we were fucked.

"I think I should get my bellybutton pierced."

!?

After much negotiation and a little pulling of her parents off the ceiling, Hannah had, with us, created a plan. If Hannah could do all the research about safety and follow-up care and present to us what she'd learned. If she could find a good place in San Jose, and if Lola approved it. If Hannah covered all costs. If she continued not to wear belly shirts.

I summarized our agreement, ticking points off on my fingers.

Hannah smiled and patted my head. "Want to make a poster, Mom?

"I could find a Sharpie . . ." said Anthony.

"Y'all are *hilarious*," said I.

The weekend before our family would say goodbye to Monteverde for good, Lola, Beatriz and I took our collective daughters to San José. We would stay with Lola's good friend from university, a psychiatrist. We would go out to dinner and to the theatre, and I wanted to look for *Harry Potter y el Orden del Fenix*. Not for me—I had finished the fourth book and felt proud and very done. But Stefan had stumbled across my highly annotated first volume one day when he'd come to work on hole maintenance. After making fun of me for reading baby books, he'd borrowed and quickly torn through all four.

Also that weekend, assuming she didn't chicken out and we could find a piercer who met Lola's strict safety requirements, Hannah had her parents' grudging permission to make herself look like a prostitute.

Most of the way down the mountain, Liliana lobbied her mother. She tried all the techniques Hannah had carefully eschewed. She begged and wheedled and promised she'd never ask for another favor. She argued it was her body and she had the right. But Lola never wavered. Liliana was a whole different ball game from Hannah. She was already too sexy for her shirt; I wouldn't have let her, either. For that matter, if the time ever came, I was pretty sure I'd laugh Ivy out of the room.

On Saturday afternoon, three floors above the bustling *Avenida Centrale,* Lola stared down a highly-pierced man in a little room. Hannah nodded knowingly; this was the same glare with which Lola had skewered the Monteverde *taxistas.*

In the Pacific Northwest, we learn to telegraph politeness no matter what the circumstances. Growing up female in Central America, Lola had learned to telegraph that she was not, in any circumstances, to be trifled with.

Lola asked Piercings several pointed questions about his practice, personal history, and the neighborhoods in which he'd grown up. Satisfied, she stepped back. It was Hannah's show now, and she conducted a brief interview. Piercings smiled and laughed and patted Hannah's shoulder. He seemed like a good guy. He took us to a little room and showed us his sterilization equipment. Hannah told him that yes, her mother spoke good Spanish and could give consent. But Piercings was cautious; I sensed perhaps he'd had some visits from furious mamas in his time.

He asked Hannah for some English before he turned to me, leaned forward, and asked, "You are fine, *Mamá*? You say yes?" Through Hannah's shirt, he pressed his finger into her bellybutton. "Sure?"

"Yes, sure. But hurry up before I change my mind," I rattled off in Spanish, then smiled so he'd know I was joking.

Hannah held my hand when she lay on the table. Lola and Liliana waited outside. I could hear Liliana begging.

Piercings asked Hannah if she was ready. *"Lista?"*

"Si. Lista."

In the moment of the needle, Hannah squeezed my hand hard. But it wasn't the pressure that had me blinking back tears.

Harry had been right. Here I was all over again, poised to say goodbye to people I loved. Listening to Lola holding firm in the waiting room, I realized how much I would miss mothering alongside her, painting with her, laughing at her Spaghetti-Os. I would miss the heart from which sprung polka-dot menageries, and the cigarette she poked in the air when she asked if I got her point. *"M'entiendes, MarGOTE? M'entiendes?"* Once we left, I might never see Lola again.

I wanted to run to Canitas, jump into our hole, and howl.

Hannah would leave Costa Rica different, in many ways. One of them was the tiny sapphire that matched her eyes but winked from her navel. Discreetly, as promised; Hannah never was a belly-shirt girl. And she was right about the tangible reminder. Each time I glimpsed that little sparkle, I thought of my friends Lola and Beatriz and the days I spent with them. Drinking coffee and speaking Spanish, making all manner of beautiful things.

35

The Big World We Found
in Our Small Pond

"Yowza. That girl is Tica now, that's for sure," Mike shouted over the bass.

I looked over at Ivy in her much-begged-for and finally procured bikini, dancing with Courtney. Courtney moved stiffly, watchful as always. But Ivy inhabited the beat, all hips and belly button.

The CEC family with the biggest house was throwing a party to mark the end of the school year, and everyone we knew was dancing. The parents and the director of the school. Little kids danced with abandon, party-animal teachers in their twenties moved sexy and sang loud, and teens and tweens did their best.

Moments later, Ezmeralda shimmied up to me, echoing what Mike had said.

"Mira Ivy! Ser Tica, ahora corre en su sangre."

I smiled. My little white girl, hot Latin rhythms pulsing in her veins. Yes, she was Tica now. All of Ivy's heat and passion, the temper that had been such a struggle—now expressed in her little body. Was it coming out less, now, as fury and belligerence? I tried to remember, but the moment was not philosophical. Hannah swooped in on Ivy and grabbed her hands. The two of them twirled and laughed.

For the last few weeks we'd been reeling our lives in, winding up loose threads in order to tuck them into a pocket of our family's memory. Here we go, from this quiet mountain town where you party with your principal and know about your teacher's weakness for Pringles because you see her buying groceries all the time, where the head of the school Parents' Association is also the receptionist at the closest hotel, and your son's friend's mom is the artist whose paintings hang in both the café and the bank, and his dad is your favorite taxi driver. All evening, watching the dance floor, my heart was full of everyone I loved in Monteverde. My world felt entirely of a piece.

I danced with Ezmeralda, who a few days ago had told me of her decision to break from the Catholic church on the issue of homosexuality. She asked me what I thought about Pedrito. Our conversation felt far more intimate than sorting out her sex life with Marcos ever had.

I took a break dancing and bumped into Mike, sweaty in the kitchen, seeking snacks. Holding a *cerveza* in one hand and shoveling mango salad into his mouth, he asked, "So you gotta go back, huh?"

"Don't gotta," I answered, also shoveling. "Wanna."

Mike raised his eyebrows, and I tried to explain.

"You know," I told him, "I'm all tanked up on *pura vida*; I think I can take it back with me. I'm so freaking lucky to have the choices I do. I can go back to Seattle and work, and my family has options we wouldn't have otherwise. We can stay here, which is a different, also glorious set of options. Believe me, I can act like a crazy person either way; this I have proven. I'm going to go back and try for sane, as much as my DNA will let me."

"Wow," he said. "That's some pretty evolved shit you're talking."

"You know it. Plus, for me to act like I'm somehow trapped in a certain kind of life? How obnoxious. But more than that, how insulting, to people who actually *are* trapped."

Poor Mike. He'd just been making small talk while he stopped to catch his breath, but I was on fire. Magda with a Barbie lecture, all teed up. Knowing her had taught me something else I needed to hold forth on.

"You know, I spent a lot of time here aware of how many people don't have the choices I have. And I want to keep looking for ways to even that out. But it doesn't serve anyone for me to be perpetually guilty and embarrassed. It's not as if, out of my guilt, I was giving everything I owned to the poor. I was just a rich white person who was also guilty and embarrassed." I paused for breath. "Magda had no use for my guilt. She wanted me to pay her on time and to leave the broom alone."

Magda and Luis needed work and I had provided it. I paid exactly what they asked for, and tipped for particularly good or difficult work. We were just people, with roles.

Mike lifted his bottle and clinked mine. "Sing it, sister. Also, god, is it possible your five-year-old is *sexy*?"

"Uh huh. That's another reason we have to get the hell out of here."

We drained our bottles and headed back to the living room, where all our friends were dancing. The pulsing diversity of that end-of-year party included taxi drivers, painters, doctors. Hotel owners and hotel maids, the directors of both schools as well as the drivers of those schools' buses. Catholics, Quakers, Seventh-Day Adventists, staunch atheists, New Age mystics, and people who never really gave religion much thought.

The friends we'd made in Costa Rica were expats who fled the materialistic States, and Ticos who wanted nothing more than a visa and a taste of all that material. They were Mike and Kelly, Magda and Luis, Lola and Beatriz.

Watching them dance, these people we'd come to love, I knew who was missing.

Back in September, I'd wanted to show my dad that I'd overcome unwed mother. And that I'd risen above being a ranting, dissatisfied breadwinner, and then a chess-playing crazymom. I had wanted to prove that I'd transcended my past, the rocky way I'd started my adult life. That I had finally left the bad Margots behind and found the good one.

But those Margots had gotten me here.

I wanted to travel back fourteen years and hug that terrified girl, clutching her peed-on stick and wondering how to survive. *You'll be okay,* I would tell her. *This baby will be a marvel.*

I wanted to call the self of ten years ago, so furious all the time, exhausted by the breadwinning. *Sweetie,* I would say. *You are earning the right to stop for a while. And when you do, the time you'll take with this family will be the most important thing you all will ever do.*

And what about that planning, overachieving chess player? Without her, would we have made it to this mountain or just fantasized about it? Back one year exactly, to that harried woman kneeling over a bathtub filled with shampoo bottles and hotel soaps. Take her by the shoulders, kiss her on the cheek. *Thank you, thank you. For organizing us into this place where we could learn to live a life less organized.*

My heart swelled with gratitude and certainty. I wasn't living a consolation adventure, trying to grasp at what had once passed me by. I was living the exact life I wanted, delivered into it by the women I had been.

I grabbed my old selves by the wrists. I tugged them onto the dance floor, and we danced with abandon.

36

Taking Our Leave

er last day at our house, I was able to give Magda our (repaired, 100% keyful) laptop. Magda had asked many questions, back in our enchanted April, about the opportunities she might have if she knew how to use a computer. I was happy to be able to gift her ours; it felt useful, and not extravagant. I also wrote up a gift certificate for twenty hours of computer instruction, which I'd bought from the man who took care of the school's rickety computer lab.

There was nothing wrong with cleaning houses, and Magda was good at it. But computer skills would give her options that she seemed to want. I hoped my gesture would be okay, and that's exactly what it was.

"Okay," said Magda when I handed her these gifts. "Goodbye."

The following morning, I took down Vic's painting of mugs and sneakers and houses, and mine of anteaters and geckos and hummingbirds. I nestled them between the hardbound pages of *Jorge el Curioso* and closed the final trunk. Marco Tulio would be here in fifteen minutes, at six a.m.

Harry had headed down the hole in the dawn's early light to tell it goodbye. Now he suddenly reappeared. Bits of rainforest, leaf and soil and twigs, clung to the fiery light of his hair. Costa Rica didn't want to let go of Harry any more than he wanted to leave. He sidled up to me and leaned in. He'd gotten taller this year, but I could still rest my cheek on top of his head.

"I'm so glad we came, Mommy." Harry hadn't called me Mommy in years. He tipped his face up to mine. "Loved and lost, Mommy. Definitely. Loved and lost."

And then regular Harry was back.

"Good call, *Madre*." He hugged me, using the opportunity to wipe some mud on the back of my shirt, and then ran off to watch for the van.

As we headed down the driveway for the last time, we turned back to watch the house disappear. It went quickly, hidden first by the steepness of the hill, then by the canopy of the forest.

At the end of the driveway Marco Tulio stopped the van so we could jump out and say goodbye to Luis, Paula, and Adolfo. We hugged and kissed and shook hands all around. We thanked Adolfo especially for the gift of *jupo*. We had shown it to every single visitor, we told him, and it made all our friends wish they lived here, too. In unison, all three of them cocked their heads to the side and said this:

"*Eh?*"

The day Adolfo had jumped up and down and said "*Venga! Venga!*", Harry had heard the word wrong. "*Jupo*" is not Spanish for vine, or swing, or death wish, or anything.

Behuco, Adolfo had said way back when. Vine. We had named our most Costa Rican, most rainforesty activity after a misunderstanding.

"God only knows," I said, "how many things we bungled that we never even knew about."

"Like, maybe Magda was just coming to say hi that day," said Hannah, "and you kept telling her to clean things. That would explain a lot."

We found ourselves so entertaining that none of us noticed when, for the very last time, we left our epic driveway.

The van was bouncing along the road past Santa Elena when Anthony sounded the alarm.

"Crazy Can Man, woop, woop!"

Marco stopped, and my husband jumped out of the van and grabbed a flattened can from the ground, putting it in his back pocket. (And the *taxistas* thought *I* was strange?)

The last thing we saw as we left Monteverde was the school secretary's brother's wife's *primo*, waving to us from the *moto* that was his again. He'd gotten out of his pickle and bought it back from us for $200 less than what he'd charged at Christmas.

"Hey," Anthony said. "Thanks for that."

37

Flying Fish

Five of us lay on our bellies on the sun-warmed deck of the freighter's bow, our heads poking out over the Caribbean. We were measuring how long a fish could stay airborne. Harry kept the count slow, giving each number its full second...*25...26...27...*

Flying fish whip their superfast tails back and forth upwards of seventy times per second to vault themselves up out of the water. Then they flap four pectoral fins to stay there. Updrafts on the leading edges of waves help them extend their stay in our world. The bigger the vessel, the bigger the leading edge, which makes the bow of a freighter a very fun place to be a flying fish.

While Harry ticked off the seconds, Ivy counted the fish themselves, how many were out of the water at a time.

"Nine! I think they're having a breath-holding contest!"

The water-cooled updraft brushed our cheeks, and our bodies stretched back amid coils of giant rope. Toes in falling-apart sneakers jumbled together in the middle, resting on twenty-inch iron cleats. We gaped at the fauna of the green-blue sea and counted seconds. The kids and I pointed and exclaimed. Anthony said nothing, but his ankles joined mine in the tangle.

The fish popped out of the water long enough that Hannah and I actually worried, gripping each other's fingers. She pointed at the one on the far right, who'd been up impossibly long.

"That one really ought to breathe."

Down for a moment then back up again. Visiting.

We'd seen no land for days. We were wholly in between.

Deep in the hold lay a new painting, carefully wrapped in the tattered clothing of our year. Lola had painted it for me on a piece of an old wooden door, the paint so thick and so cheerful I couldn't see the slats. A woman on a swing stretches her toes heavenward, surrounded by a flock of white birds. Stars shine and moon gleams. Polka dots; a riot of color.

Our world was open now, to all the possibilities of the ways we could live. It would never shut. We were rooted. We were free to explore.

There are a million ways to live a life.

I felt my feet, tangled in the sunshine with the feet of those I loved best in the world. We watched the flying fish. In, out. Exploring, returning.

Some people dream of sailing away. I just dream of sailing. With these exact people, for as long as we can.

Acknowledgements

The number of people without whom this book wouldn't exist is higher than I know how to count, and the gratitude I feel toward each of them flows wider and deeper than I can ever express. Bad news for the Acknowledgements.

First: I would never have picked up a pen had Nia Michaels, Pam Mandel, and Julius Sommer not sat in our dining room and said "Yes. Do it. NOW," when I told them I might, maybe, take a writing class. Thank you.

Theo Pauline Nestor and the members of the 2010-2011 UW Certificate in Memoir class got me started and kept me going (even though I lamed out and never got the certif). Thank you.

From that class sprang friendships and a writing group. Anne McTiernan, Rosemary Gregory, and Joyce Tomlinson: For your encouragement, faith, and constancy—thank you.

Many people opened their quiet homes when mine was noisy. Then they lurked in the background and brought me snacks: Carol Brown, Knox Gardner and Victor Chudnovsky, Kristi Skanderup, John and Sheila Valentine, Joyce again and Nia again and especially Erin Page—thank you.

Bob Shacochis, Steve Almond, Christine Johnson Duell, and Jennifer D. Munro told me—early and with authority—that I *could*. Carmi Parker, Hannah Page-Salisbury, Joyce, and Kristi told me—all along—that I *must*. Thank you.

Claire Dederer said those things, too, but was forced to say them MUCH MORE and WAY LOUDER. She also told me to grow out my bangs, which turns out to have been an excellent call. Thank you.

Luke Abrams, Eric Doerr, and Jay Fluegel provided managerial support in all manner of situations. Niyantha Shekar asked me to sign my first published piece, then put it in a frame and hung it where our whole team could see. You all are what's best about Microsoft. Thank you.

To Beth Davey, who tried her best; Karen Gordon, who read for Monteverde; and Beth Rutherford and Kate Willette, who read just because. And to Lyn Stultz, who makes me read out loud. Thank you.

Ivy Page-Salisbury, Renay Frendshuh, and Luis Antonio Santamaria, for some critical last-minute *Zona* research. Thank you.

A lovely group of people prevented my book from being titled *I'm Not Sure: Something about Costa Rica, I guess.* They are Aliza Corrado, Amy Nathanson, Anne Phyfe Palmer, Anthony Salisbury, Beth Rutherford, Beth Speck, Brandon Duran, Carmi, Carolyn Gronlund, Cathy Bronsdon, Clay Martin, Doralee Moynihan, Emily Lieberman, Hannah, Harry Page-Salisbury, Ivy, Jennifer Castle, Jennifer D. Munro, Joan Griswold, Jocelyn Coit-Durland, Jules Cohen, Lisa Huycke, Luke, Marti Reinfeld, Maura Roberts, Niyantha, Rachel Paris-Lambert, Robin Wehl Martin, Robyn Hicock, Susan Ford, and Theo—thank you.

Diana Dunnell, Erin, and Hannah provided beautiful work and late-night help in the end game. The last-minute production magic performed by Liina Koivula of Gorham Printing and Randy Winjum was heroic. Thank you.

Ana Barrientos, Aliza Corrado, and Pam. For art that I want with me always—thank you.

Cecily Gray and Susan Eisman. Though not named in these chapters, you are everywhere in them. Anything I do that I'm proud of is traceable back, somehow, to things I have learned in my decades of admiring you.

Erin, Mom, Dad—my first family. I love you so much. And John, Linda, LoraLee, Lisa, Mike, Sarah, Kale, and Susie—my wonderful more family. You all are the roots that pulled us back. Thank you.

Hannah. You made me believe that at least one person wanted to hear the stories I wanted to tell. "Mama, read me something from your book!" Over and over. Thank you.

Ivy. For confiscating my phone and marching me upstairs, for closing solitaire and KenKen (even though I am very, *very* good). For looking at me sternly and saying "Do I have to sit right by you? Is that what it's going to take?" Thank you.

Harry. Who hugs so hard and so strong and so always. Thank you.

What a lucky, lucky planet, I think, every day. *To have those three upon it.*

And finally. There isn't a sentence on these pages that would have been true or could have been written without Anthony Salisbury. For parenting solo during a year's worth of weekends and even some long weeks. For cleaning up after me, whatever the mess. For "Hmmm. Yeah. Let's," and all that those words imply. For all of it, forever, and no matter what: Thank you.

Made in the USA
Lexington, KY
25 February 2014